ANDY MACVANNAN, ench   his father, experienced his first Hibs game at   ooked on the phenomenon of football, he became an avi   porter of the Hibees, regularly attending matches both home and away.

At the beginning of the 1990s another passion took hold in the shape of punk rock. Embarking on a journey of discovery, his enthusiasm for playing and writing about music saw him enter into the world of the music fanzine.

Football was temporarily kicked into touch but still tugged at his heartstrings from the sidelines, eventually leading him back to the club he loves.

We are Hibernian
the fans' story

ANDY MacVANNAN

Luath Press Limited

EDINBURGH

www.luath.co.uk

First published 2011
New edition 2015

ISBN: 978 1 910745 30 4

The author's right to be identified as author of this book under the Copyright, Designs and Patents Act 1988 has been asserted.

The paper used in this book is recyclable. It is made from low chlorine pulps produced in a low energy, low emission manner from renewable forests.

Printed and bound by CPI Antony Rowe, Chippenham

Typeset in 10 point Sabon by Main Point Books, Edinburgh

In loving memory of my dad Bobby, who took me to my first Hibs match.

Contents

Acknowledgements

I especially wish to thank Gavin and all the staff at Luath, my interviewees for their time, help and enthusiasm and especially Don Morrison, Tom Wright and Gordon Munro, Estefania (for encouraging me to do this), Dave Gilchrist, Jennie Renton and Alan Laughlin. I am grateful for permission to reproduce Gordon Wright's photograph of Irvine Welsh (www.scottishphotolibrary.net) and Genia Ainsworth's photograph of Dick Gaughan. Thanks are also due to Joe Tree, Davey Johnstone, the Hibs Supporters Club and, of course, my mum.

Hibernian Football Club
a brief chronology

1875	Hibernian are formed by Father Hannan and Michael Whelehan.
1891	Sir Tom Farmer's grandfather and great-uncle meet with others in the High Street to set up a fund to resuscitate Hibernian.
1893	Hibs move to the current site of their stadium in Easter Road.
1902	Hibs win their second Scottish Cup.
1903	Hibs win the League Championship.
1911	Jimmy Hendren signs for Hibs.
1941	Gordon Smith joins Hibs.
1945	Lawrie Reilly debut with Hibs.
1948	Hibs win the Scottish First Division.
1951	Hibs win the Scottish First Division.
1952	Hibs win the Scottish First Division.
1954	First game played under floodlights at Easter Road.
1955	Hibernian are the first British team to enter the European Cup.
1957	Joe Baker makes his debut with Hibs.
1958	Lawrie Reilly plays his last game for Hibs.
	Hibs lose to Clyde 1-0 in the Scottish Cup Final.
1959	Gordon Smith leaves Hibs to join Hearts.
1961	Hibs beat Barcelona in the Fairs Cup.
	Joe Baker joins Torino for £75,000.
1971	Eddie Turnbull appointed Hibs manager.
1972	Hibs lose 6-1 to Celtic in the Scottish Cup Final.
	Hibs beat Celtic 2-1 in the League Cup Final.
1973	Hearts 0 Hibs 7.
1976	Pat Stanton transfers to Celtic.
1979	Hibs lose to Rangers in the Scottish Cup Final.
1980	Hibs relegated for only the second time in their history.
1982	Pat Stanton returns as manager.
1985	Hibs are beaten 3-0 by Aberdeen in the League Cup Final.
1990	Wallace Mercer takeover attempt – the 'Hands Off Hibs' campaign begins.
	Season 1990–91 Sir Tom Farmer becomes the majority shareholder.
1991	Hibs win the Skol Cup 2-0 against Dunfermline.
1998	Alex McLeish appointed as manager.
1999	Franck Sauzee joins Hibs.
2000	The Easter Road slope is levelled.
2004	Tony Mowbray appointed manager.
	Hibs lose to 2-0 Livingston in the CIS Cup Final.
	Formation of the Hibernian Historical Trust.
2005	Hibs fans form the Dnipro Kids Appeal (to help Ukranian orphans).
2007	Hibs open East Mains training ground.

	John Collins becomes manager.
	Hibs beat Kilmarnock 5-1 in the CIS Cup Final.
2009	John 'Yogi' Hughes appointed manager.
2010	Hibernian FC open a Learning Centre at Easter Road.
	Colin Calderwood appointed new manager.
2011	Pat Fenlon appointed new manager
2013	Terry Butcher appointed new manager
2014	Hibs are relegated to the Scottish Championship
2014	Hibernian appoint Alan Stubbs as new manager and Leeann Dempster as new Chief Executive.
2015	A new fan-based share scheme (Hibernian Supporters Limited) is announced by the club. Hands on Hibs fan group reject the scheme citing a lack of transparency by the club.
2015	Hibernian begin their second season in the Scottish Championship – the second tier of the Scottish league system.

Introduction

THE FANS INTERVIEWED for *We are Hibernian* all talk frankly and with honest emotion about the impact the remarkable football club called Hibernian has made on their lives. Despite their widely varying backgrounds and circumstances, they share an equal passion for the club and the book's title is intended to reflect this sense of loyalty, belonging and ownership.

I missed witnessing many of those great teams and those vast Easter Road crowds of old, but they have come alive through the recollections of others. I wanted to know how we acknowledge the club's origins and whether people think they are relevant in the modern age. Do those roots dating back to the 19th century still have resonance for today's fans? Are there real differences between Hibs and local rivals, Hearts? Do our closest neighbour's help us to define our identity, or are we so different after all? What is it we really remember about watching football and why is it we often remember the strangest things?

Throughout the book, feature boxes pick up on themes touched upon and carry a direct quote from the interviewee relating to the subject matter. As well as historical reference points, I have included topics such as Lees' Macaroon Bars and Subbuteo to give an extra flavour of football's sights, sounds and even tastes.

Many of the original chapters in the first edition of *We are Hibernian* (2011) have been updated to reflect some of the significant events that have taken place in the last few years of the club's history. New interviewees have also been added to the last three chapters of this second edition. As in the first edition, every effort was made to chose fans from varied backgrounds and varied opinion. My own story of coming to love Hibs might be the best way to demonstrate what brought me to the point of conceiving this book.

When I was a kid my dad worked abroad for many years. I too lived out of Scotland for a short time and greatly missed Edinburgh and my friends. One of my father's pals used to enchant me with his stories of Leith, Edinburgh and the Hibees but although his stories would always interest me, it was my dad's recollections of going to Hibs games in the late '50s and early '60s, which fascinated me. He talked about the crowds and the expectation he felt when Hibs ran down the tunnel onto the pitch. Of course I heard about the great players and the Famous Five but it was the story of the fans that most intrigued me. Little snippets, like his description of tiny bursts of light dancing over the huge East Terrace (actually fans lighting and smoking cigarettes) transported me to the scene. I believe that those tales cemented my connection to the club before I ever set foot inside Easter Road.

I had a certain feeling of trepidation before that first Hibs game, for understandable reasons – my mum had told me that my dad had come back from the football soaked in urine after a trip through to Hampden Park. Apparently he was forced to endure 90 minutes of piss-filled beer cans being chucked back and forward all around his head. I'm glad to say that my first game was not quite as dramatic in that way. It was a friendly tournament against Coventry at Easter Road in 1980. I don't remember much about the actual game, apart from the fact that Coventry played in a dull brown strip but the stadium and the sense of occasion are imprinted on my memory. My dad took me to the Centre Stand with its creaky wooden floors and benches, in a ground that had barely changed in 40 years. As we reached the top of those stairs, the vast terracing opposite was dramatically revealed to me, although only a quarter full. It was exactly as I imagined the stadium of a big football club would be like. Although huge and impressive, it was in reality a crumbling shrine to decades of domestic and European success. But that was in the past; the crowds that it craved had yet to return.

I think my mum only ever came along to one game, down in Ayrshire against Kilmarnock. I remember nothing about the game itself but I retain the image of the friendly old woman who served us a tasty pie at half time and the impressiveness of Rugby Park's pristine pitch still remain in my memories. When I listen to the Proclaimers song 'The Joyful Kilmarnock Blues' it takes me back to that game:

I'd never been to Ayrshire
I hitched down one Saturday
Sixty miles to Kilmarnock
To see Hibernian play
The day was bright and sunny
But the game I won't relay
And there was no Kilmarnock bunnet
To make me want to stay...
© (Reid/Reid) Warner/Chappell Music Ltd.

I have to confess that in the days before I could truly distinguish between right and wrong, I requested a Celtic top for my Christmas. My wish was granted and I got one. I still console myself that I was only half way through my 'green revolution' and it was a minor blip on my true course to becoming a Hibs fan. That unfortunate phase didn't last for long and my passion for the colour green achieved its rightful expression not long after that when the next window of opportunity came a few months later: for my birthday I requested a Hibs strip. Its first test came a few months later when my dad took me to watch an East of Scotland select game at Tynecastle. As we walked along Gorgie Road towards the stadium and I realised that I was not just in the minority, but was the only one wearing green. At only nine years of age perhaps I can be forgiven for my naive assumption that because this was essentially an Edinburgh select team, both Hibs and Hearts fans would be there, backing the same cause. I was soon relieved of this illusion, for as we walked along Gorgie Road every Hearts fan who passed us muttered 'fucking shite!' under their breath. I felt scared but mostly I couldn't believe that my dad didn't tell me it wasn't a good idea to wear green in the first place. Or maybe I had chosen selective deafness and blocked out his desperate pleas?

As a young man with a rapidly growing interest in Hibs I wrote a letter to the club. The previous week I had been at a Hibs v Celtic game and was annoyed at the state of the crumbling stadium. The late Kenny Waugh replied to my letter, point for point, which I found quite impressive. He closed: 'Finally, regarding your rather cheeky postscript, money is indeed hard to come by and the money from the sale of Gordon Durie has already been reinvested in the club, both for the purchase of players and the general running of the club. I can assure you that we do not need your advice on how the club should be run and I hope that having answered honestly all your points that no further correspondence will be entered into.' Needless to say, I did not enter into any further correspondence.

By the age of 14 I had loads of friends that loved to go to games but, being more compliant to their parents' demands, they didn't go to the bigger matches against Rangers and Celtic. On Saturday afternoons I would often say to my mum I was going to a pal's for the afternoon. I would wave goodbye and jump on the number ten bus down to Leith. I can't recall whether my mum ever checked if I was at my friend's or whether I had an elaborate excuse ready in the event that she did. In fact, only recently did I tell her about my deception and her reaction was as shocked as she might have been 30 years ago. Looking back, I find it strange that I was quite happy to go to some of these games on my own. I suppose I was just so sold on the experience back then that nothing would stop me.

I would get off the bus half way down Leith Walk and then walk to the ground along Albert Street. That street became very familiar to me on Saturday afternoons. From Easter Road I would return by the same route and nearly always get myself bag of chips. On one occasion a half brick crashed through the window and landed on to the chippy floor and I was astounded at the staff's lack of reaction – they barely raised an eyebrow. Only the understated, slightly disgruntled murmur of 'That'll be the fitba oot then' seemed to pay recognition to the fact that, at the very least, one of us could have been nursing a large lump on our head.

Adults would affectionately laugh at my bad language. I assume that the sight of a little boy with a high-pitched voice shouting, 'That's fucking shite, Hibs!' was the source of their amusement. At a game against Morton in the early '80s I found myself in the enclosure underneath the old Main Stand. It was quite an unusual place for me to go as I usually frequented the East Terrace. I seem to remember that we got beaten and that it was another bad result in a longer run of bad results. When the game finished, frustrated at yet another lacklustre performance by the team and unable to contain my anger, I quickly walked down to the front of the crowd barrier and hurled my scarf onto the pitch. Any football fan will tell you that this is a last resort and not something you should ever take lightly. I was instantly made to regret my decision. A voice behind me said, 'Come here, son!' I turned to find an old man in a wheelchair who seemed extremely concerned by my behaviour. He urged me to go onto the pitch, pick up my scarf, and keep my belief in the team. 'I've been following the Hibs for a long time and dinnae you worry, son, they'll come good again,' he said. Sheepishly I clambered through the gate, picked up my scarf and returned it to its rightful place round my neck.

I was an avid Subbuteo enthusiast. I played every day. I had my own leagues and I commentated on my own games. It goes without saying that Hibs were generally amongst the cup winners, I always made sure of that! In a 'small' way I got about as close as I would ever get to actually playing for the club. I believed that I should challenge my skills further and so I entered the Scottish National Subbuteo championships, downstairs in the Princes Street John Menzies toy department. Of course I had my mini-Hibs team with me and I was quietly confident of making it to the final. My confidence took a knock early on as I made my way down the escalator. As I reached the bottom I saw two of my competitors methodically polishing and buffing the bases of their players. I remember thinking, 'God, these guys take it even more seriously than me.' In my first game I took a two-goal lead in the first five minutes. Perhaps I shouldn't have allowed my opponents comment of 'this guy's really good' to go to my head. He clawed back the goal deficit and scored a late winner. I was eventually knocked out on goal difference. Ah, that familiar feeling...

Later on I became one of the original 'Hibs Kids' and I remember that my membership would get me into games for free – about three or four times a season. I felt like I had been plucked from my traditional standing place on the East Terrace and maybe I was starting to think of myself as a man and not a 'kid'. My membership unfortunately reached an early termination when me and my pal Stevie got thrown out the ground because he had chucked a Mars Bar onto the pitch.

We are Hibernian sets out to remember some of the great characters connected to the club. There was one large guy with a black beard who always wore a black donkey jacket and carried a mysterious, black sports bag. Me and my football-going mate, John, nicknamed him 'The Doctor'. For some reason we always thought that there must be something potentially lifesaving in his bag and that this must be the reason he attended each and every game. We were almost worried when we didn't see him at a game, in case his absence might have some dire effect on the team's fortunes. Equally, there used to be a very old guy who always stood exactly on the centre line at the front of the old East Terrace. On one occasion when Hibs scored I watched him become beside himself with glee. He wore his scarf round his neck but clearly his limbs were more than a touch rigid, yet he managed to do something that he probably hadn't managed in 20 years. Within seconds of that ball hitting the net he was physically assisted in lifting the scarf above his head by two young fans standing on either side of him. They slowly forced his arms up so he could enjoy that simple act of raising his scarf above his head. It was almost painful to witness and I remember wondering whether he would manage to get his arms back down again. Maybe he'd forever be frozen in that goal-scoring moment.

Some people who told me their story for this book say that football opened their eyes to the adult world. I think that was also true for me. I wonder whether going to games as a kid was a way of trying to identify with my father and trying to understand what he saw. It was definitely a way of accessing the adult world, rallying to a single cause and being accepted as an equal.

I took Hibs so seriously, at the point of third year in secondary school, I even stood up one of the cutest girls in our year. I had decided to go and see Hibs against Aberdeen and promised myself that I would leave the game early to go and meet her. But once I was over the threshold, the old stadium got the better of me and I was hypnotised by one of the most toxic atmospheres I have ever encountered. Brutally, the linesman was hit on the head with a large stone and had to be replaced. Jim Leighton, the Aberdeen goalkeeper, could barely take his bye kicks because of the myriad of missiles raining down on to the pitch from The Cowshed. There had been a simmering sense of violence prior to the game and now it broke into something akin to a frenzy. I was so utterly compelled that I just couldn't leave the ground.

Ugly moments for some people sometimes throw up comical moments for others. I remember a small minibus full of Rangers fans getting rocked back and forward by a large crowd of Hibs fans, on St Clair Road. I bet the driver wasn't a popular man when they realised he had parked in the wrong place. It was amusing because the Rangers fans inside acted like they were still driving along the M8 from Glasgow, desperately ignoring the fact that they were being rocked back and forward. It eventually took the intervention of the police to get them on the real road home.

At the age of about 14 I attended Ian St John's football school in Redford Barracks. The reward for our hard work was to meet Ian St John and then play five-aside with players from Hibs and Hearts. I vividly remember the moment that I skipped past Walter Kidd of Hearts, like he wasn't there. Please allow me some exaggeration. Before I knew it, he had obliged me with a scything chop to my right leg, sending me nose down on to the cold, wooden floor. I looked up expecting a sympathetic hand to pull me back to my feet. Instead I was met with a vengeful glare, as though to say, 'Dinnae try that again!' I met some of the young Hibs team that was later to be part of Alex Miller's side – Mickey Weir, Kevin McKee and maybe Paul Kane were there. My only previous encounter with Paul Kane had been one winter night at a reserve game. Me and a friend from school went along to an unremarkable reserve match at Easter Road – our implacable hunger for anything Hibs knew no bounds. At games for the second team you could freely walk round the empty terraces but the other people at the game generally did the sensible thing and took advantage of the seats in the Centre Stand. Picking a temporary spot behind the corner flag at the Dunbar End, Kano sauntered up to take a corner kick and Stuart shouted, 'C'mon Kano, fucking hurry up!' Kano instantly turned round and snarled 'Fuck off!' It made us think twice about shouting at a player again.

One season in the mid-'80s I missed just one game home and away. I was proud of this at the time and that was the point where I still believe that I earned my 'colours' for life. I'm not sure this would have applied had it been in the glory period of the 1950s, but following Hibs in the '80s was not necessarily a pleasurable experience. Going to away games in Glasgow was sometimes pretty scary as well. I went to Parkhead once with a broken arm freshly set in a plaster cast. Me and my pal walked towards the ground, assuming that we were blending into the green and white tapestry of the approaching crowds. Somehow a group of youths of around our age seemed to smell our allegiance wasn't of the Celtic persuasion and started throwing stones and rocks at us from the other side of the road. Naturally a broken arm is a wee bit of a hindrance when you are trying to make a quick get-away, but we somehow got away unscathed.

In 2001 we played Celtic in the Scottish Cup Final and our woeful record in the competition was to continue for yet another year. We were beaten 3-0. We were determined to enjoy the occasion while we wondered what the outcome of the match would be. The usual ritual of going for a 'few' beers was rigidly adhered to and 'a quick pint for the road?' inevitably delayed our journey to Hampden. We rushed to find a taxi. An unusually willing taxi driver picked us up straightaway but soon the driver's chat turned to. 'Aye boys, it's an all-Fenian final! Nae Huns at Hampden this year...' I remember wondering whether the driver would be so jovial if we were to beat them. I very much doubted it. Sadly, we also had to endure a 20-minute monologue about his love of Edinburgh's 'sauna scene'. That was a long journey but at least the sun shone brightly, as it always seems to when cup final day comes around. The scene really was set. 'We were first to wear the green, we were the first to wear the green' was belted out from the Hibs end and I will never forget the uncomfortable murmuring sound from the Celtic end as they desperately tried to think of a suitable retort. They obviously knew a wee bit more about their history than I suspected.

I was fortunate enough to have the incredible experience of playing bass guitar with a band called The Process in Tokyo at a venue called Waseda Zone B. Me and the band became engaged in conversation with some Japanese guys upstairs in the bar. 'You are from Edinburgh? That is Scotland, yes?' I was initially surprised at their knowledge of geography but was shortly to be even more astounded at their knowledge of Scottish football. Flabbergasted would be a better word to describe my reaction to their next comments: 'I hope you are no Jambos! You must be Hibees... yes?' 'How the fuck do these guys actually know this?' I thought to myself. What are the odds of finding three Japanese football fans who have taken on Hibs loyalties at an underground Grindcore gig in Tokyo? It turned out that they had adopted Hibs as their favourite team due to the introduction of Shunsuke Nakamura into the SPL. As we exchanged enthusiastic handshakes, the surreal nature of this encounter was not lost on me. I briefly indulged myself in the thought that Hibs must be the club I always thought they were – known the world over but still appealing to those involved in extreme, underground music from the heart of Japan.

Back in the 1980s when I was in my teens I went through to Dens Park to watch a League Cup Semi-Final against Aberdeen. I used to travel to away games with a big group of people. I don't remember much about the game but I do know we were well beaten. At half time we heard one of our names being read out over the tannoy system. You have to remember that this was in the days before mobile phones, so it was important that your folks knew exactly where you where. 'Would Gerald Aitken please report to a police officer as soon as possible.' Naturally we thought something really bad must have happened. Gerald quickly reported himself and was hurriedly escorted up the touchline, down the tunnel and into the bowels of Dundee's Main Stand. As he entered the control room, a phone lay off the hook in front of him. Expecting the worst, he picked up the phone. 'What are you up tae the night, Gebbo?' asked his pal. I have to take my hat off to the person that made the phone call because it had us laughing for the rest of the day and helped to mask a bad defeat for the Hibees.

Of course the main reason we watch our team is for the football. We may have other reasons for our allegiances but it is the game itself that draws people into the stadium every second week. The 2007 CIS Cup Final win will always live with me. I think everyone that day felt a huge sense of emotion and relief at having finally lifted a trophy after so many years. I really was choked up when we beat Kilmarnock. I just remember thinking about all those people who are sadly no longer with us and how they would loved to have been there. I am not remotely religious but I did have a feeling that somehow, from afar, they were contently smiling to themselves. That game seemed to mean more to me than just what happened on the day. It was almost like my time as fan had somehow been validated. I had often missed out on entire seasons of Hibs games through other interests, apathy or circumstance – but the Hibees were never far from my thoughts.

We believe that we have clear memories of players gone by but when I try to recall a distinct moment or action of play it is much harder. There is something almost ghostly that is engrained somewhere in my memory when I try to remember my favourite Hibs players. You will read more about many great players in the chapters ahead but I still feel duty bound to mention some of my favourites.

Ralph Callaghan was a player that passed the ball with true distinction and complete conviction. I just remember that he seemed to have so much time on the ball in an era where tackles came thick and fast and challenges were never shirked. Eric Schaedler was another that relished the physical side of the game and he was a true winner. He competed like his life depended on it and if anyone played with more passion and commitment for Hibernian then I have yet to see him. I often content myself with being lucky enough to see players like these even though they were coming to the end of their career in the early 1980s. Despite the fact that Andy Goram later signed for Rangers he was simply an amazing goalkeeper who could have played for any club side in the world. I always had a soft spot for Alan Rough and Jim Leighton too as they also performed magnificently for Hibernian. It is the players of my childhood, and early teens, that seemed to impact most on my memories. Perhaps my pickings are not as rich as many other fans in this book, but if I had to choose an all-time favourite player it would have to be wee Mickey Weir. Fans use to sing, 'He's here, he's there, he's every fucking where, Mickey Weir, Mickey Weir...' and he was everywhere with his weaving forays on the wing. I am extremely proud to add Mickey Weir to the 2nd edition of this book and I think that he would have found a place in most of the great Hibs teams.

Since the first edition of *We are Hibernian* (in 2011) the club has endured a torrid time on the field of play. This is best illustrated by the fact that Hibs have been led by three different managers in the last four seasons. We suffered the hellish torment of a 5.1 Scottish Cup Final defeat to Hearts in 2012 and were then defeated 3.0 by Celtic in the 2013 final. But the most defining moment of recent times came for the club came in 2014.

It followed an extremely poor season where the only possible consolation for Hibs fans lay in the strong likelihood of Hearts relegation to the Scottish Championship. But we found ourselves sucked into the Gorgie vortex and facing a relegation play off. After leading by two goals in the first leg, Hibs returned to Easter Road and were ultimately relegated by the last kick of the ball in a penalty shoot out against Hamilton. Any gloating rights over our city rivals evaporated in a split second and Hibernian reluctantly joined Hearts for the start of the 2014 Scottish Championship season.

For most of our long suffering supporters this was the final straw. Demonstrations against the board of directors quickly followed that game and a large rally was organised just a couple of weeks after when several former players such Paul Kane and Pat Stanton led a supporter ultimatum for change and control of the club. There is no doubt relegation was one of the darkest days for the club and we have a very long road to travel before we can recover from it.

Just prior to the beginning of the new 2014–15 season, Hibs appointed Alan Stubbs as their new manager. In all my time as a Hibs fan I don't recall a new appointment being met with less enthusiasm. Not for the new manager himself but perhaps by a lack of faith in whether the club had the ability to make a successful appointment. Maybe Hibs fans had not counted on new Chief Executive Leeann Dempster's ability to competently recruit a manager who could at least breathe some life into a demoralised and humiliated squad of players. Many before Stubbs had spectacularly failed and some fans had begun to question whether the club itself had a hand in being unable to foster a winning mentality or adequately invest in a higher standard of player. But of course the football world is an unforgiving beast and their appointments will tell their own story in the years to come.

Hibs failed to gain instant promotion from the second tier in the 2014–15 season but they did finish runners-up ahead of Rangers. We therefore qualified for the play offs but ultimately failed in our first knock out round against a recently rejuvenated Rangers side. Many fans applauded them off the park that day, perhaps in recognition of a team who had finally begun to entertain and fight for the jersey. In reality they had failed to beat a very poor Rangers team who ultimately failed to gain promotion, as they were comprehensively beaten in the play off final by Motherwell.

We are Hibernian is packed full of opinion about the way that Hibs fans see their club in the modern day. I think we should cherish the history of this remarkable football club but we should also encourage the clubs benefactors to open their doors and give access to their facilities. It is the supporter that gives so freely every week to watch the team that they love. We should remember how important our club has been to our past but enthuse about the positive role they could play in uniting our communities and paving our future.

There is no doubt that Hibernian have made some strides forward in reaching out to their immediate community and to those whom have recently settled in Edinburgh and Leith. This is more important than it first may seem. Hibs were ultimately born from Edinburgh's emigrant Irish population so perhaps the clubs efforts on this front can be seen as an acknowledgement to its roots and contemporary identity.

Hibernian can always do more. They can ultimately reinforce and build a genuine sense of community spirit. Scottish clubs will never consistently compete with the glamorous and much hyped fare served up by the English Premiership or the Champions League. Our strength surely lies with cementing genuine links to its supporters. This is the path that will likely endear Scottish clubs to potential fans of each new generation and it was an issue highlighted by many of my original interviewees in the first edition of the book.

Other fans expressed their opinions on the rivalry between both of Edinburgh's football clubs. Some say that the rivalry appears to have become more hateful and intense over the years. Perhaps this is true on a visible level but I believe that this rivalry was just as strong in days gone by. Perhaps the way that it manifests itself has become more defined by the type of song that supporters sing or even the fact that we live in an era of crowd segregation where tribal affiliations are allowed to flourish. I suspect that Hibs fans celebrated just as much in the 1950s with a win over Hearts than they do in the modern day. I would imagine that they also felt equally as disappointed with a defeat.

The team we support has an influence on the way we learn how to interact with others. Particularly our close family and friends. The journey we enjoy supporting a club usually begins as a child, but what may be overlooked is this rare opportunity for children to bond with their parents. It certainly helped me to recognise that my dad was an individual and that he had his own life experiences. It also made me connect with the past in a way that no history book could ever do.

My father passed away a couple of years after the first edition of this book. He suffered for many years with Alzheimer's but I will always remember how much he enjoyed attending the launch night of We are Hibernian. He seemed to be revitalised by the occasion and his connection to the club – it was his last social occasion in public. The whole evening left me in no doubt that football is much more than just a game and it has a positive influence that reaches far deeper and wider than many people can possibly imagine. Behind it there lies a rich seam of stories that recount moments of joy, humour and sadness. Supporters of the game routinely nurture and often centre their friendships round their attachment to the game of football and the team that they love.

I thoroughly enjoyed hearing what other supporters had to say on their own connections to the club and how Hibernian played such a huge part in forming their identity. Hibernian is living, breathing and it is important. It has a remarkable past that is alive within every single one of us and we all have a story to tell about it. So the next time you catch a glimpse of Easter Road Stadium try to stop and think about its history. Imagine the thousands who have sat and stood in its stands and terraces. Remember the players of bygone days who played for the love of playing and for the love of entertaining.

Consider the events still to happen and the stories that have yet to be told.

Andy MacVannan
wearehibernian@gmail.com

Charlie Reid

Musician, born 1962.

❛ I still think about that match every couple of days, and what it means to me, how it shaped me. ❜

I FIRST STARTED going to games with my dad in 1972. At the time we lived in England and we were up visiting family in Edinburgh, so we went along to Easter Road. Hibs were starting to have an excellent side again and we watched them beat St Johnstone 7-1. It had such an impact on me. I still think about that match every couple of days, and what it means to me, how it shaped me. I had never been to a game before. My dad came from a family that mostly supported Hearts, but he was kind of more Hibs-leaning. After the Second World War he used to go along and support Hibs and he even had trials with them – he played a bit of juvenile football.

From that win against St Johnstone onwards, that was it for me, I thought they were fantastic! I wanted to learn a bit more about them. My dad had told me about the Famous Five, Joe Baker and all those guys because he had watched them on a regular basis. I read about the history of the club back to its foundations and I found Hibernian to be a unique and groundbreaking club in so many aspects. Not just in the way that they were founded, but how they struggled against the prejudice there was against them. I view the club as forward-looking, progressive, a force for good. Over the time that I have supported them the football has often been pretty poor, although when it has been good it has been great! My favourite period, even more than the 1970s, was when that team came through under Mowbray. It was like a golden age. It might be many years before we see a team like that again at Easter Road.

That first time I saw Hibs, as a ten-year-old boy, they attacked a lot and I particularly remember Pat Stanton and the young John Brownlie with his surging runs up the wing from the full back position. But St Johnstone were also a pretty good team – Willie Ormond was managing them and he had done a tremendous job. I think they were in the Fairs Cup that year. I remember very clearly the old high terracing, the way it looked in front of the flats at the back of Lochend. There wasn't a huge crowd at that match, maybe 11,000. Hibs were just starting to become a very interesting team and you felt something was beginning. Within the support there was a real sense of excitement, especially given the way they destroyed St Johnstone that day.

After we moved back up to Scotland towards the end of the 1970s me and my brother used to go and watch them, but the team wasn't as good by then. I still felt they were a better side than Hearts, I just found them an altogether more interesting club. I mean I have been to Tynecastle many times – funnily enough, my dad, the week after he took us to Easter Road, took us to Tynecastle and we saw them beat Falkirk, with Donald Ford and players like that in the team. But I just found in all the times that I went to Tynecastle, and I don't believe in putting down another club, that Easter Road was a more stimulating place and the football was more interesting.

I think Hibs are at their best when they remember that it isn't just about winning. I know that we don't concentrate on winning often enough but it's really important to play proper football and Hibs are at their best when they do that. If you look at the League Championship Winners statistics it's all square between Hibs and Hearts; if you look at the European record, then Hibs are probably still ahead. When it comes to the cups, particularly the Scottish Cup, then Hearts are more successful. It's interesting that up until they won the Scottish Cup in 1998 Hearts hadn't won it for something like 37 years, so they have gone through long periods without winning anything. I do think there's a different ethos at Tynecastle. Hibs are more about playing football and there's more of an emphasis on how you do it. It has to be said that when Hibs have had more money invested in players they have had the better team. Equally, when Hearts have had more money invested in players, then they have had the better team – it is quite simple!

It's important to understand the background of the last few games against Hearts, since the bulk of our good side has been sold. You get what you pay for. Although Hibs are well run off the park there is a lack of ambition that comes from the owner and the chairman. They have done a good, efficient job in terms of a business but there is a lack of drive to win. We need a bit more of that back. Tom Hart, who owned us in the 1970s, wanted to win and although we didn't win much then either, we came close on a number of occasions. We also faced a Celtic team that was probably as good as the Lisbon Lions and still had several of them left in the team. Celtic were a team who made European finals and semi-finals – that's how good they were. Had they not been as good then Hibs probably would have won a couple of league championships round that time. I think Hibs lack ambition at the moment. That's not to say we should win at any cost in an Old Firm or Hearts kind of way, but I think we need new investment. I think we have needed it for a long time.

Nowadays I go to watch Hibs at Easter Road every weekend I can, although I don't tend to go to the away games as much. I buy a season ticket but I rarely use it because I'm away most of the time. I think the stadium has really changed for the better. I remember talking to my dad about when they put another level on the terracing, in 1948 or 1949, and made it into a huge bowl with the massively high concrete terracing – I loved that stadium! When they cut down the East Stand it was never the same, so I was glad to see it knocked down recently. It's funny looking on the internet because you can see bits of film of it when it was full and when it was empty. When they put up The Shed, after they cut the terracing, it wasn't great, so I'm glad to see the back of that.

The atmosphere was tremendous at the last derby – the Singing Section has really worked. It's a good idea and I hope its going to grow, as hopefully the support will grow over the next couple of years. Hibs have done really well keeping their average crowd up. Some of that is down to the better facilities they have now, so really I'm very much a 'new stadium man'. I'm ambitious for the club. Eventually I'd like to see us add another 10,000 seats, but if the club has real ambition they'll maybe have to look for another site. At the moment the stadium's capacity is more than adequate. For all of the criticisms I have of the board, on the business side they have got it right and they also got the training facility built quickly. Unlike Hearts, they managed to get the new stadium finished. It's now an excellent medium-sized stadium, but let's see some ambition on the park. I should say that the ground's looking really good though, so the club should be commended for that.

I'm glad the club is acknowledging its roots – in the past there's been some reluctance to do so. The club is now at peace with its culture in a way that maybe some other clubs are not and I would like to see more done to acknowledge our history, without that 'greeting into the beer glass' thing that so persists at Celtic. Hibs can do it with a little bit more dignity. As a Scottish football club with Irish roots, that identity should be celebrated and integrated into what we all are as Hibs supporters. I have no problem seeing the Irish tricolour at the ground but what I really love is seeing the Irish harp. I don't think the tricolour says 'Hibs', whereas the harp does – to me, the harp symbolises the club. That's what it's about, not ancestry or nationality.

Hearts supporters will piss themselves laughing at this: my brother and I always try to keep Scottish Cup Final day free. Why the fuck do we bother doing that, you might think. But one day Hibs will make the final and one day we will win! Scottish Cup semi-finals I can bear to miss. There have been many times my brother and I have said, 'Damn it, we have a gig booked that day!' and I always get frustrated if there are big games that I can't see, but it really would hurt if I missed a final.

When we were out in Australia we were asked us along to a sports event. Football is a minority sport there, it's a cricket, Aussie Rules or Rugby Union country, so we felt a wee bit like outsiders. Aussies are always friendly though, and they said to us, 'Get up and do your club song.' We said, 'Yeah, alright!' Stuart, the guitar player at the time, and Stevie, our keyboard player, who is also a Hibs supporter, loved it. We got up and did a verse of 'Glory to the Hibees' and it went out on Australian TV. I think some people knew that we were going to play it because there is quite an active Australian Hibs supporters branch and there were definitely a few of them in the crowd. It was funny doing it there – we'd never been asked to play it in Scotland. I don't think that as the Proclaimers we have any songs that have a direct reference to Hibs as such, but if a club means as much to you in your life as it does to us, it's likely to come through in your songwriting. Not necessarily in any other than a humorous way, but it does come through. The likelihood is that, hopefully, we will make a few more records before we die, so at some point I would imagine there will be references to Hibs.

At the CIS Cup Final when they played 'Sunshine on Leith', it was kind of surreal. You can understand that to see them in a final is amazing, but to see them score five goals and winning it is something I will probably never see again. What moved me the most, apart from the singalong at the end, was when the players came over with the cup. I was in the main stand, quite close to the centre line (Craig was behind the goal that day), and when I looked down at Scott Brown and Whittaker I just realised how young they were, and I really felt how old I was, because when I first started watching Hibs these boys weren't even born. I actually got a wee bit tearful on that subject – it wasn't because the song was being played, that felt very uplifting to me and I was extremely grateful that all the Hibs supporters have taken the song up like that. I just felt a wee bit old in the realisation of the many years that I have watched Hibs, and how this was a high point I hoped to be repeated. Who knows when, given the history of the club, and how long it had been since we had seen them win anything, and how long it had been since they had really, really performed brilliantly? I speak to people who were there in 1958 when we lost to Clyde, a match nobody ever thought we would lose. We had beaten Rangers and Hearts on the way to the final and Hearts were the best team in Scotland at the time. We beat Rangers in the semi-final and that was it – it seemed destined we were going to beat Clyde, but we fucked it up! We fucked it up against Aberdeen in 1947 as well.

‘I just felt the whole takeover idea was wrong and I reckon that a lot of Hearts supporters thought that as well.’

A Hands Off Hibs campaign sticker.

Christ, the one final I have missed in my lifetime was the Livingston one in 2004 – we were away in America at the time – and I'm really glad I missed that! I'm also glad Hibs came back a few years later with the bulk of that same team and beat Kilmarnock. That felt amazing. And we were also still in the Scottish Cup, although that ended in disappointment. But there you go, swings and roundabouts.

At the Dunfermline final I felt pretty tense because the expectation was huge. There must have been 40,000 Hibs fans there that day, it was an amazing crowd. We all knew beforehand Hibs' tendency to screw things up in finals, but I thought we deserved to win on the day and it was a very exciting game. Walking away from the match I said to someone, 'The club will survive now.' You have to remember, it was still very touch and go. Sir Tom had taken over and the situation had been stabilised, but it was still touch and go. I felt that because the debt was being managed and the club had won something, that it would put some much needed money into the coffers. Winning that game got us in to Europe the following season but the most vital thing of all was that the club would survive.

I don't know what other Hibs fans feel, but I always feel that the club should have young players coming through and playing their football on the deck. So what, if occasionally Clyde beat you 3-0 or you get hammered by Celtic 3-0; it's disappointing, but I don't want Hibs to be like other clubs where it's only about winning and staying in the league and hating the opposition. I think Hibs should be much bigger than that. To me Hibs is an international club, albeit a small international club, and should embrace new ideas. The two things that the supporters are entitled to in a league that is pretty poor are decent attacking football and bringing through young players.

I lent my name to the 'Hands off Hibs' campaign and through that I got to know an awful lot of people, like Kenny McLean, junior and senior, Willie McEwan and George Stewart, who are all real stalwarts of the club and really

In 1990 Hibernian were to face one of their toughest tests. Wallace Mercer – the then Hearts Chairman – proposed a merger of the two Edinburgh clubs. Hibs fans believed that in reality this was nothing more than a takeover attempt that would ultimately swallow Hibs whole. Fans quickly rallied to form the Hands Off Hibs group and set about campaigning to save the club. High profile celebrities lent their weight to the campaign and John Leslie even appeared on *Blue Peter* sporting a Hands Off Hibs T-shirt. The campaign united all Hibs fans in a last stand to save the club.

When Sir Tom Farmer was persuaded to take a controlling interest in Hibernian, which he did despite the fact that at the time he had no great interest in the game itself, the campaign reached its rightful conclusion: the club was saved. The huge sense of relief turned to outright elation when the team went on win the League Cup in 1991.

good people! I just felt the whole takeover idea was wrong and I reckon that a lot of Hearts supporters thought that as well. Mercer, being originally from Glasgow – and for all the time he had been involved with Hearts – still didn't really get it that the Edinburgh rivalry is older than Celtic and Rangers. You just don't do that to people and I wouldn't want it done to them either. At some point there will be a reckoning at Hearts because of their debt. I don't want to see them cease to exist and equally I wouldn't want to see us take them over. But potentially the next takeover could come from us, because they could be on their arse with no ground or anything. I wouldn't want to see it because it's the wrong thing to do and Edinburgh is a more interesting place when you have that rivalry. For all it was upsetting to see Hearts beat us in that semi-final and then win the cup, at least a couple of years later we won the League Cup against Kilmarnock. I think Hearts' success provokes the Hibs board, players and supporters into wanting a bit more, so it's not necessarily bad if they win things occasionally. Mind you, I may get strung up for saying that! I would like to see us get to the stage that we were in during the 1970s, where we were ahead of and beating them more than they beat us, but that would require more investment.

George Best was one of the top players the world has ever seen. We had him when he was well past his peak but he was still a hell of an amazing player. It's hard on Jim Leighton and Alan Rough, who were both good keepers, but to me Goram was perhaps the finest goalkeeper I have ever seen. Rangers maybe got a couple of better seasons out of him than we did, but his last two seasons at Easter Road were as good as anything he did in his career. I remember when he kicked the ball down the slope and it went over the other goalie's head, at the last game of the season against Morton. He was utterly, utterly brilliant – an absolute world-class player! John Brownlie similarly, but for the leg break, would have been a more successful player than Danny McGrain and arguably he was more skilful. Guys like Pat Stanton and Alex Edwards were absolutely brilliant. John Collins – what a total professional and a fantastically gifted player! Paul Kane was a good player and guys like Michael O'Neill, who was maybe not the hardest working, could certainly play. Mickey Weir, Yogi Hughes, Brown and Thomson were all outstanding players as well but I will stand up and say it, I think Derek Riordan is the most naturally gifted footballer I have seen Hibs produce since Pat Stanton! I was a massive Riordan fan, he was an extremely gifted football player, but his relative lack of success is disappointing, I can't help thinking that he could have played at a much higher level, and had he been advised correctly, or maybe if he had more ambition, then he would be doing a little bit better than he has been doing. For those who criticised him – they will look back and be hard pushed to see anyone from that tremendous bunch of players who contributed more to Hibs' game than he did.

Steven Whittaker was fantastic as a goal scorer as well, and Gary O'Connor – what a player! He slipped down a wee bit when Brewster left because he was a help for him when he first came through. And Alan Gordon was some player as far as goal scoring was concerned. If we had a guy like that coming through for

Hibs now he would definitely be on the Scottish team. We've had some fantastic players, but out of all of them the best to watch was Stanton, so I think he's my favourite.

When I first started going to watch Hibs I always stood on the main terrace. When I came down from Fife with my brother we'd get to Edinburgh at about one o'clock and we'd go into the stadium and just walk about, maybe get a pie or whatever. We loved being in the place. I'm sure a lot of supporters feel like that at their football clubs, you love being in the ground. I like the fact that they've widened the pitch and it really looks like a modern stadium. It's got a really good atmosphere about it.

We used to go to away games at places like Tannadice or Dens Park and I remember going to see a semi-final just at the start of the great Aberdeen team. They beat us 1-0 or something like that in the semi-final of the League Cup in about 1979 and I remember the fantastic atmosphere in The Shed at Dens Park with the Hibs support. Turnbull was still manager then. For the Cup Final against Rangers in 1979 we were behind the goal at the old Celtic end. It wasn't a great game because it went to two replays and then we got beaten. McCloy brought down one of our guys – Colin Campbell (who ran the sports shops) was pulled down about five minutes from time and there's no doubt it was a penalty. It was a penalty, a stonewaller, and we didn't get it! I don't believe in the conspiracy theory thing and I don't believe referees, or the bulk of them since the war, have operated an absolute pro-Rangers agenda but you did have your suspicions after watching that. It was outrageous. We were robbed. I told myself we'd win other finals, but we didn't. It really would have been nice to win that one. Maybe if we had, we wouldn't be talking about a hoodoo on the Scottish Cup for Hibs.

I think it's up to all football clubs to involve themselves in the community that has given birth to their support. You've got to remember that Hibs were quintessentially an Old Town Edinburgh team from the slums of the Cowgate. However, I've always felt Hibs' natural constituency to be Leith, North Edinburgh and East Edinburgh, but of course there are Hibs supporters all over the world. The club's job is to reach out to the community in the city of Edinburgh and beyond. I advocated the 'Kick for Kids' campaign for years before they actually started it and I would like to see them expand massively on that. Maybe the average gate at Easter Road is 15,000 per season, so why not give away a thousand tickets every game? There would be an obvious danger if you did that for the Hearts, Celtic or Rangers games, but with the vision and the investment to back it up, people could be bussed in from as far afield as Lanarkshire, Glasgow and up to Fife for home games against the smaller teams. You've got to be very pro-active building the next generation of Hibs support. Entry to games is overpriced in Scotland and we need to take a look at what we are charging per game as well – I mean, the Bundesliga is massively successful with their cheap ticket system. The problem is that clubs would need to get their budgets sorted out, look for more TV money or bigger gates to compensate for the loss from the actual ticket price. A lot more could be done, an awful lot more! We have to stop talking about it and we have to start doing it!

It's not the fault of Celtic and Rangers that they are the biggest clubs in Scotland but they do suck more life out of the game every year, so we have to totally rejig how we approach the game in this country. We need to get more people playing football, improve the facilities and work at getting kids involved. Surely we should also take a look at what we are paying the players?

It's one thing the English Premiership lopping off the best players in the world, but it's not necessarily the best thing for Scotland. I'd like to see a more skills-based league where you relegate a few more, freshen it up every year, integrate the associations in Scotland, maybe abolish the junior leagues – and basically have Scottish football organised a wee bit better with a wee bit more common sense. You could still have the same number of clubs operating but there should be a trap door for, dare I say it, the East Stirlings of this world. If Gala Fairydean have got ambition they should be allowed to rise and if there are clubs without ambition, then they should be allowed to fall...

The funniest thing that I have ever seen at Easter Road was someone throwing a rugby ball onto the pitch in a match at Tynecastle around the time Hearts were talking about moving to Murrayfield. That was witty, I like that. So often it can be moronic, but when it's funny it's great! Another funny moment was a game against Rangers in the late '80s. A guy dressed as Santa Claus had been arrested and as he was being led round the pitch, the Hibs support were singing 'Santa's a Catholic, they tell me Santa's a Catholic!' The whole place just collapsed in laughter. Even some of the Rangers supporters were laughing. When it's witty and digs at the culture of bigotry, that's the kind of thing I love. I hate personal abuse of players and I used to cringe when John Robertson got abuse. He was a good guy and, fuck it – he was a great player! But I do think funny chants are great. The humour at Hibs is a bit above most clubs and I think the fans are a bit wittier than Hearts supporters. My brother was at a game a few weeks ago, he's not got a season ticket anymore, but he took his daughter along. They were in the East Stand, a couple of rows along from the Singing Section. They started singing 'Shoes off if you hate Jam Tarts' and there were apparently hundreds of these guys throwing their trainers about. To me that is funny – it sums up the better aspects of the Hibs support and that's what I love about them!

Colin Whitson

Support Worker, born 1965.

‘ Once the crowds started arriving, you were in! If you got caught and thrown out you could still try and get a lift over. **’**

'WHAT'S THE SCORE with Hibs? What's the score with Hibs?' you'd always hear my family saying when the football was on. So I was brought up thinking, 'What's the score with Hibs?' and it was a while before you even realised it was football they were going on about.

The stadium's only a five-minute walk from where I was brought up. In the 1960s we lived in an area that wasn't recognised as Restalrig, Lochend or Craigentinny, and this could create all sorts of problems when you had that gang-orientated shit. As a youngster I'd get, 'You're no' from Lochend', 'You're no from Craigentinny', that kind of thing. So I would always say, 'No, we're from the high flats and there's about ten of us that live up there.'

You could see the stadium from my window. My grandad was a founder member of the Hibs club and my mum used to tell me stories about them buying two cases of beer, emptying the bottles out and sitting them upside down to use as chairs. They would then have meetings to discuss how to raise funds to afford a charabanc, as they called it at the time, to go to away games. My grandad passed away before I was born and I never met him. My mum's family came from the Canongate but she grew up in Lochend and my father grew up in the Southside, so I think my family are steeped in Hibs connections all the way back to the beginnings of the club.

My mum used to tell me stories about when my grandad would come home and ask any young guy that was hanging about with her, 'What team do you support?' If they said, 'Hearts,' he'd say to my mum, 'Right you, up the stair!' If they said 'Hibs' he'd go, 'OK, well, dinnae you keep her oot too long.'

On Saturday mornings my dad took us swimming and then we kids would always go to see our gran in the afternoon. One day, that didn't happen. Instead, he took us to see Hibs reserves – the 'wee team'. Actually going to see a game, seeing how big the football pitch and the goals were, how big the players were – it was like... Wow! You could hear old guys calling the players by their first names, which I thought was amazing – I was too young to realise that there was a fucking team sheet that comes out and everyone could get a copy.

When I was about seven or eight we moved on to going to first team games against your Clydes, Airdrieonians and Ayr Uniteds but we weren't allowed to go and see Celtic, Rangers or even Dunfermline because the crowds for those games were that big.

There was a bunch of us that would play together – seven aside, first to ten goals, or next goal's the winner – we'd have played football all day, every day if we could. We were mostly Hibs and Hearts fans, a few of us supported Celtic and Rangers. Us Hibs fans would talk about the game all the time and eventually the talk evolved to going to the actual games together. That would have been when I was about nine. We used to sneak into the ground up an old TV cable pipe. There was this great bit up the back of the seated enclosure, a space between the lamp post. We used to put one foot on the wall and one foot on the lamp post and climb up Spider-Man style. A taller guy would go first and lean down and help to pull you up. You would get in for about one in the afternoon and hide in the bushes up at the back of the East Terracing. Once the crowds started arriving, you were in! If you got caught and thrown out, you could still try and get a lift over. 'Geez a lift over, mister,' you'd say. You'd sometimes get, 'I cannae even lift masel ower son.' But more often than not, it worked. With the midweek and European games there were crowds everywhere and you were always toiling to get a lift over, and the longer you left it the less chance you had of getting in because there was that many police about.

On numerous occasions we got caught. Even if you went to the length of hiding in the toilets, the police would just come in and throw you out. But you would just go to another part of the ground and try again. We sometimes used a ladder that some older guys had stolen off a van, and after the game they would take it back and stick it on the van again. One time the guy who owned the van appeared just as we were putting the ladder back on, and asked, 'What the fuck are you doing?' 'We were just borrowing it, nae harm done.' He never found out that we were using it every second Saturday.

On one occasion when we were still walking about trying to find a way of climbing in, I remember seeing a Celtic fan getting kicked to shit right outside the ground. It was in the days when people would wear crash helmets and scarves round their waists and wrists. It wasn't until later on that somebody said, 'He's a Hibs fan.' And right enough, he didn't have any hoops on or anything like that. I remember thinking, 'That's just fucking wild.' You were that young that you didn't realise people were that drunk, you just thought adults were complete nutters! There was no cotton wool wrapping you up, you were seeing all sorts of stuff; people falling over drunk, pissing in the street, fighting and arguing with the police, the crowds, the huge spectacle, the big massive roar...

I remember beating Ayr United 8-1 not long after the 7-0 game (my dad was at the 7-0 game but unfortunately we had to go to our gran's that day. And the European nights, beating Rosenberg 9-2 or something like that, those spectacles were just amazing. Obviously being at the East End of Princes Street to see Hibs coming back with the League Cup in 1972 is high in my memories. Me, my mother and my brother stood at the Waterloo statue opposite the Bridges. The whole place was mobbed. We saw the bus come past and head down to Leith and then we waited for the team to return. The players entered the hotel and eventually appeared at the window with the cup.

Every few months we would climb into the stadium, just to see the ground with nobody in it. One time I saw a bunch of other guys from Leith who had broken into the main stand, were wearing the attire of the day, jumpers with initials on them and flared trousers – running about on the pitch with the League Cup! I'm not completely sure if that's an actual memory or if I've just got a picture in my mind from a story that went round. But there were definitely times when we would go into the ground and kick a ball about on the pitch with our mates.

Football was everywhere when I was growing up. I remember people asking what my English team was. I'd think, 'I'm a Hibs fan, why did I have to have an English team as well?' I did like Arsenal but only because they won the double in '71, I liked Liverpool later into the '70s, glory hunting, I guess. My brother was into Leeds United because they had loads of Scottish players. On *Match of the Day* on a Saturday night you would only have a Scottish game on for the last five minutes, so it was very unlikely that, for example, you would get to see Motherwell against Hibs. The European games were shown though.

I remember one particular time I had climbed into the ground and got into the match. I had a white polo neck jumper on. Where I stood, just before the corner flag at the Dunbar End, there was a wee square bit at the bottom and I was right in the middle of it. I was all excited telling people later that night, 'That's me on the telly.' At another game that was on TV you could see my brother jump up with his parka on and throwing the ball back over the fence. We'd all be down at the bottom of the terrace when there was a corner, just so we could get our faces on the telly. Sadly the best moment with my brother, when he headed the ball back onto the pitch as it came into the enclosure, wasn't on TV.

Loads of people used to go to Easter Road one week and Tynecastle the next because they supported the Edinburgh teams and all that, but at the same time they would be affiliated with one team or another. I remember lots of folk at the match with carry-outs (not me) and guys holding up their glasses of whisky in the rain to add water to their drinks. I remember one away game at Tynecastle around 1975. As usual we swapped ends at half time, and you would hide your scarf under your jacket. We kids were all walking with large lumps under our jumpers. You would go round to one end to hopefully see your team score and therefore it was obvious you supported that particular team. I remember both Hibs and Hearts fans standing on the terrace at Easter Road with nip glasses and filling them up to wish each other a 'Happy New Year' at the derby. The football scarves of the time were just one colour and it was just the same for

Hearts. You would have families all standing next to each other supporting either side.

My grandad was a staunch Hibs fan and my granny was a Hearts fan. Because he was a Catholic, the priest wanted him to bring his kids up in the Catholic faith. He was up telling my granny, 'You will be damned to hell and your kids will go to purgatory unless they are brought up in the Catholic faith.' When my grandad found out about this he went and blackened the priest's eye and threw him down the stairs. It was the end of the religious thing for my grandad.

To this day, I'm totally anti-authority myself and I don't really know where that comes from. The Troubles in Ireland were very much brought to the fore at the football. Rangers fans would sing about the UDA and Celtic about the IRA. Small pockets of Hibs fans would sing IRA stuff. I thought that was a political, antagonistic thing and it was only as I got older I realised there was an Irish connection for Hibs going way back. With my own family there is that link to Ireland but I've never traced the family history.

Everything evolves. I can't see why anybody today would want to be associated with the atrocities that happened during the Troubles, but there's still a small pocket of Hibs supporters who advocate that Irishness in a way I think is detrimental to the club, because it's got nothing to do with football, which is basically 11 guys on a park. I grew up playing football and when you're playing football against somebody you are not bothering your arse about race, colour, religion, or whatever. At the 125th anniversary do for the club we were all talking about how we had to change the old badge with the crown on it because it wasn't registered as an official coat of arms. There was also a portcullis badge at one point, although they never had an embroidered badge on the strip when I first supported them. The first embroidered badge that I remember was 'HFC League Cup 1972', after we beat Celtic. I like the badge as it is now because it represents the stages and roots of the club – the Irish immigrant connections and the move to Leith – with Edinburgh Castle representing the bigger picture of the city. You get some really pedantic people saying, 'We're not actually in Leith because the boundary is there and doesn't go past that.' Let's face it, if somebody farts in Leith you can smell it in Easter Road. At the end of the day, at least we're definitely not in Gorgie.

If you watch the footage of the 7-0 game, you'll see how the Hearts fans singing 'I was born under a Union Jack' were quickly silenced by Jimmy O'Rourke. The Hibs fans were singing 'I-I- IRA- IRA, IRA rule OK.' That sort of thing has died away nowadays although there has been a resurgence in buying the 'Éirinn go Brách' flag, but you can only really get those when we go to Hampden. A homage to Hibs' roots is fair enough, but only the misguided find the whole IRA thing relevant. When I was growing up, Hibs supporters using the Republican card were really polarising the club.

It can be quite an eye-opener when you're on a bus going to various finals and semi-finals. Some songs are sung on the bus that are never sung on the terracing but they are still there in people's hearts and minds, as it were. A mate of mine used to sing one about a Rangers team in the 1960s: 'The boys in blue got fucked 6-2'. It never fucking happened. I had an argument with a guy who said, 'Aye it fucking did,' and I was like, 'It rhymes and that's fucking fine – but it never fucking happened!' I handed out a song about the 6-2 Hearts game but unfortunately it never really caught on. It was to the tune of 'A Partridge in a Pear Tree' and it went '6 fucking 2, a peach fi John O'Neil, cracker from Zitelli, super strike fae Russell and a hat trick from super Mixu.' With the ground being all seated now, you can't just walk up from the pub on a Saturday and meet your mates because Mr A will be sitting in one seat, Mr B will be sitting in another seat, and maybe Mr C and D will be together. If you've got a season ticket you're split up over the stadium unless you go *en masse*. The only people that go en masse are usually young guys that are getting their first income, but even then they might be sitting in one row where the guy sitting in seat 100 can't speak to the guy sitting in seat 107. At games before, if you'd not been for a while, you'd go and meet up at the stand, next to the floodlights or underneath the cameras. I remember being under the camera gantry in the '80s when someone burned a Union Jack. Lots of people were gobbing on the cops after they put the fire out and folk were flipping their hats off. I'm sure the police thought, 'Fuck off! We thought this was an easy shift and we'd get to watch the game! So now we've put a fire oot, we're covered in gob and we're getting abuse.' Then they tried to catch the guy, the guy runs away and the whole thing's a farce. Eventually the police huckle somebody else and say, 'You're going oot,' so that was it. That kind of thing doesn't happen now but nor is there the same camaraderie on the terracing and that sense of having a laugh. You would meet people at the game that you never met in any other context. Now you can't get a family just deciding, on the spur of the moment, 'We'll all go to the game on Saturday together.' You're all going be sitting in a different part of the ground, because you can't get fucking tickets together. You have to register your name and address to get a ticket. I think it all affects the atmosphere and the numbers of supporters that still go. There are a lot of them that can't be arsed buying a season ticket but they're up for going to a couple of games. When the team's doing well, they might say, 'I'm gonnae go along and see that, it sounds good,' but they can't go along and see it with their mates. They can meet in the pub but then it's 'See you later then.' They had 'pay at the gate' recently for a game with Rangers and Newcastle and to me that's fucking excellent because you can just go as a group.

There were times in the 1980s and early '90s when, depending if I had money, I would go to the boozer and think, 'Fuck it, I'm gonnae go along to the game the day', and go round to the ground with some folk that I knew. That option isn't there anymore. Some say, 'Aye, you should go to every game.' Some games can be absolute murder and even if you're a season ticket holder you might think, 'Cannae be arsed, I'll miss next week.' Now you've got to get a ticket in advance and I think it affects your type of fan. If it's pay at the gate then you can just go along as opposed to; 'In that case I will have to get my ticket first and I cannae be arsed.'

I don't think Thatcher understood the whole dynamics of football and the whole mindset for a whole fucking load of people in this country that she was meant to govern, she had no fucking idea about what their social habits were. Even by just meeting for the release of football on a Saturday afternoon and shouting and swearing until the veins come out their necks didn't mean they weren't going to use that whole anger and energy to rise up against the state in some way. She thought, 'Oh right, there's a few people creating hassle,' so now as a result, everybody's got to sit down.

When my laddie was younger I got a season ticket for him and we used to go to the children and adults section. Loads of other people I hadn't seen for years were also going with their kids, and are not going to the pub before or after the game. Depending how it worked, I might go for a pint and then meet my laddie in there. We were surrounded by a lot of people who were older and younger, as well as faces you could remember from the terracing in my school days.

People from 18 to 25 are busy indulging in other aspects of growing into an adult and football is a prime focus for that. A lot of them maybe drift away, but when they come back it's changed. There have been times in the 1980s and '90s when I've thought, 'Do I sit here and get pished or do I go to the game and watch Hibs scrape a fucking 3-2 win against Partick Thistle on a pissing-with-rain afternoon? Actually... No! I think I'll get pished!' At that time the football wasn't all that good and the entertainment wasn't there. There's a whole new generation going now who can't remember the icy, windy terraces – and they can't remember a macaroon bar, spearmint chewing gum or a pie served in the Hibs colours because it's gone off.

Kids have no chance of a lift over or climbing the wall like I used to do. If you're taking kids along it's a financial strain on people who are on a lower wage. Generally I think it's people with better paid jobs that are going now.

I've always found Hibs more orientated towards the working-class ethic and ideal. The club was set up to keep Catholic young men on track, as it were, giving them something to get interested in away from the slums. We've always

❛ They can't remember a macaroon bar, spearmint chewing gum or a pie served in the Hibs colours because it's gone off. ❜

had that family, community interest, and I think the fans have always been more to the left rather than the right wing.

I've heard people saying, 'My laddie's a great fitballer but I've told him there's no way he's signing for Hearts.' Are Hibs and Hearts both catering for the working classes of Edinburgh or are they on two different sides of a divide? Starting off with a religious divide, over the last couple of years on various websites there has been this ' big' and 'wee' team thing, the implication being that Hibs are the poor neighbours. What the fuck does that have to do with football? Fuck off with your golf jumpers and your middle-class ideas! I don't spend all my money going to games, I don't spend all my money on merchandise and I don't have to have a Hibs number plate. If Hearts guys I know are at the same level supporting their club as me, then we can have discussions about football, rather than: 'We've got more money than you'; 'Vlad' s a fucking idiot'; 'Rod Petrie's giving you no money'; 'Your manager's ugly'; 'Your manager's uglier'; and all that shit. Alternatively, we might have a discussion about football rather than point scoring: 'That's a good player you've got there in that position, but if you played him in this other position then he would work with such and such a player.' A mate of mine who's a Hearts fan once told me, 'When I was younger, the League Cup was a cup to go for but now, because you've won it and we've won the Scottish Cup then the Scottish Cup becomes better. You play the same teams but the Scottish Cup, is for the whole of Scotland and the League Cup isnae.' They've taken away its European qualification, but if I was playing football I wouldn't look at it like the 'Mickey Mouse Cup', I would be looking at it like it's a major fucking trophy! I also don't know if Hearts fans really believe it's a 'Mickey Mouse cup' (which they've not won for years and years); it's just they won the Scottish Cup, but just three times in 50-odd years, which isnae such a great thing to bleat on about. I don't think we'll ever win the Scottish Cup. There's so many people in my family that have said it's got to be won before they die and, yeah, they have all fucking died.

Football grounds across the Scotland of yesteryear were regularly filled with a familiar, booming voice: 'Macaroon ba-ars! Geyyer macaroon ba-ars!'

The word 'macaroon' derives from the Italian *maccarone* and the Scottish variety is a sweet confection covered in chocolate and topped with roasted coconut. Production of the Lees Macaroon Bar started in 1931. The recipe was devised almost accidentally by confectioner John J. Lees while he was actually trying to concoct a chocolate fondant bar.

For decades Lees' Macaroon Bars were considered the ideal accompaniment to a pie and Bovril on a cold Saturday afternoon at the football.

I don't know if it's so much a case of 'pressure' but just a case of every time Hibs get the chance to make a difference there's always some fucking stumbling block.

I remember one of the first games I went to away, Celtic hammered Hibs 6-1. I was in the old stand at Hampden, looking along where the dugouts were, and the whole stairway stunk of fucking pish. I remember the old wooden seats, with the grooves moulded into them so you could get your wee bum on them. At that game I was about five years old and when Celtic scored the fifth or sixth goal, a guy stood up and started shouting. He had swooshy hair, sideburns, Eric Morecambe specs, winkle-picker shoes, a big overcoat and his can of Lamot Pils which he kicked over when he jumped up. He spilt it over my brother's seat and I remember my dad saying, 'Oh!! Fuck you!' It was just a step too far for him. My mum and my aunty were both saying to my dad, 'Calm doon! Calm doon!' So the guy started saying, 'We're all the same, we're all brothers, wearing the green and all that.' My dad replied, 'How dare you patronise me!' I think we left shortly after that, down the staircase that stunk really badly of pish. I wasn't aware back then that we hadn't won it for 60-odd years, and at the time, we'd got into the Scottish Cup Final. I think Hearts were there in 1976 and we got back there in 1979. That was it for fucking years, it wasn't even mentioned. I remember cracking the joke about Hearts only having plastic knives and forks because the bastards didn't know how to lift silverware. Then the bastards won the cup in 1998 so it fucked up that joke!

I remember going to my gran's at New Year and all the men, me and my brother and cousins were upstairs. My gran stayed downstairs and my aunty stayed up the stair in the tenement. We were all watching the 7-0 game, so everybody was jumping about mad apart from my great uncle whose face was fucking tripping him. I was saying to my brother, 'Maybe he's a fucking Jambo?' Apart from him the whole house was jumping about. What a party atmosphere, it was brilliant! The highlights were on at something like 9.30 and we were all watching this wee black and white TV with my uncle and his cigars in the tube. He was blowing smoke into the tubes, putting the stopper on, and saying to me, 'Keep that, it turns into diamonds later on,' and my mum quickly responding, 'Just put that in the bin, son... fucking idiot, dinnae listen tae him.' This wasn't like the normal party where 'ssshhh, uncle is singing, aunty is singing' because it was like the whole house was singing!

I took my laddie along to the 6-2 game, I actually had a bet for Hibs winning 5-0 that day and also had them down for a 3-0 as well. I remember Durie took a throw in and Hearts scored but I kept saying to my laddie, who was about ten, 'It's still a matter of time, son.' The second half was fucking immense and big Mixu could have had a hat-trick before half time, he had one chalked off and then he got the two headers. It was superb, I'll never forget that!

There's a social member of the Hibs club who is actually a Hearts fan. He doesn't frequent the place during the week, mostly only on Sunday afternoons, and his wind-ups really piss people off but he's tolerated by the members who he drinks with. He was my downstairs neighbour and after the 2-1 game at

Tynecastle when Shiels and O'Connor scored, I sang through his letterbox. I thought, 'Fuck him, my turn to wind him up.'

I've heard people say, 'You can slag my wife and family but dinnae slag my football team!' I've seen people get really fucking upset just because someone's slagging their team and they say, 'That's my fucking team you're talking about!' They take it as a personal slight because they feel they are part of the club and it's a real deep insult to them. Maybe it's a build-up of frustration like, 'I go there and I fucking pay my money, I watch them week in, week out.' Some people say, 'I've watched them taking me from being that excited to that fucking low, and I go back and I watch them kick me in the fucking head again and again and again. Then it takes you, who supports another team, to say I am watching shit because I know I'm watching shit, I don't need you to fucking tell me!'

I sometimes think I was spoilt seeing Turnbull's Tornadoes during such formative years. I remember European games in the '70s against Juventus, Leeds, Liverpool, Rosenberg, Sporting Lisbon and teams like that. When you saw Arthur Duncan run like a whippet up that fucking wing it was superb. A lot of people my age could rattle the team off just like that.

There was a different wage level back then so players would say, 'We're happy here, why move?' Whereas now the players come and go, they're in and out. We had Whittaker, Brown, and Thomson who were quality players for us but they never actually made such an impact on the league.

There are a few games I would want to erase from my memory that were just terrible. The Livingston CIS Cup Final is definitely one that was a real kick in the balls. That same team which had so much potential after knocking out Rangers on penalties gave us a belief that we had already won that cup, which was shown by the fact that about 40,000 Hibs fans turned up. I still thought, 'Dinnae take this so lightly.' And losing to Liverpool away was such a disappointment after getting a not bad result up here and then capitulating to them something like 3-1, I think Toshack had a hat-trick. That was a totally different time in my life as well when you would be thinking, 'Maybe we can do something, Hibs are fucking great, because they played mighty Liverpool off the park at Easter Road!' You think, 'We can definitely do something this season.' The games come round and you play Rangers off the park, you get a result and you think, 'Great, we'll beat Celtic away.' We fall away – for example, how can we get beaten at places like Falkirk? I always think that we should be streets ahead of them, as I do if we draw against Partick Thistle and get knocked out of the cup by some team like Arbroath. I remember getting beaten by Arbroath in something like 1978 and it was a fucking nightmare! And they got back to Easter Road for the replay, they won and they had fucking Hearts strips on in to the bargain. I just felt so deflated and pissed off – how dare they do that to Hibs! It was looking so good but you think back and reflect, 'Well, that's fucking Hibs.' They build you up and pull the rug from under your feet!

On match days I normally come to the Hibs Club and then leave about quarter to, get round there and get in, and then the game spoils it! I remember a number of seasons ago when after eight seconds Stokes scored against Rangers and we played them off the park for 20 minutes. Then Riordan, back in defence, lost the ball and 'bang bang' Rangers score. Then 'bash', again and again. I thought, 'I dinnae believe this.' And I remember being 3-1 up against Rangers and they came back to win 4-3 when Gascoigne was still playing.

I used to work with a guy who was on the Hibs Pepsi advert. I knew where he stood because you could see him a mile away. He was a big fucking huge guy with grey hair and he always used to shout out 'HIBEES, HIBEES, HIBEES', and there would be nothing happening on the pitch at all. But you could hear him wherever you were and people would be like, 'Oh right there's that fucking guy again.' I also remember the 1979 Cup Final replay and two guys for the whole of the second half just singing constantly. It was a hell of a long time to sing 'There's only one Jackie MacNamara'. One would start to peter out and his mate would start up again, 'One Jackie MacNamara' just at the point you expected them to stop. It went on and on, and on and on, and on and on and I was like, 'Fucking hell man!' So I had to walk away from them. It was at Hampden and it was pissing with rain, there was sludge on the terracing at the so-called ' Celtic End' – although I preferred to call it the uncovered end because I didn't see why Rangers had the right to have an end of the stadium where it was covered.

There was one guy who used to go to all the under-19s, and apparently he went to a game where he managed to blag his way on to the team bus and then sit down with them all for the pre-match meal. Rumour has it that he ate Alex Miller's meal while he was off doing other stuff, so when Miller came back he was like, 'What the fuck have you done with my meal?' That guy had apparently never worked his whole life but he'd blag tickets off the players for tours to Europe. I once asked him, 'Where did you get your jacket?' And he was like, 'Aye, Mixu gave me this one'. It's always a leveller when you think, 'At least I'm no that fucking extreme.' But do these guys get any more disappointed than you when the team lets them down? Do they get any more elated than you when the team wins? I don't know if they do.

There are fans that collect the pin badges and scarves and cover their walls with them. I remember one guy – he used to spray 'Vodka rules' everywhere before he stopped drinking – he had every scarf you could get. He used to wear a full Hibs strips to games back in the days when it was unknown for people to even wear a replica top, and he always took a giant Hibs teddy bear to matches.

One guy was always shouting and bawling at the ref right through the whole game, he even started before kick-off. Sometimes you'd wonder if we were watching the same game. Hibs would be on the attack and he would be shouting at the linesman in front of us, he'd come up to the halfway line to continue shouting, and he'd still be shouting when Hibs were up at the other end skimming the bar with a shot. My dad told me about one time ages ago he'd bought 'black' tickets for the corporate area at Parkhead. Celtic had loads of nuns attending games back then he got up and shouted, 'C'mon Hibs, get into these bastards that are hiding behind white hoops, we are the ones wearing all the fucking green!' So he got chucked out.

In the '93 Cup Final I went on the 'Four in Hand' bus with my dad and the driver thought he was going to Hampden, then getting back on the route to Celtic Park he took us past loads of Rangers fans, so the word went round to hide the colours and keep quiet, and up steps my dad, opens the skylight and starts singing, 'We are Hibernian FC, fuck you, you dirty orange bastards.' I was sitting there thinking, 'Oh no!' when the whole bus started singing 'Coco's Dad, Coco's Dad, Coco's Dad...' There'd been a lot of talk of forged tickets and halfway up the stairs into the ground the Police were checking tickets. And there was my Dad saying, 'How do I ken you're not on the way back from a fancy dress party? How do I ken you're a real polisman? Where's your ID card? How do I ken that's no a forgery?' Meanwhile I was saying, 'C'mon Dad, let's just get in.'

I remember my uncle telling me about one time he was at Easter Road with a friend and it was a really mobbed game. They spotted a big space down at the front and started making their way there when my uncle suddenly stopped halfway down. There was a single guy standing in the middle of the space and the crowd was actually backing away from him, he was shouting such vitriolic abuse. Then my uncle started moving down again. 'Nah, it's all right' he told his mate, 'I know that guy. He's my brother in law.' It was my dad!

Despite everything, when I set foot in Easter Road I still feel a total vibe of expectation. What's the score gonnae be? Who's gonnae play? Who's no gonnae play? It's all about the tension and the trepidation!

Liz and Bill McBain

Liz McBain, born 1941.
Bill McBain, born 1936.

‘ One of my cousins had cigarette football cards and one of them was of my dad. I desperately wanted it and he wouldn't let me have it. ’

LIZ   We were away staying at Crieff Hydro once for the weekend and we thought, Och, it will be quite nice to go to the Hibs game in Dunfermline. The thing was, we missed a turning to Dunfermline, and where did we end up?

BILL   In Alloa or somewhere like that...

LIZ   We struggled on to get to the game. But that's the kind of thing that seems to happen to us. Even if you don't physically go you are always there in spirit, you always feel part of it and you always watch out for the score. We were talking to each other recently about the big matches that we had been at. We were reminiscing about the Leeds game, which wasn't on television or the radio. Back then I was very worried that night because Bill didn't appear home at the usual time. He was just late because there was extra time but I was so worried because you couldn't tune in and find out that the game was running late.

BILL   We were both at the Barcelona game in the Fairs Cup when the referee got attacked. Barca didn't have a Messi or anyone like that but they were still a top class side and yet against all odds, we won it. In those days my dad was technically neutral because we went both to Easter Road and Tynecastle, but we were more inclined to the Hibbies. We were standing on the terracing... I don't know how many were at Easter Road that night, there must have been 60,000... there was certainly a huge crowd. It was just such a great atmosphere.

LIZ   It was nail-biting.

BILL In those days Hibs had a decent team.

LIZ Yeah, but we still didn't expect them to win.

BILL It was a different type of football that Hibs played, none of this defensive stuff – you adjusted your team to suit the occasion and went on the attack.

LIZ I was about seven when my dad first took me to a game. It was against Celtic and of course the crowd wasn't segregated. We were behind the goals, packed in together. This Celtic supporter started swearing quite badly and I can remember my dad saying, 'I've got the wee one here!' And right away the guy said, 'I'm sorry, pal, I'm really sorry.' It was lovely that he apologised like that. There never appeared to be anything nasty, even though there was rivalry. We always went to the Hearts v Hibs games at New Year and there was never any bother, even at those matches.

We hadn't gone to a game for a good while but then we started going along again, it must have been maybe 20 years ago. The club had put up big wire meshes to separate the supporters! We were sitting there and it was a dire game for Hibs. Hearts scored and this poor soul on the other side of the wire, at the Hibs end, couldn't resist jumping up and down, and these horrible men were trying to climb over their seats to kill him! He obviously couldn't get a ticket for the away end. It was just a horrible thing to witness. When I used to go to matches first the fans were never separated and we never had any problems. I mean you weren't very happy if your team was getting beaten but you didn't take it out on the people beside you. You just accepted it and I think that's the way it should have stayed. We sometimes go to the rugby as well and there's no segregation, and there are never any problems.

BILL A real disastrous game was the Scottish Cup Final against Clyde. But it has to be remembered that Clyde were a better team in those days, they weren't quite as lowly as they are now.

LIZ We must have been in our teens because we had just got together.

BILL Christ, that's a long time ago.

LIZ Thank you, Bill! I've still got old pictures of my dad, who was the secretary of the Tynecastle Branch of the Hibs Supporters Club when we played Clyde in that final. My dad came back from the war pretty badly disabled so he got involved with organising the branch for something to do. We were on his bus, all pretty miserable at the end of the game, and we got into trouble with him because Bill and I were having a wee canoodle at the back. Dad was furious. It's a wonder he allowed him to marry me after that! He was embarrassed because one of the frosty wee ladies on the bus had made a comment about us, but it was our way of recovering!

My dad played for Hibs as an amateur before the war. My brother told me he used to get called Jumbo Johnston – Dave Johnston was his real name. One of my cousins used to have cigarette football cards and one of them was of my dad! I desperately wanted it and he wouldn't let me have it. I asked him about it relatively recently and he didn't know where any of these cigarette cards were now. It was so annoying. They were wee caricatures of the players, I think they may have been drawn by a cartoonist called Earl Wright.

BILL I'm not sure about that. Your dad was a friend of Earl Wright I think. The picture of him was a framed metal etching. Remarkably, Liz's dad also had a trial for Blackpool as a professional!

LIZ Yes, it was in the time of Stanley Matthews playing at Blackpool as well. I think the club had been asking him to come down to play for them but he was the youngest of a very big family and I think his dad had died recently. His mother didn't want him to go. My father lived in Waverley Place so he was steeped in Hibs from a very early age and although we lived at Carrickknowe we always went to Hibs matches. We never went to Hearts matches at all.

BILL I did because my dad went to see both teams, week in and week out, and I just tagged along. It was good, I enjoyed that.

LIZ I can't remember going to a Hearts match apart from if they played Hibs. Our middle son is a Hearts supporter now, he's a Jambo, can you believe it? It's really because we lived in the west of Edinburgh, and a neighbour who was few years older than him would take him to the Hearts matches, so he got used to it. I'll never forget going to the school to speak to a teacher about something and my son didn't know I was coming in. There he was, resplendent in his Hearts strip! I said to him, 'Have you just been to gym or something?' Then the teacher said, 'He always comes to school like that.' So the wee devil would leave the house in the morning, walk round the corner and change into his Hearts strip. That was back in the time when kids wore their ties and blazers so I was quite amused. He was a good footballer himself and he chose to support Hearts instead of Hibs. Maybe that's significant? I don't think he's so bothered now, he doesn't go to matches because in his early teens he was involved in a pitch invasion at a Hearts game. There was a lot of trouble. Although he wasn't really hurt, he never went to another match after that incident.

BILL Liz's dad, being secretary of the Tynecastle Supporters Club, became quite pally with Gordon Smith. Gordon gave him his cap and a shirt so we gave it to the Hibs Historical Trust. Seemingly they now have it in the boardroom.

LIZ Gordon Smith and my dad were really friendly. In fact, my dad introduced him to his wife to be, she was an Orcadian, like my dad. Everybody used to laugh when they heard that he was secretary of the Tynecastle Branch, for obvious reasons, but they used to organise some good dances and family events. I think you need people like him in this world, people who are prepared to organise things. The branch had quite a following. The young wives of the branch members at our local church had a fundraiser one time and my mum and dad came along. This wee lassie that I didn't know said to my dad, 'Davie! Hello!' Her and her friends had been camp followers, they were only about 15 years old and went to all the games on the bus. She said to me, 'Your dad always looks after us on the bus and makes sure we're alright.' That made me realise what a caring character he was. I remember him saying Hibs were playing against, I think it was Leith Athletic, and they had to have the police right round the pitch because they were such dirty players. He used to play the big drum in the Boys Brigade band. That might be why he was called Jumbo Johnston, because he wasn't fat, he was really thin. I don't think he was ever very musical but he could certainly bang a drum.

You don't ask the right questions at the right time with your parents. If you don't remember bits of information they tell you, they are forgotten forever. You keep meaning to tell your children things as well, but you end up being just as bad. My dad was a good storyteller and my daughter used to sit beside him on a pouffe beside his big chair, and listen intently while he told his stories about the war and the past. I wish I had recorded those conversations back then, I really do. The reason we don't have anything left from my dad was because my Auntie Mima hated photographs of herself so she just burned everything! That's what some people do. There was nothing of my dad apart from what we had, but I think that happens in families quite a lot.

Unfortunately he became ill, but he was never well really after he came back from the war. He had so many things wrong with him and then he had an accident where he damaged three or four vertebrae in his back. As a result of that he had to wear a corset and every so often he had to get a plaster cast put on from his torso all the way down to his groin. There was one very funny moment when I was at a match with him in the Centre Stand. He got into an argument with a fan of the opposition team. This particular chap said, 'Outside, now! Just come outside!' challenging him to a fight. My dad got up with his two walking sticks, he could hardly move with this damn plaster cast and of course the chap backed off: 'Sorry, mate...' It was one of those things you really remember because it was so funny! That's the kind of situation when things could have gone wrong. Deep down, I think people are really nice. Dad kept going to games up until not that long after me and Bill got married. Then he developed rheumatoid arthritis really badly, mixed with all his other problems. He was 51 when he had to retire so he wasn't old, and it got harder for him to go to games, but he was always following the Hibs on the radio and he still had a good relationship with some of the players. Gordon Smith came to visit him regularly. I was at the match when he had his leg broken. My dad was very upset because people called Smith a 'pansy' just because he wasn't the macho man type. I can remember Gordon was saying to the trainers, 'It's broken, it's broken!', and they still made him walk off the pitch! It was horrendous, it really was, you could tell it was broken and they had this attitude of 'Gordon the softie' or something like that, because he was never a player that really tackled too much.

BILL His hair was always immaculate! Gay Gordon didn't have the same connotations in those days...

LIZ In those days a leg break was much more serious. They didn't have all the physios and everything they do now. Gordon was always being attacked by other players. I'm trying to remember the Rangers player that was always fouling him... I think it might have been George Young. We had this picture of an overhead kick that Gordon Smith did, he gave it to my sister and inscribed it 'To Elizabeth with love from Gordon', but we can't find now. My brother David thinks that when he was a youngster he traced it so many times that he might have ruined it. David is a guitarist with Elton John and he played a big part in getting him to come and play at Easter Road in 2005. There were cartoons in the newspapers with 'Hibs sign up Elton John' and things like that. We took a big 'Welcome Home David!' banner to the gig.

 Going back to our childhood, once my brother came along, my sister and I were kind of out of the picture as far as being taken to games by our dad was concerned. But I still have some great memories of the matches he did take me to. In particular I remember Joe Baker being absolutely wonderful. There was a match way back, I think it must have been during the Famous Five times, Tommy Younger was in goal and it was so foggy he couldn't even see to the half way line, so he was yelling, 'What's happening? What's happening?' But they kept on playing, regardless! That proves they would play a game in any conditions – you genuinely couldn't see a damn thing!

BILL Tommy Younger was a big character in every sense of the word.

LIZ He was a big, cheery kind of chap. We got to meet some of the other players, like Lawrie Reilly, for example. You would see them at different events but we're not the pushy types who went up and tried to speak to all these guys. Back in the '50s I think we maybe weren't paying that much attention to the actual football. The kids today are the same. We've got two girls who sit in front of us in the stadium and they never look at the actual match, they're too busy preening themselves or whatever. When I was that same age I was more interested in the crowd standing on the terraces. I couldn't see much anyway because I was quite small compared to everyone else.

BILL Kids would usually get lifted up on to the barrier so that you could see.

LIZ We did, but it wasn't very comfy from what I can remember. You would also usually go to the end where you hoped they would be scoring goals.

Somebody said to me the other day that they wished Hibs had kept the slope. You know, if they win the toss nowadays, in the second half they still shoot down the down the slope, even though it doesn't exist anymore.

We're Church of Scotland and the minister at our church in Carricknowe was a great Hibbie. One time he had gone to the match straight from a funeral and the guy at the turnstile said to him, 'Father, just come in.' He was really embarrassed at being taken for a priest but I think he just went along with it and got in for free because that was the way things were back then. When you think about it now, with so many children lifted over the turnstile the official crowds must have been much smaller than the reality. They wouldn't think of asking you to pay for a youngster, whereas now there are probably wee tiny tots getting charged money to get in.

I don't remember much about people drinking at the game, maybe because my dad didn't partake in alcohol. I suppose it didn't even occur to me that people were drunk. Everyone gets so miserable now at games compared to games in the past, but was that only because Hibs used to be such a good team? I think because it's more comfortable now at games it maybe lacks something. We are in the West Stand and when I first went to our seats, I was shocked! There was a chap behind us, quite a nice chap, at the game with his grandson, and he couldn't stop himself from venting his spleen. The language of that man was just disgraceful. I was expecting him to have a heart attack, he would get so upset. So about a couple of years ago I turned round and said to him, 'You don't need to talk like that, there are youngsters around.' 'Other people were swearing as well as me!' he replied, almost like a wee boy, but he has never done it since. We have some quite nice people around us, quite a mixture.

The wee chap beside us gets really excited and always screams, 'Up the park, up the park!' But he goes off on cruises regularly and then we get one of his pals who comes in his place, he's quite a character as well. I thinks it's exceedingly important as a release of energy for people. I used to be very involved with politics and things like that, but I'm now more interested in the football. It somehow means more... is that a terrible thing to say?

BILL I think, as well, it's good to be able to get out of the usual routine, to belong to something and meet people along the way.

LIZ Yes, the belonging is really good. I would have loved it if I could have taken my children along when they were kids but we simply didn't have the money. I think they are actually very good with the kids at Hibs and there are free entry schemes now and things like that. A great-nephew of mine was one of the mascots and they were really nice to him, he's going along to the training ground near Tranent now.

When we seriously started back to watching Hibs, there were players like Scott Brown, Dereck Riordan, Brian Whittaker and Gary O'Connor. It was like the young team was somehow running free. It was just lovely, even if they got beaten at least they played exciting football. But at the moment, we are always saying,

'Oh come on! Pass the ball!' The thing is I don't mind getting beaten if we have played well and if we have really shown some good football in the process.

BILL   The current pay structure is against Hibs – they have a ceiling to how much they can pay players, they don't pay out-of-the-ordinary wages and that's why they can't attract the bigger names. I think that money kind of spoils the game now. It must be terrible down south with the salaries that they pay these guys. It's just outrageous! So that's why Hibs struggle to attract the good players.

LIZ   You sometimes look at some players who've gone to bigger teams and you wonder how good we could have been had we kept them all.

BILL   That's going to be an ongoing problem, they're not going to be able to attract the top players.

LIZ   But you keep hoping! We went to the European game against Maribor and when Maribor scored a chap near us stood up to leave. His pal said to him, 'What are you doing?' and he said, 'I cannae cope, I just cannae cope!' He had come to the game and then left within minutes, he just couldn't bear the ignominy. Not long after that Hughes was sacked. Poor John Hughes. We have known John for a long time because he played football with my son and he was an awful lad but a lovely lad as well.

BILL   The problem was his mouth. He was hard and fair but his mouth was the biggest problem.

LIZ   It's been proved since that nobody was going to be able to sort out that team. I always say, it surely doesn't take much just to get the ball in that net – why can't they just do it? Everybody is so absolutely over the moon when they

Davey Johnstone – Melody Maker football tourney, 1969.

'David is a guitarist with Elton John and he played a big part in getting him to come and play at Easter Road in 2005.'

score – it's so funny that every goal gives us all a shot of adrenaline. There was a time, being a Hibs fan, you expected to do well; but now we don't expect it, we are always just hanging on. For example, when we were 2-0 down against Dundee United recently, half the ground was already leaving, I don't think it was even half time. I hate that!

If you're a real supporter then you should support them through and through and you shouldn't boo them. When they booed Nish I though it was terrible. I prefer the tradition of booing the manager rather than the players. The thing about John Hughes was that when we were doing badly he wouldn't make a substitution or he would substitute players that were doing well. It seemed as if he didn't really know what was needed. I've got this feeling that when managers are on the touchline they can't really see what's happening. The rugby coaches sit up in the stand – it's probably better to be out of the way rather than have all these things happening around you.

BILL Me and Liz always stick with them until the end and something I've noticed is that there are more women going to games these days.

LIZ   Yeah, I've noticed hardly any women used to go, probably because the facilities were practically non-existent. All the men stood against the wall to pee so it wasn't really all that wonderful for women. Also, the enclosure didn't really provide you with much cover from the rain under the old stand, never mind the rest of the ground.

Regards the club's history, I'm only aware of its roots because of my dad but even then we still didn't know a huge amount about it. Some people believed that if you were a Hibs supporter then you must be Roman Catholic and we used to get annoyed about that. If someone made a comment you would say, 'We're just Hibs fans!'

Liz McBain's brother, Davey Johnstone, has been the guitarist with Elton John's band for over 30 years. He also plied his trade alongside the legendary Meat Loaf and Alice Cooper and still holds Hibs close to his heart.

'My earliest Hibs-connected memory is of Dad taking me to Gordon Smith's grocer's shop at Willowbrae when I was five. I remember he had great teeth, great hair and he gave me a Mars Bar!

'One sight I'll never forget is of Joe Baker running flat out trying to stop a ball going across the touchline. He didn't make it. I was right behind the goal and I heard him puffing and blowing (he was carrying a few extra pounds), and wheezing, 'Bastard!' I'll also never forget the friendly against Torino when my all-time idol, Denis Law, brought his special glamour to Easter Road. Strangely enough, the smell of beer and the sight of guys pissing into empty bottles are my other main memories of those times!'

BILL But it wasn't very often you would come up against prejudice.

LIZ I think it's always been there though. Even now, people usually show surprise that you are Hibs supporters if they learn that you are not Roman Catholic. There's a Jambo chap at our church who always makes funny comments about it. There's also a terribly vitriolic aspect to how Hearts feel about Hibs, and we have a Hibs chap in our circle who is exactly the same in reverse. He seems to hold a real personal grudge against Wallace Mercer. He says he tried to deliberately destroy Hibs – didn't just try to be better than Hibs, but actually tried to destroy the club! And there was one chap who lived opposite us – you couldn't have got a nicer, more intelligent and wonderful person – who was absolutely vitriolic against Hibs, really nasty when he spoke about them. It was most peculiar!

BILL He lived until he was 94 years of age. That's a long time to be so bitter!

LIZ If anybody said anything about supporting Hibs he would start. I think it's related in some way to religion. I'm very much against the sectarian aspect of the game. It seems funny to think of somebody supporting a team because of their background or their politics. And in terms of songs, I am absolutely fed up with 'Glory to the Hibees', it's so out of touch with what Hibs are now.

BILL I don't remember much singing on the terraces in the early days, even though they had plenty to sing about back then.

LIZ Usually though, I love to hear the young lads singing songs at the games even if I can't understand the words. Maybe we would join in if we could understand. I don't know if our attitudes have changed from when we were younger in terms of being beaten, Bill's still not a happy bunny when that happens!

BILL I don't carry it on from day to day though.

LIZ It's such a little thing to score a goal and make everybody go crazy, so why can't the team do it more often? But whatever happens we are Hibs fans. And there's a real community aspect which is a great thing. A friend of my daughter's for instance had a bad accident – he lost his legs and was badly burned. The supporters were really good to him and he still goes to watch Hibs every single week, it's still a wonderful thing in his life.

BILL That support through thick and thin that Hibs fans give the club is a big part of what it's all about.

LIZ The best atmosphere I remember was when we won that CIS Cup Final. It was really good, even though the weather was miserable – it was snowing. The

Barcelona game way back, and even the one at Murrayfield recently with Messi playing, these games had great atmospheres. I think Barcelona had said before the game that they didn't want any injuries so Hibs didn't go in too heavily. It was just lovely to see such great players. It was something else to watch Messi, he was just incredible!

BILL Yes, the Barcelona game first time around was quite a match.

LIZ We don't get a good press a lot of the time. I remember when Calderwood was not interested in re-signing Riordan. He came on the pitch head down, because he very easily gets upset. To me players like that need to be nurtured rather than knocked down all of the time. (I see the players almost like my children, I'm pleased if they're trying hard and doing well.) Anyway, after that there were big headlines in the newspapers: 'Riordan Sulks'.

The act of following Hibs would best be summed up as having been wonderful. It really has. And as 'old fogies' we can still happily go to these matches and enjoy them like we did when we were young. Mind you, when I was young I cared a lot about how I looked and now there's me in my furry hat not really caring too much about style any more. At our age, as long as you are warm, then who cares?

BILL I think you just have to keep cracking on, giving them your support and hoping that better times will come for Hibs.

LIZ Every season we get another chance at the Scottish Cup, so maybe it's our year. It would need to be a miracle but you never know, because miracles can happen.

Bruce Findlay

Music Business Manager, born 1944.

' By comparison to war, football was like rivalry between a bunch of pussy-cats. '

I WAS BORN in Chesser Grove, which is essentially Gorgie. When I was about four years old I remember being really excited on Saturdays when the street was mobbed with buses bringing visiting teams' fans to Tynecastle stadium. To me, at the age of four, this all seemed very exotic – at that time most people didn't even have cars!

Aged nine or so, I started to go to Tynecastle with a bunch of other kids – we'd get lifted over the turnstiles. The reason we were there wasn't so much to watch the Hearts as to collect bottles inside the ground, we'd fill a sack with 20 or 30 and take them to the local grocer's where we got about two old pence for each one. I remember those crowds of 30,000 or 40,000 people from the west of Edinburgh all cheering together. It would be wrong to say I was ever a Hearts fan though, they were just the local team.

My mum and dad got divorced when I was about six so I only remember my dad vaguely. My mum died in 1968. She was a fabulous woman. What a massive influence she had on me! She not only got me into the hippest football team the world has ever known, she also got me into music – the hippest business you could be in. How lucky am I? And I don't even come from Leith!

My Hibs eureka moment happened in 1951 or 1952. There was a live cup game on the radio at home and my mum was shouting, 'Come on Lawrie, come on Lawrie!' Then she shouts, 'Yes! Yes!' Not only was this a woman shouting about football but this was my mum. She was very artistic and I had never once heard her refer to football before, so it was all quite bizarre. I said to her, 'Why are you so excited?' and she said 'Lawrie has scored!' – this was Lawrie Reilly, a Hibs legend (although I've since learned that as a player he had to have a part time job to keep his wages up).

I said, 'Mum, I can't believe you were shouting along to the football, for Lawrie Reilly and Hibs!' Hibs were the enemy because they came from the other side of town from us. It turned out she actually knew Lawrie Reilly. She told me that he was the man who had painted my bedroom the year before and that he worked for Armstrong Sinclair (a local Jambo painter-decorator, Lawrie was his apprentice).

I went to school the next day a Hibs fan! At Stenhouse Primary, football was the big thing. I remember it was almost like being a born-again Christian, I went straight in and announced, 'I'm a Hibs fan!' Immediately my two mates, Alan and Dougie, both piped up and said, 'So are we!' It was a total identity, particularly for Alan, whose nickname was Nally Gordon. We ended up going together for the next few years. Even kids as young as seven went to football matches on their own in the early '50s. Alan, Dougie and I caught the tail end of the legendary Hibs team when they were still the best team in the world. Forget Celtic *circa* 1967, that Hibs team were the best team the world has ever seen!

At Tynecastle, while collecting bottles, I'd caught glimpses of the football but when I went to Easter Road I never ever looked for bottles, I watched the games. Easter Road could hold nearly 70,000 people and it would regularly fill up for Hearts, Rangers and Celtic games – 25,000 was a poor crowd. The squash could be pretty tight but we kids would get in for nothing, we'd get lifted over. We always stood at that corner where the old Cowshed was. It was absolutely brilliant, you could sit with your legs over the wall. The stewards would come over and say, 'Put your legs over.' They were worried the wee boys would get their legs bashed. Those were the days when old men – they could have been dirty old men but never were – looked after you. Fights and all sorts of heaviness would go on but I never, ever felt frightened. I felt excited, thrilled, slightly nervous, but never frightened, because whoever 'Mister' was would always look after you. There was a respect for old and young. It was a genuinely fabulous time, you were watching poetry in motion as the 'Gay Gordon' came waltzing down the wing. The pitch sloped – it was known as the Easter Road slope – and when Hibs won the toss they would always kick down the hill for the second half. No matter what happened in the first half you thought to yourself, It's OK because they're kicking down the slope next half. If they were 1-0 up at half time it was dangerous because they might take it easy but if they were losing they always stood a chance of winning the game.

When we got to the age of 10 or 11 we sometimes joined the coaches to go to away games. Hibs became an obsession. We had a great football team but slowly it was changing. Lawrie Reilly, my hero, kept on getting injured and there was one season he hardly played at all. I wasn't aware it was 'political' and that he was fighting for a testimonial. Gordon Smith had got a testimonial and was still playing, Willie Ormond was still playing but Bobby Johnstone had been sold. The same 11 players would play every week; if they didn't, it was because they were injured. It wasn't as if the manager was playing 'fun and games' with a pool of 16 players, they didn't have pools of players in those days. If you weren't playing that meant you were dropped, you weren't just 'rested' and all these expressions they use nowadays – you were just fucking dropped! It was a kind of honesty and the players just accepted it.

Gordon Smith was the best football player I have ever seen in my life and still today I can't think of anyone better. Johann Cruyff was good, Pele was good but Gordon Smith was a genius! He played keepy-uppy – the only other person I saw doing that was Jim Baxter at Wembley in 1967. Gordon Smith never took the piss, he didn't think he was showing off but that's what made it even better because the reality was that he was showing off! He would do keepy-uppy with his head, knee, shoulder and all the legitimate parts of your body that you could use. He would keep the ball in the air and run 20 yards with it, he was awesomely good! Gordon Smith got so much stick from other players because he was such a genius and he was also taller than Lawrie Reilly. He was an incredibly handsome guy, I thought he looked a bit like Gregory Peck.

I never met Gordon Smith and I only met Lawrie Reilly a few years ago for the first time in my life, him at 84 years of age, me at 66. I nearly cried when I met him, I was choked. It was at an awards night at the Corn Exchange. I asked him, 'Did you once work for a guy called Armstrong Sinclair?' And he confirmed, 'Oh yeah, he was my uncle.' I told him that Armstrong's wife was my mum's best friend and mentioned how she had been electrocuted with an electric kettle in her kitchen on Gorgie Road – I can still visualise my mum coming into my bedroom in floods of tears and waking me up. So here was I trying to recount the story to Lawrie, and Lawrie, at 84 years of age, correcting me – it had been an iron. I thought that was fabulous.

It was only when I read his book that I understood the ins and outs of why he didn't play towards the end of his career. It had nothing to do with age, he retired at only 29. He was dropped because he was arguing about his wages and his testimonial. And also he'd got injured a lot latterly, they couldn't fix him and they used to put him back out too soon. But he was a genius. He was just great to watch, he was like a terrier. Gordon Smith, though, was majestic,

Lawrie Reilly (centre) playing for Scotland v Sweden, 1953.

'Lawrie Reilly, my hero, kept on getting injured and there was one season he hardly played at all.'

like a pedigree horse running down that right wing, going inside and outside; weaving, ducking and diving. He would ultimately cross the ball on to Reilly's head: Bang! Or on to Eddie Turnbull's foot: Thunderbolt! Eddie had the hardest shot I have ever seen in football. I saw a guy being knocked out by one of his shots, it was so thundersome. And Willie Ormond could score a goal from the byline, I've never seen anyone score goals like Willie Ormond did. So catching the tail end of the Famous Five was magic for me. It was downhill after that because all we got was Joe Baker. How good was Joe Baker! Even Lawrie Reilly admits it.

Joe Baker was kind of my age, he was handsome, he was hip, he was cool. We weren't interested in the players' private lives, who their girlfriends were, whether they were straight or gay – it was all about football. What you saw was what you got! My life and my career has been showbiz, rock'n'roll showbiz, but showbiz nonetheless. What you get on stage or what you get on the football park is one thing and what you get off the park can disappoint or impress. It shouldn't really be important because the poetry is what it's all about. I would describe Gordon Smith as the best poet I have ever seen.

My second favourite Hibs player, when it comes to pure football, is Alex Cropley. He was sold far too soon. That was the beginning of the era of Hibs selling great football players. They let Gordon Smith go because they thought he was old and then he went and won the fucking championship at Hearts, *they* let him go and he went and won it with Dundee. Come on! Nowadays it's different because David Beckham was being offered something like £50,000 a week to play at 35 but Gordon Smith was still a kid at that age – he retired at 39 or 40 I think. He got kicked to death though. His cure for his ankles, which got broken and certainly bruised and bashed lots of times, was running in the sand dunes at Gullane. He argues to this day how it strengthened his ankles running in the sea and the sand, that's what he believed so therefore I believe it. If you've got an injured player anywhere in the world, come to the east coast of Scotland!

Signed from juvenile side Edinburgh Thistle in 1944, Reilly went on to hold the record for Scotland caps of any Hibs player before or since. He earned the nickname 'Last Minute Reilly' after scoring a last minute goal for Scotland against England in 1953 and he was Hibernian's top goalscorer for a remarkable seven seasons between 1950 and 1957. During that time he also collected two League Championship medals, scoring an amazing total of 185 goals in 257 league appearances for Hibs. Towards the end of his career he became embroiled in strike action over the club's refusal to grant him a testimonial match. Due to continual injury problems, his career ended in 1958 when he was only 29 years old. In his final game he helped Hibs achieve a 3-1 victory over Rangers at Easter Road.

I always thought the Hibs strip was better than the Hearts one. It's sexier, so I can understand why girls might like Hibs better than Hearts. Maroon is a 'dead blood' sort of colour. Green is about springtime and life, it's about rebellion and all kinds of other things. There is a huge difference between Hibs and Hearts! Hearts = right, Hibs = left, Hearts = establishment, Hibs = anti-establishment. I have been totally aware of that from day one, from Lawrie Reilly, from my mum who was anti-establishment and from my dad who was total establishment and a Hearts fan.

In fairness, Hearts were awesome in the late '50s. They had Willie Bauld and Alfie Conn, so we have to give credit to them. As far as the derby matches went, Hearts tended to win them and that's why the 7-0 game is such a legend in Hibs folklore. Hearts used to stuff us even when we were the best team in Edinburgh and were playing well. The rivalry back then was big-time but it was just friendly banter. In those days there was no segregation, there was a traditional Hearts end and a traditional Hibs end, so that was where you would stand at first until they tossed the coin and then you thought, Fuck it – we'll have to move to the other end. You can't imagine it now but three-quarters of the crowd, apart from those sitting, would move round. When it was a sell-out, as when Hibs and Hearts played, the crush in the middle was just amazing! Did I hate Hearts? Of course I did, but I was still best pals with a lot of Jambos. People talk about being at rugby matches, screaming and yelling for your team, and afterwards going to the pub together for a drink. One of you might be a wee bit happier than the other and then there is a wee bit of you drowning your sorrows and 'The drinks are on me!' or whatever. Football was like that as well back then.

All the kids were down the front. You could squeeze through the crowd no problem, you would even get a lift on people's shoulders. It would still be like that today if it wasn't for the Ibrox disaster. They talk about crowds swaying but seeing Hampden on television in the late '50s was incredible: 130,000 people swaying in that stadium. I was in those crowds and it was brilliant – I never felt like I was going to die.

Hibs were doing reasonably well in the late '50s but probably by then Hearts were the better Edinburgh team. Lawrie was coming to the end of his career, Joe Baker was coming in and scoring goals – but then again, he scored every time he touched the bloody ball! Joe Baker was a goal machine like nobody has ever seen, forget that guy Boyd who played for Rangers last year because Joe Baker pisses over him. Baker was dangerous but he could also play football. Everybody back then wore those dirty grey boots you used to have to screw the studs into. They even used to play with leather footballs that deliberately got weighted down. If you see photographs of the crowd, they are still wearing those old-fashioned hats and twirling those rattles. There was cheering and yelling, you still got fights and rivalry, but the fact that you were still able to swap ends of the ground tells you a lot. There was a 'self-policing' type of thing going on that helped a lot. Nowadays, there are sometimes four rows of separation.

I can understand people who don't come from Manchester being fans of

Manchester United because they are a great team. Likewise, tell me someone that doesn't admire the Real Madrid of the '50s? But I don't think Hibs ever had the benefit of that kind of support; to be honest, I don't even remember people with Fife accents at Easter Road unless we were playing Dunfermline. So I think it's a wee bit romantic to suggest that people travelled from all over to watch Hibs back then. But we were famous for our style of football and I do believe that we inspired players in South America. We introduced floodlights and undersoil heating and we were also the first team in Scotland to have regular off-season tours to the rest of the world. Forget about Rangers and Celtic, they were parochial crap, very rich football teams who didn't do anything like that because they had no imagination! They just thought that they were 'the people'. Unlike them, Hibs have always understood internationalism.

In the 1950s we were still in the aftermath of the war, so there was this sense of togetherness. By comparison to war, football was like rivalry between a bunch of pussycats. It was genuine rivalry and just as fierce as today, but much friendlier. It's hard to believe that I used to go to the 'enemy' end of the ground and not feel physically threatened. You might have felt verbally threatened – I tell you, the banter in the 1950s was ten times better than it is now. The ribaldry, or the rivalry, in verbal abuse that we gave each other absolutely dominated. I am very 'political' with a small 'p' but I believe in community and I have a sense of that when it comes to articulating what we really mean. Give me Bob Dylan, John Lennon or Billy Connolly, give me comedians, poets or rock'n'roll lyricists over football pundits, commentators or politicians! Humour is a wonderful way of getting over your venom without offending. Give me, any day of the week, the word over the sword!

The adult world did sometimes seem a bit scary. I remember one time when I was not quite shaving, I was at a Celtic v Hibs match. We got beaten and I was crying at the end of the game. As I was leaving a bunch of Celtic fans that were all joyous with each other turned to me to encourage me to be part of their 'joyousness'. They saw I was crying. They also saw that I was a wee laddie and to this day I remember this guy who had a flat cap on. I felt threatened as he cuddled me and pulled me in because he was a hard looking man. 'Dinnae cry laddie, your team have got nae class; he said. 'You know the difference between your team and my team? Your team have got nae class!' I instantly hated him!

I had been brought up under the influence of art and culture to think I was intelligent and bright, and to believe that these things were more important than physical power. This was the first time I thought: 'I hate Glasgow, I hate Celtic, I hate flat caps, I hate you.' Looking back, that was a terrible thing to think, and I can see that being from Edinburgh, perhaps I thought we were the 'bosses' of those guys from Glasgow, so there was a wee element of that.

Another time was when I took my kids Sally and Ollie to their first football match when they were six or seven. Hibs were 'enjoying' fifth or sixth place in the league and the game was against Celtic. It was a big crowd and I was at the Celtic end of the stand. Hibs won and the Celtic fans went ape shit and invaded the pitch – if Celtic had won then I think they might have won the league, certainly it was a crucial game for them. Before the end of the game the crowd got really volatile and they were f'ing and c'ing. I'm a bit of an f'r and c'r myself but not when kids are around. My kids were frightened. They started saying, 'Dad, I'm not liking this.' Even though we were winning I took them away about ten minutes before the end of the game. Those were the two moments where I didn't like football and where I sensed a kind of 'violence' in the air.

Funnily enough, if there's another team in Scotland that I quite like (apart from Falkirk of course as I'm a wee bit of a 'Bairn'), it's Celtic. I have a certain sympathy for them because I used to think that they adopted rebels. One reason Hibs are the best team in the world is because we also take on rebels, down-and-outs, weirdos and nutcases. There is no racism at Hibs. I'm proud of Edinburgh and I'm proud of Hibs because we attract people from any part of the world and it doesn't matter whether they are lower, upper or middle class.

People say they support Hibs because of the 'Catholic thing' but to me it's nothing to do with that, because I am an atheist. My dad was a total Wee Free from Helmsdale and my mum was more of an atheist. She did encourage me to go to church but I think that was to get rid of me on a Sunday morning for a bit of peace and quiet. My mum was my inspiration, she understood bohemia and to me Hibs are a bohemian team full of romantic notions. People might say, 'Yeah, but they have never proved it on the pitch,' but yes they have and I live to remember it, not once but a second time around in the 1970s. As a manager Eddie Turnbull was a hardnosed wee bastard and we all know that famous story when he said, 'Gordon, the trouble with you is that your brains are in your heid!' I was at school with Alan Gordon for a short while and we bonded immediately. By the time I was running my record shop in Rose Street, he was playing alongside Jimmy O'Rourke, Alex Cropley, John Brownlie and that crowd, and what a fucking team that was. If it wasn't for Joe Harper being imported for £180,000, they would have gone on and won the league because we had just won the League Cup and we had also won a Summer Cup. To my mind we may have been the best team in Britain. We were certainly the best team in Scotland. We didn't win the league and we didn't win the cup but that's because we expected that we should. We became a bit flamboyant but we're bohemians for god's sake... so we got carried away! There's nothing ruthless about us and I think that's another reason Hibs don't win very much – because when we are good we begin to enjoy it too much.

I discovered rock'n'roll and Kerouac's On the Road in my late teens and went hitchhiking around the world but I always keep in touch with what was happening with Hibs. You hear about fans that have emigrated and the first thing they do is check the results for the Hibs score. If I had emigrated myself I doubt if I would ever have become as big a fan of any other team.

One of the great moments for me was standing outside the Balmoral Hotel looking up at the open-top bus and seeing Alan Gordon up there looking down at me. We hadn't seen each other for years but he recognised me. I got a wee thumbs up from him. I was so thrilled we won something, I don't care if it was just the League Cup, in fact it actually takes the same amount of effort to win it. But until we win the Scottish Cup we are going to get the piss taken by all sorts of people. I almost hope we never win it because we will always be more attractive than any other football team in the country and that's what it's all about.

Some of the Hibs players used to come in and buy records at my shop. It must have been crap they bought because I can't remember any of it, it was probably stuff like the Moody Blues. I got quite friendly with some of them and there are stories that I could, tell, to do with cannabis, but I won't. If players came into the shop I never asked if there was any chance of getting on the guest list and I never went 'back-stage' at Hibs until the last ten or 15 years and I was never part of the Hibs showbiz set.

My shop became a success within months of opening and I had such wonderful staff there that I could take Saturday afternoons off to go and watch Hibs. I used to go with Andy Scappaticci, who ran the King Thistle restaurant in Thistle Street, and Owen Hand, who was a folk singer and is sadly dead now. The three of us went to Easter Road virtually every week and also to some away games. Scappaticci is one of the funniest guys I have ever known in my life who didn't become a stand-up comedian – he must have influenced Robbie Coltrane, comedy-wise. Owen Hand was a poet and a songwriter. So standing on the terracing with these guys and watching Hibs with them during the period 1969 to the mid-1970s, was joyous.

In the old days players were allowed to live out their careers. In the '80s we still had the likes of Eric Schaedler and Arthur Duncan – guys who deserve legendary status because of what they were doing in the '70s, but who were 'dead' football-wise by that time. Nowadays players are playing on longer, partly because of advances in medical science. Also they can get rested because teams play with pools of 15 players. Back then teams had 11 players plus 11 reserves. Arthur Duncan was famous, like Arthur Sproule in more recent years, because of his pace. In fact he was even faster than Sproule, he could probably run a hundred metres in ten seconds. He couldn't really dribble that well but he was so fast he would beat five players and he would get down to the byline and you would shout, 'Cross it, cross it! Cross it!' before he ballooned it into the crowd. Most of the time though, he did get good crosses in. I think he must have had more games for Hibs than anyone. The players played for their shirts back then. They never kissed the shirt and they never threw it in to the crowd because they didn't need to do that to prove that they played for their team. If I was a football player today, with 66 years of experience in life, and I scored the winning goal in 2011 that kept Hibs in the Premier League, I would take my shirt off and I wouldn't throw in to the crowd, I would leave it on the ground and I would jump into the crowd. I would be so in love with the fans and they would be in love with me so I would want to make love to the crowd! There is something not very genuine about some of these guys who are pretending to do something similar and still making their money at the same time.

I'm a fan of Hibs' last best team – the Duncan/Alex Cropley period in the early 1970s. Around the time Punk Rock happened,independent record shops were dwindling as giants like Virgin and HMV moved in, and so I got into managing bands. While I was managing Simple Minds I opened an office on Frederick Street and always went to Vito's, the Italian restaurant downstairs. I'm talking the late '70s and early '80s. Wallace Mercer also went there on a pretty regular basis and although we both differed so strongly when it came to football and politics, I liked him. He liked the banter.

I remember going down to the restaurant and asking him, 'What's this I have been reading about you wanting to take over Hibs?' And he said, 'I don't want to take over Hibs.' I said, 'You do really.' And he said, 'Bruce, you and I are both business people, you understand from an economic point of view that combining Hibs and Hearts together, with a new ground holding 30–40,000 people, would be a good idea. We could compete with Rangers and Celtic.' So here he was talking like a mathematician. And I said, 'You're misunderstanding the heart and you're misunderstanding the point of football. Don't you understand how important Hibs are to Leith and the whole East End of Edinburgh? It won't double the crowd and you will kill both communities – both communities!' He smiled and we agreed to disagree but I do think my comments registered. I'm sure I wasn't the only one that said that to him. Wallace Mercer said a couple of years later, 'It wasn't a takeover, it was an amalgamation of two clubs.' But it was a takeover. It was 'Edinburgh United'. But I would say that, perversely, what Mercer did has worked out for the best.

I understood absolutely where he was coming from but I don't think he was a football fan so in that respect he was a wee bit like our man Farmer. He was a business man, and business people are not that emotional. Perhaps that's why I have never been the most successful business person. Hibs today are unique in Scotland because of their financial structure. They have re-invented the club. Apart from Ibrox and Parkhead, we have the best football ground in Scotland. It's a huge achievement, given that we have barely won anything in 20 years, that we have a wonderful, compact, ground of international status and facility. And we don't have a massive debt, whereas every other club in Scotland does. Petrie, for all that a lot of fans hate him, has got the finances right. That's one of the things that's comparable with the 1950s, Hibs being progressive.

Derek Riordan was a maverick wee character and the best thing he did was coming back to Hibs. The worst thing he did was leaving for big money at Celtic, where he was stuck on the bench. To me, that was shocking! Derek Riordan was no Alan Gordon, if you know what I mean, and I don't want to say anything derogatory about him because he was my hero at the time and to be honest I loved him! Lawrie Reilly was not the most intellectual and I don't know if Gordon Smith was either, but he looked smart, like Franck Sauzee did. With other players you think, 'That guy is a smart player.' With 'Big Yogi' John Hughes I wish in many ways that he had been given another couple of months because he was definitely passionate enough. What do we want? Do we want some intellectual to manage the club or do you want some passionate guy? I want a balance between the two, if you know what I mean.

There is a romance about Hibs. I like them because of what they stand for

– the outsider, the downtrodden, the rebel. They are anti-establishment but not blindly. We are always a modern club and that is the point of Hibs I think. Hibs stan for something that is much broader than that. I love the fact that we have imported players, not because we can afford a fee of 20 million pounds but because we recognise the talent in the guy, his of spirit and passion for the game. They might not necessarily understand Leith but someone like Zemmama does now. I loved that guy. And I loved Latapy as well – he is still a genuine legend in his own country. I bet that one of the best periods of his life was with Hibs. It was the same with Sauzee, he was kicked out far too soon. These guys seemed to get the notion of what Hibs are about. Home-bred players like Reilly, Riordan and O'Connor can get sucked away by money. But I know that if it was me getting £1,000 a week with Hibs and I was offered ten times that with Rangers, I would tell them to go and stick it up their fucking arse because I'm getting enough money!

Hibs are arguably the most disappointing team in Scotland right now – we are hurting. At the end of the day Hibs could go down to the division below or even the division below that, but I would still be a fan. For me, life is all about the love of family, the love of friendship and the love of going to a Hibs football match. Hibs mean more than sport, Hibs are a community! There are fans who would say that Hibs are their whole life but that's never been the case with me. Buddy Holly, John Lennon and Bob Dylan had as big an impact. Essentially I'm a rock'n'roll man, which is one of the reasons Hibs is my favourite team – they attract the same kind of people, the mavericks, the wild and the rebellious. I think that's why I identify with them.

To use a music metaphor, Hibs are not Arcade Fire and they are not The Clash, although there's a bit of that in them. Hibs are the Flaming Lips... I daren't say The Proclaimers. I love the Proclaimers and they are pals of mine but I think even they would agree with me. If The Proclaimers had the 'Gay Gordon' in their band, then yes, they might be.

If Hibs were a band they would be the coolest band in Britain and they would never go to number one in the charts except by a fluke – but they would continue to survive.

Eilidh Munro

Graduate, born 1989.

' The 2007 CIS Cup Final was one of the best games I've ever seen. It had this inexplicable feel about it that this time everything was going to be different. '

THE REASON I am a Hibs fans is pretty simple really. My dad is a Hibs fan, and the reason he was a fan was because his dad was also a Hibs fan. It's just been passed down through the family, but I didn't actually start to get interested in football until I was about 11 or 12 when we watched a game on TV, and I really enjoyed it! My dad never forced me into supporting Hibs, but at the same time, I never really thought of supporting anyone else. I never thought, 'OK, I'll see who's the best team in Scotland right now and choose them.' It was partly the football side of it that appealed to me and partly the excitement of just being a fan and getting behind your team. It was possibly a Scotland match that I first watched, certainly it was a game where it seemed to be clear cut who you were supposed to support. I don't remember a lot about going along to that first game, but I do remember it was just really exciting to see the players performing in real life, and I felt that sense of community sitting beside other fans, supporting your team together. It was much, much better than watching football on TV because you can experience everything around you. You kind of miss out on that real atmosphere when you watch it on TV. I still go with my dad and we buy our season tickets for seats beside each other. It's definitely a way of bonding with him.

I still have the first scarf that I bought and I wear it for most games. I'm pretty sure it's never been washed, which I suppose is pretty disgusting really! It's not really made any difference either way, so I don't know why I continue to wear it, I just do... I don't really have any other superstitions but I did have a cap that I wore to a few games and we lost every single one, so I have never worn that one again since then!

When I first started supporting Hibs it was around the time that we played

AEK Athens and that particular game was my first one at night. It was a totally different atmosphere and it was a European game. I felt that sort of bitter-sweetness of winning but not actually going through to the next round. It was back at a time when you could be proud of watching Hibs play.

The 2007 CIS Cup Final was one of the best games I've ever seen. It had this inexplicable feel about it that this time everything was going to be different. It just felt like it was our time to win something. I distinctly remember that I didn't want to presuppose anything until the final whistle went. Because it was Hibs, the outcome could have gone either way. That feeling is probably not unique to Hibs but equally I don't think anyone would like to curse their team by thinking, 'OK, we've won now.' 5-1 was a pretty convincing result but because you can be 2-0 down and still come back from it I felt apprehensive. If Hibs are losing, I constantly have the hope that they are going to turn it round: 'C'mon! There's ten minutes left, we could still score three goals!' It's physically possible, even though it's unlikely, but you still have to have hope!

We sit in the lower West Stand behind the home dugout. You get to hear the managers shout instructions to the players. John Hughes was constantly shouting at the team, he was always up off the bench gesticulating, whereas other managers have been much more reserved. I don't know if that was him as a person or if that is just the way that he worked.

I really like the new ground. It's a proper stadium now, but it's a shame we've hardly ever seen it full. You've got to see a change on the park before you can get more people to come back. We do have fans that are out there – in the CIS Cup Final there were more fans than I've ever seen in my life. Why they don't come along every week has to be a money issue, because it's not cheap to go to the football and it is a lot of money for a season ticket. The club does have a payment plan now – it was a massive one-off payment before – but I think it's still a lot for people to pay in a few months and even individually the games are quite expensive. I'm not really aware of how the old ground looked. I do know that they used to have standing before it was seated. I know that my dad used to go with his dad and he talks about starting the 'Hibees Bounce' in the old East Stand and getting a lift over into the ground when he was a kid. I think my dad is pleased that I am interested in Hibs but he doesn't really make a huge deal out of it. I guess he gave me the option that if I didn't like it then I could just give up and so it has always been my choice. I have nobody to blame but myself!

There are a few games that I would prefer to erase from my memory. The CIS Cup Final against Livingston in 2004 was pretty shameful. I was thinking, 'This is our time to win something.' I didn't see any reason why we shouldn't win and I was gutted when we lost! I just wanted to leave and forget it. I didn't hang about to see Livingston lift the cup.

I really liked Franck Sauzee, he was a great player and you could tell he had a real connection with the club, he wasn't just a 'pay cheque' kind of guy, which I think is the problem with quite a few of the players nowadays. Not that any of them are ever going to get big bucks at Hibs, but I think Sauzee did genuinely care about how well he played, and the way he spoke about the club was very affectionate. It's not fair to say that all the players don't care. Probably the younger ones that have come up through the youth system do care and are a lot more attached to the club than some of the older players. You don't hear many of them saying that they have affection for the club like Sauzee did, or talking about the honour of playing for the club. I mean, that's what you hope for and what you want to hear, one of them saying that it's been a boyhood dream of theirs to play for Hibs, but you just don't hear it! We, as fans, want them to be fans as well. We want them to care as much as we care, so if they turn round and say, 'It's just a derby defeat, what does it matter?' your reaction is, 'You just don't understand!' You want them to feel the same passion that you do for the club. The thing is, none of the players seem to stay for a long time. I still think that they should have some kind of attachment even if it's a little naive to expect them to. In an ideal world they would all care, but it's too much to expect every single player to have grown up as Hibs fans.

In terms of recent players, Riordan should have been a favourite of mine – he was with us for quite a long time and he scored a lot of goals but he was not a favourite because of his poor attitude. I always felt like his heart was not really in it. Maybe it's because he didn't make it at Celtic, or maybe that's unfair. I do think he cared about the club, but maybe not as much as he did about himself, which is a common trait among players nowadays. The younger players like Wotherspoon and Stevenson, I always think that they tried, and for me that effort is more important than actual skill. Obviously you would love to have someone like Messi on the team. That is my real criticism of Riordan, that he just didn't seem to put in enough effort. When he was good he was really good and you wouldn't have swapped him for anyone, but there's so many times that you felt like he couldn't be bothered and didn't care... it was so disappointing! If he had always tried, he would undoubtedly have had the full support of all the fans.

I haven't watched Hibs long enough to have a favourite team because we are

6 I really liked Franck Sauzee, he was a great player and you could tell he had a real connection with the club. **9**

constantly changing, but I think they played at their best under Tony Mowbray, which kind of goes without saying. I'm not sure that he had the best team but I think he got the best out of them. Celtic and Rangers just grind out a win because that's just what they always do. But I don't know how much I would want to support a team that goes out to win everything by any means possible. I would say skill and entertainment is really important and that's something that Hibs became known for. Sometimes they play really well and it's really exciting and good to watch, it's nice football, and sometimes it's just dire and you can't bear to watch it.

I haven't thought a lot about the differences between Hibs and Hearts. I would say that there are probably a lot more similarities than differences, because other than who you are supporting, the fans have a lot in common. You are still watching a team that doesn't win every league and cup every year, so you get used to failure. I haven't ever really thought about what Hearts fans expect of their team. I wouldn't expect that they demand to see 'silky soccer' as much as Hibs fans but maybe that's just my own personal bias coming in? Hearts aren't as well known for that kind of football but they are doing a lot better than us, so they probably don't care. The atmosphere at derby matches can sometimes be more bitter than against the likes of Celtic and Rangers, but at the same time, it's a relatively friendly rivalry. I have never seen any 'bad' incidents, although I know that they happen. I would say for the vast majority of fans the derby match is special, it's one of those games that you just have to win!

After we won the CIS Cup Final in 2007 we were coming back through from Glasgow to get to the City Chambers. My dad knew that there was going to be a small reception there and that the team was going to take the bus down to Easter Road before parading the cup round the stadium. While we were racing back through in my uncle's car, my dad was very eager to get back before the team did. We got through in plenty of time. My mum and my sister were there as well, the glory hunters that they are… The players were piped into the

Franck Sauzee made an early start to his senior career, making his debut at the age of 17 for French club Sochaux. However, it was at Marseille where he first tasted success, winning two consecutive league championship medals in his first two seasons. After a brief spell with Monaco, he returned to Marseille and helped them lift the European Cup in 1993.

With 39 caps for France under his belt, Sauzee joined Hibs in 1999 and quickly fell in love with his adopted club. Famously, his front teeth were knocked out as he was scoring a goal in a 3-1 victory against Hearts in March 2000 – such was his commitment to the cause. Sauzee was regarded as a true gentleman and a man who really grasped the importance of pulling on the famous Hibernian jersey. 'Le God' was his nickname and Le God he will remain, forever written into the folklore of the club.

building and they paraded the cup around. There were lots of photos taken with the Lord Provost and various councillors. Me and my dad got our picture taken with Rob Jones and the cup – we looked like dwarves alongside him. There was a bus that the players, the manager and the support staff were on – the bus with the cup. Then there were two buses behind that and the second one was also an open top bus, it was the one playing music, so I went with my dad onto that one, but apparently we were supposed to get on the one behind that, which was a normal coach. Anyway it was great fun and the bus was bedecked in all the flags and scarves. It's something I'll never forget, especially as we hadn't realised we were not supposed to be on that bus! I just blindly followed my dad and it was brilliant! Otherwise, we would just have been sitting looking out the windows and you wouldn't have got quite the same atmosphere, seeing all the people in the streets cheering as the team went past with the cup.

The people who sit behind us at the games are really moany, it kind of annoys me sometimes. You think, 'Why do you even come?' And there's a woman that sits near us, she shouts loudly at every single game, trying to spur the team on. Her voice rings out above all the others. But being beside the same people for a season has never really been an issue for me, there's never been anyone so bad you have to move away. I guess you forgive them, because you understand their passion and frustration. It's probably a good way for people to vent their anger and it's always related to the football, it's never a case of hurling abuse at players for no reason at all and it's usually for a good reason. Its been a bit of an escape for me watching Hibs, but it sometimes makes you wonder why you do it, especially when they are losing every week and you come out of the ground thinking, 'Why did I watch that?' But it's an escape being there, focused on your team winning. So you also come out of the ground thinking, 'OK, it was only a loss, so get over it.' Coming away with a victory puts you in a good mood for the rest of the day. My mum always moans about how we come back with long faces after a loss. I wouldn't say that I was that affected after the game, but I suppose I must be. That's why it's good when you're winning.

I don't place a great deal of importance on the club's roots but I do know a priest started the club and then took some of the team across to Glasgow and started Celtic. I don't think that the Irish connection is hugely important. When I watch Hibs, I don't think this is a Catholic team or an Irish team, that has nothing to do with why I support them. It's probably the same for most Hibs fans, it's certainly not got the same importance as it has through in Glasgow.

I would also say that Hibs don't do as much in the community as they probably should do and that's probably something to do with it being more of a business than a community team. They make an effort, but it's not their number one priority. They could reach out a bit more and allow youth teams to practice in the training centre and suchlike.

I would like to think that you can set Hibs apart from any other team because of their exciting football, but you can't really claim that at the moment. I would like to say that we are a club that cares more about entertainment and playing the game rather than winning every match, but that's not really being supported by the performance on the pitch. You can pretty much guarantee that Celtic or Rangers will usually win the league. Does it mean as much to them as it would to us when they win cups, or do they just take it for granted that they ought to win? Hibs always ramp up their game against the Old Firm, and against Hearts to a lesser extent. It means more to you to beat them because they are who they are. You do feel like the odds are stacked against you. It is possible that another team could win the league, and that's why when the managers set out their stall at the beginning of season, I always feel that they should be aiming higher. I mean, the fans don't expect you to be top of the table, but there's no excuse not to try to be.

I don't watch much football outside of watching Hibs. When I watch *Match of the Day* I just don't care as much what happens or who wins. If I had a team in England that I supported then yes, I would be urging them on.

I like the way the league is at the moment, to have a smaller league isn't going to stop the dominance of Rangers and Celtic, so a bigger league would be better. There are a lot of First Division teams who are good enough to play against the teams in the Premier League. To play teams just once would make it a bit less predictable, it would be more up in the air as to what the result would be.

To describe what being a Hibs fan, I would say it's just part of who I am – a Hibs supporter through thick and thin. It can be hard work, but you do have this strong sense of who you are, and a strong connection to all the other fans who are supporting them. There's always hope!

Dougray Scott

Actor, born 1966.

❝ When I walk into Easter Road I am full of memories of going there with my dad, seeing great matches, and of my childhood in general. ❞

MY DAD WAS from Barrhead in Glasgow. His uncle was a scout for Hibs and he would take him along to the matches when he was a boy. That's how he became a fan. My dad started taking me to matches when I was five or six and that was it really... I fell in love with the club!

I was born in 1966 so I was lucky that I started watching Hibs in the early '70s when we had Turnbull's Tornadoes. We were a pretty good team at that point. We had Blackley, Schaedler, O'Rourke, wee Joey Harper, Gordon, Duncan – a string of really good players. It was really exciting going to see them. We always had great tussles with Rangers and Celtic, so it was just a brilliant club to follow. I loved the colour and the stadium had a great atmosphere – looking at Arthur's Seat during the game always seemed pretty magical. So I loved it, I just loved it! We went to away matches as well. We were pretty hardcore Hibs fans and we've been to pretty much every football ground in Scotland over the years.

One thing I remember about going to Easter Road with my dad was that if people were swearing, which was quite often, my dad hated it. He would turn round and say, 'Hey, there's a boy here. Mind your language!' I would be looking at those guys from Leith and thinking, 'I don't think they're going to stop swearing dad.' I would get hugely embarrassed while he was still shouting: 'You there! Stop that swearing, we're at a football match!' He was very much into 'proper' behaviour at the football. He was very critical of Hibs when we played badly. Ultimately, though, he loved them as much as I did.

There were some Hibs fans at my school in Glenrothes but not many, it has to be said. It was usually Celtic or Rangers, Raith Rovers, East Fife or Dunfermline that people supported. But there's a Hibs Supporters Club in Glenrothes and I went on their bus to matches a couple of times. I would usually go with my dad, but as I got older I would sometimes go on the train to Edinburgh. Up until the age of 18, when I left Scotland, I would almost always go to matches with my dad, or sometimes with my brother or friends. Later I would fly up from London to see the matches.

This season I haven't been to any matches because it's dire, just dire! Financially we're in a great position, but it seems that Petrie is very tight with the money, so who are we going to get? I don't know the ins and outs of the finances of the club but, to me, it said a lot about Hibs when they got rid of John Collins – or John Collins left because of what happened with the players complaining about his training methods. If the rumours are true and they actually went to Petrie's house, he shouldn't have given them the time of day. Not everybody is an Alex Ferguson but I think John Collins was great in the way that he had them playing and the results that they were getting. He was re-establishing a very similar playing style to what Eddie Turnbull had for us way back. Alex McLeish also had us playing in a very exciting formation and it was great to watch but I thought Collins was fantastic and what happened with him was bizarre and very disappointing! I was friendly with McLeish, it was good times when he was the manager. I was enthralled when he talked about Hibs, although he would never tell me anything about the tactics he was playing. I don't know a huge amount about tactics but I've been around football all of my life and I have friends who are in football and talk a lot about football. I think in the case of John Hughes he tried his best but it was the players that weren't responding to what he was asking them to do.

I went to Athens to see Hibs against AEK and that was pretty amazing! I was at the second proper game because the first one was cancelled. Franck Sauzee was injured, that's the main thing I remember, but I thought we did OK in the end. Just travelling and being around all the Hibs fans was pretty intense, as you can imagine. I think some of them looked at me and thought, 'Fucking poofy actor – what the fuck does he know!' Once I actually talked to them and relayed the fact that I have been following Hibs since I was a wee boy, they kind of understood that I was OK. It was a real laugh. They wanted to do things that I didn't want to do, so it was pretty amusing!

As I live in England now, I watch a lot of their football on TV. I went to see Arsenal v Birmingham the other week at the Emirates Stadium – what a stadium that is, it's unbelievable! I love the atmosphere of football matches, there is nothing quite like it, and going to the Emirates Stadium, which is probably one of the best stadiums I have ever been to in my life, was great. You just can't beat the live experience. I love the ritual of it all. I have to say that I don't like watching matches on a Sunday or a Monday, at a stretch I don't mind the 12.45pm kick-off, but I much prefer it being on the traditional Saturday afternoon.

There is a completely different feeling when I go to watch Hibs because I have an emotional connection that I don't have with any other club. People sometimes say to me, 'Who's your team in England?' and I will say, 'I don't have a team in England.' I like Man Utd and I follow their results, mainly because of what Fergie did with his commitment to the youth system. Also, the way he dealt with the media is hilarious. However, a Man Utd defeat doesn't affect me in the same way as it would if Hibs get beaten. Hibs is what matters to me. I can still get the blues about a bad result.

When I walk into Easter Road, I am full of memories of going there with my dad, seeing great matches, and of my childhood in general. That connection to my father is very much with me whenever I watch Hibs. Being a Hibs fan is in my DNA! I remember once I had to attend the premiere for *Enigma* at the Edinburgh Film Festival. I had seen the movie three times anyway, so I thought, 'OK, I'll say a few words and then I'll go and watch the match.' I went over the road to watch it in a pub, and some American took offence that I didn't stay for the premiere.

I have watched Easter Road change over the years and now we have a great stadium. In the East Stand there used to be quite a big standing area, all open. I think the capacity of the ground when I was watching in the '70s was something like 40,000, it might even have been a lot more than that. There were a lot more people going to see football in those days so the atmosphere was a lot bigger and noisier. I remember going to see Hibs playing Celtic at Easter Road one time. We were winning 2-1 when the referee abandoned the game because of the fog, with only ten minutes to go! What I specifically remember was when John Blackley turned round and flicked the 'v's at the Celtic fans. He got into real trouble for that. I was also there for the 6-2 game against Hearts.

For me there's a huge difference watching Hibs to any other team, it's the same for any fan watching their own team. Trying to explain to someone why you support a team that loses all the time is sometimes really difficult. I once told my wife we hadn't won the Scottish Cup for over a hundred years, but all she remembered was me saying, 'We haven't won in over a hundred years.' She actually said that to someone: 'They haven't won in over a hundred years,' and I was like, 'NO, NO! We haven't won the Scottish Cup for over a hundred years!'

You can't change your team and nor would I want to, because I love Hibs. I think that we have a great tradition going way back to when we were formed with these young kids being taken off the street by the priests and the Hibernian Boys Club being formed. Initially there was the youth club and then out of that came the Hibs. Then Celtic stole all of our players and they had to start all over again. It's a great history and I love that side of things! The Irish connection is part of Hibs' identity. That's what the club was born out of. It is ultimately a compassionate club, which may not be so much the case today, but it certainly has been in the past, and that is very attractive to me.

I'm not interested in bigotry and I've witnessed so much of it in Scottish football that it's scary. The whole Celtic and Rangers thing is still intense and has hardly changed over the years. I've been to quite a few Old Firm matches and I really dislike being in that atmosphere, it's not a great advertisement for Scottish football. Thankfully it's not the same in Edinburgh with the Hibs and Hearts derby, there is still a rivalry but we both need each other.

I like Hibs and I don't particularly like Hearts. I think that Hibs represent the 'rag boys', the 'orphans' and the 'outsiders', but not in the political sense. Traditionally Hibs are a caring, anti-establishment club, whereas Hearts lean more towards the establishment. I don't like seeing the Union Flag in the crowd. There's nothing wrong with Great Britain, but the connotations of seeing a Union Flag at Ibrox or at Tynecastle are something different in that context.

Hearts don't have the tradition that Hibs have in terms of playing style. We have always been known for our attacking flair, that's what the Hibs fans want to see. When Bertie Auld was manager it was like, 'What the fuck is this? We don't want to see this type of football!' I didn't want to go to Easter Road to watch players who didn't have attacking skills. Even McLeish, who as a former defender has got a great defensive brain, had a fantastic attacking team. That's the kind of football I want to see. Every club has its traditions of football styles. Hibs traditionally have a more attractive style of play than Hearts. Celtic have a similar tradition to Hibs. I always remember Rangers being really tough, especially when John Greig was the captain in the 1970s. They had a few players with attacking flair, but in general they were a defensive team. They proved that on the way to winning the European Cup Winners' Cup in 1972.

At the time of the Mercer takeover, I was doing a theatre job in Chichester, and my dad was sending me the press cuttings so that I could follow what was happening. The takeover would have been a disaster. The idea of Hibs being merged with Hearts was just too much to bear – thank God it never happened! We were in a really, really bad way. But today we are one of the most successful clubs in Scotland in terms of our books being in the black, but I would like to see Hibs hold onto their younger players for longer and to attract a few more high quality players – at the moment we just seem to be a feeder club for Celtic and Rangers. So if we can somehow stop that from happening and show some ambition for the club, or find a little bit more money for these players to maybe stay on, that would be a great thing. We have a great youth policy, we have always had great young players coming through, but they leave too quickly. Times have changed. In the old days, teams were on a much more even keel as there wasn't so much money in the game. The clubs were reliant on what crowds they could attract and back then Hibs had a great support. Wages were lower so there wasn't much of an advantage in a move to a bigger club because the wages weren't that much better. Now when players move to England the wages are just astronomical, but within the system that we have in Scotland there is a chance, a possibility, that we can create a successful team that can realistically hope for maybe third place. If you are a financially successful club like Hibs, then you should start to expand and increase your ambition.

Someone once asked me what would I choose, between winning an Oscar or Hibs winning the league. And I said, 'Can I not have both?' I would really just love to see Hibs winning the Scottish Cup! One of my most vivid memories is of that 1979 final against Rangers when it went to a third replay. We so nearly won it in the first game. I was there for the second game and it was really, really close. That same year we were in the semi-final against Aberdeen and we won 2-1 but I remember the replay of the final. I had a ticket for the Rangers end for some reason and when Hibs scored it was so, so difficult not to jump about, screaming! I am the eternal optimist and a romantic when it comes to

Hibs. Nothing would make me happier than seeing Hibs lift the Scottish Cup. Realistically, that is what we could do, as opposed to winning the league. It's a long, long way away until we can even begin to challenge for that. A good few seasons ago Hibs had that fantastic run and were talking about being title contenders. The 6-6 game against Motherwell was kind of indicative of the club because your heart was in your mouth and you didn't know whether you were coming or going – you've got to be a bit of a masochist to be a Hibs fan, but we will always be Hibs fans despite that!

In terms of the strength and the depth of the squad, we don't have what Rangers and Celtic have. But if all the players are in sync and listening to what the manager wants them to do, I think that there is even further that Hibs players can go. I don't think they even know that they're capable of doing it, I think that they freeze at some points. Players sometimes seem to think, we're not supposed to be in this position. What's going on? I think they can surprise themselves. It's like watching Scotland play against Spain – if they had played like that against the Czech Republic then it would have been an entirely different result. That 4-6-0 formation or 6-4-0 was just ridiculous, I've never seen anything like it, it was very disappointing. If teams go out to play these matches away from home, and if they have a bit of muscle about them like Aberdeen had when they won the European Cup Winners' Cup, then they really have a chance. Aberdeen had great belief in themselves and they weren't scared of anyone, and that's what those Hibs players have to have. They have to have a belief that they can go to Celtic Park and Ibrox, and take it as an inspiration that they are at these grounds, rather than being intimidated. Ferguson made other teams feel intimidated by his teams – that's what he's good at. There is no reason why a team like Hibs can't adopt that mentality and become like the Aberdeen of the early '80s. They might lose a couple of games, they might not beat Celtic and Rangers, but at least those teams will feel like they have been given a really good game.

Edinburgh's Cowgate area, 2011.

‘ You can't change your team and nor would I want to because I love Hibs. I think that we have a great tradition, going way back to when we were formed in 1875. ’

I would say that John Brownlie definitely has to be one of my all time favourites because he was such an amazing wing back and I also thought he was a phenomenal footballer. Also Pat Stanton, he sums up everything about Hibs that I love. Another player who has a special place in my heart is Franck Sauzee! He was a really nice guy as well. And then there's John Collins and Joe Harper. We've had some great players over the years. I was there when George Best played for Hibs against Partick Thistle in that first game. I remember thinking what a remarkable player he was. Even though he was the worse for wear with drink and didn't even train, still I had never seen a player like him. He just created space out of nothing, it was quite extraordinary. And of course he scored that amazing goal against Celtic. I remember that goal very vividly and it was just so exciting when Tom Hart dug into his pocket and said, 'Just come and play – don't even train.' It was fantastic, just fantastic!

I have a son who is also very passionate about football. He's a Man Utd fan. I've tried to get him into Hibs, and there's still time. Unfortunately the first Hibs game I took my kids to was against Dundee and it was a 1-1 draw; you could actually hear the players talking to each other, that's how bad the game and the atmosphere was. I once took my American publicist to see Hibs at home against AEK Athens. She was blown away by the experience and was saying to me, 'What is this? It's unbelievable!'

There are so many great memories but some bad ones too – I've watched Hibs playing appallingly bad football. I remember the good times though, that's for sure. I couldn't make it to the CIS Cup Final but I was watching it on the TV and I was like everyone else in being so relieved to see us lift the cup after so many years. The other one that we won when Keith Wright scored was great too, but getting beaten by Livingston was truly awful! Being at Hampden for the Scottish Cup Final, when we got beaten by Celtic, was not a good memory either, especially as Celtic had Larsson who was magnificent that day.

When I go to see Hibs I'm usually just there on my own, I don't need to go

Hibernian were formed on 6 August 1875 by two men of equal vision, Father Canon Hannan and Michael Whelehan. After watching football matches on the Meadows, the two men put their case for forming a team at a meeting for the Catholic Young Men's Society in St Mary's Street Halls.

With no outlet of representation for the immigrant Irish community of the Cowgate, the newly formed club attempted to gain a level footing on the field of sporting achievement. It was also suggested that football could provide an alternative to the lure of less 'healthy pursuits'.

Hannan and Whelehan were proud to base the name of the new club on the old Latin name for Ireland, and so Hibernian Football Club, the Edinburgh Irishmen, was born.

with anyone else to get an experience out of it. For me it's not a social outing, I love the whole day and the ritual of it – I like getting there at least 20 minutes beforehand to get a pie and sit down with the programme. I hate missing any part of the game and I prefer not to have to chat when I'm watching it. First and foremost I just want to go to the match, watch the game and leave. People mean well but sometimes you just want to go and be a fan, I am the same as anyone else at Easter Road, I love the club just as much as anyone else does. I am the same as I was when I was little kid, there in spirit with the team on the pitch, and I feel every goal that goes against us. I feel the same elation when we score a great goal and I get depressed if we get beaten. There's nothing better than when we have won or played well, it's fantastic, and the desire to see the team do well will never leave. I have a huge belief in them, misguided as it may be at times, but that will never leave me no matter where I am in the world.

Jim Slaven

Chairman of the Connolly Foundation, born 1970.

' The history of the club is extremely relevant to me as an individual and to why I support Hibernian. '

I MADE A conscious decision to be a Hibs fan. I was born into a Celtic-supporting household but I saw Hibernian as very much part of the community that I was from. As someone of Irish ethnicity growing up in the Southside (and later in Gilmerton) I felt a natural affinity with Hibernian and there was never any animosity with my family over this. My sense of being working class, from an Irish background and from Edinburgh all fitted very nicely into me being a Hibs supporter. From an early age I knew that the football team you supported was about much more than just the football on the park: it was a part of who you were.

For me, being a Hibs supporter is like being working class and being a republican, it is part of my identity. In the sort of post-modern world that we live in now, it's recognised that people's identities are made up of a whole lot of different factors, but when I was young it wasn't all that thought out. Going to a match was a great day out with your pals, but I did see the club as very much part of my identity and from quite early on, going to matches was as much an issue of class and community as it was about the sporting event that was taking place on the pitch.

I remember standing in the old stadium with the floodlights on and how everything seemed absolutely massive. I seem to remember the games I went to as a kid always being really busy. My memory is of going with your friends and being surrounded by all these adults in jam-packed stadiums, everybody standing and everybody being together. The atmosphere gave me a buzz then, and it still does to this day. It doesn't matter how long you've been going, before kick off you can still feel that electricity. The standout moments for me are the games that involved players like George Best and Franck Sauzee –

George Best playing for Hibs was something incredible, something that will stick with me forever. But taking my daughter to see Hibs win the League Cup is a great memory as well. I'm a season ticket holder and I go to most of the away games. I still go with my friends and get that buzz before the game. But the actual experience within the stadium has changed completely. There's been an incredible improvement in the facilities, but that has somehow diminished the atmosphere. It used to be a working-class experience and it's less so now.

The social aspect has definitely diminished because of all-seater stadiums and all-ticket games. There's a lot of spontaneity that's been taken out of football in terms of fathers just deciding on the morning before the game, 'C'mon, let's take the kids to the football.' Nowadays you have to get tickets in advance, you have to pick what games you can go to and it's quite expensive as well. The other problem with all-seater stadiums is that if one person gets a ticket for one bit and another person for another, you can't just gather together with your mates during the game like in the days of the old terracing. Now we tend to congregate before kick-off, at half time and then after the game. So during the game itself people are much more isolated.

Everyone looks forward to a European adventure or the pre-season friendlies. It's as much about having a trip away with your friends as the football itself. You meet some amazing characters at the football and when you go to away games or trips abroad, you get to spend a lot of time with them.

We were in Ireland a few years ago for the pre-season friendlies and went to Maribor for the UEFA Cup game. Everybody wanted to make a special effort to get to Maribor, despite the fact it was quite an awkward place to reach. I'd just returned home from holiday on the Sunday and we had to leave on the Tuesday to go to Manchester, Vienna and then Ljubljana where we hired a car to get to Maribor. We had to come back exactly the same way after the game and so after a fortnight off I needed another fortnight to recover from it! Loads of other people had arduous journeys but it was well worth it. It's

James Connolly memorial – Cowgate, Edinburgh, 2011.

6 It was people in his community that founded Hibs and it was a connection that was important to him throughout his life. 9

inspiring witnessing the lengths that people go to watch Hibs and the absolute commitment they've got to the club. Maribor is a skiing resort, so there were nice bars and restaurants, and it was off-season. The local people were really welcoming, which is not something you necessarily get in Scotland where a lot of places are reluctant to have football fans in. But about five minutes into the Maribor game we knew we were going to have a long, difficult season ahead.

The history of the club is extremely relevant to me as an individual and to why I support Hibernian. It's a story of an immigrant community of 'Little Ireland' who were excluded by the Edinburgh FA and the Scottish FA from getting involved with indigenous teams, so they decided to start their own football team. Now that is an incredibly powerful image. It would have been easy for that community to turn in on itself and to isolate itself from a Scottish society which viewed it as the 'other'. But rather than that, they chose to integrate into wider society, taking a positive role through football and sport. This is a story of working-class immigrants organising themselves very successfully, despite all the barriers that were put in the way and the struggle they had. Why that history is a problem for some people a hundred-odd years later I think says more about Scotland than it does about Hibs.

In Edinburgh today there are no visible signs of Little Ireland, apart from St Patrick's Church in the Cowgate. There is no acknowledgement that the inhabitants of that area were almost exclusively Irish immigrants, no acknowledgement of the contribution immigrant communities and working-class people have made to the city. Hibs are the most important remaining visual signifier that the Irish community came here and made such a positive contribution, building a magnificent football club – one of the biggest in the country. Not only did they achieve that, but they had an idea which spread around the country to create other little Hibernians in order to encourage other immigrant and working-class communities to organise themselves.

Immigrants the world over have developed different strategies for dealing

Baptised at St Patrick's Church in 1868, the birthplace of Hibernian, James Connolly's pivotal role during the Easter Uprising is much celebrated and still recognised in Ireland. However, in Edinburgh very little evidence of his contribution to the socialist and republican movement exists. Connolly was born to Irish parents but he spoke with an Edinburgh accent.

During his time in America he regularly asked how the team was getting on in letters he sent back to Edinburgh, and he remains one of Hibs' most famous and remarkable fans.

James Connolly was executed by a British firing squad in Dublin in 1916. The brutal nature of his death outraged many Irish people and served to politicise a whole generation.

with hostility and discrimination from host communities. One such strategy is to deny, or attempt to hide their collective history. I believe we have to recognise history as it was, not how we wish it was. Hibs are now tentatively trying, through the Hibernian Community Foundation, to organise educational processes with school pupils and adults and generally to uncover some of this hidden history of Edinburgh and Hibernian. The contribution of people like James Connolly and others in the Irish and immigrant community who started newspapers and trade unions, deserves to be recognised. They organised people to fight for basic human rights for all. Knowing this history would give people a better understanding not only of where Hibs came from but also of the history of the city. Hopefully this would also lead to James Connolly being seen in a more positive light. In the 20 years that we had the James Connolly march we repeatedly wrote to Hibs asking them to acknowledge the fact that he was at the founding meeting of the club and used to be one of the ball boys and carried the strips. Perhaps not unsurprisingly, they were very reluctant to engage with us. Nonetheless, his contribution is a fact and unless the club are prepared to acknowledge the reality of how it came into existence then we aren't going to be able to move on.

In *The Making of Hibernian*, Alan Lugdon identifies James Connolly as being one of the people who was present at the founding meeting in St Mary's Halls. There are references to Hibs in Connolly's letters home from America and during his speeches he used to make light-hearted comments about Hibs games and results. It was people in his community who founded Hibs and that was a connection that was important to him throughout his life.

While it's wrong to generalise, I always associate Hearts with the establishment of Edinburgh and see Hibs as being the outsiders, the underdogs. But the supporters aren't a monolithic block. There's a section of the Hibs support that are uncomfortable with the origins and name of the club, just as there are people who have Irish-Catholic roots who are uncomfortable about recognising that part of their identity. Given the sectarian and anti-Irish nature of Scottish society we perhaps shouldn't be surprised by that. It can be seen as part of a strategy devised just to get by in Scotland.

In the mid-20th century efforts were made by the Hibs board, Harry Swan and suchlike, to separate the club from its Irish roots. Edinburgh, like many parts of Scotland, was then a deeply racist and sectarian place. You had Cormack's Caledonian Clan – an organisation which styled itself on the Ku Klux Klan – picketing St Patrick's Church and making attacks on the Irish community, and Protestant Action, which had several Edinburgh councillors. So there was a perception engendered that it wouldn't necessarily be safe, or wise, for people to express their 'Irishness' at football matches.

The club was announced publicly to the world on the centenary of Daniel O'Connell's birth, so there has been an interest in Irish politics from day one at Hibernian – the idea that it's a new thing is a misunderstanding, like the view that because this space is occupied by Celtic we should avoid it. In fact Hibs are the original Irish team and we should be very proud of that.

There are many misconceptions that surround the club's origins. For example, the tricolour flag is actually the original non-sectarian flag. It stands for the green of Catholicism and the orange of Protestantism, with white for peace in the middle. So the notion that it can be seen as 'inflammatory' is a bit odd to me. For one thing, it's the flag of a nation-state within the European Union. The people who complain about the tricolour being flown at football games are the same people who would tell you there isn't any anti-Irish racism or that there isn't any sectarianism. Yet if the tricolour is waved at a football game these people use that as a justification to blame the victim for attacks on them.

What we are trying to do now is to recognise the history of the club and create a space where people can freely express their ethnicity. There has to be a way of doing that which isn't seen as being provocative. We need to create a space where Hibs can acknowledge its origins and those who want to can express their ethnicity, within the football stadium and within Edinburgh, without feeling somehow that they are doing something wrong or that it's illegitimate. We haven't got there yet. The more the Hibs story is known, the more it will act as an inspiration for today's immigrants and marginalised communities.

Getting the harp back onto the club badge was a step in the right direction, as was the setting up of the Community Foundation to engage and put something back into these working-class communities. I would like the club to go still further and its website and publications to be more explicit about the social, political and economic conditions that existed when it was founded. But I realise we still need to take some people with us as we go on that journey. In the last few years Hibernian has tried to use the history of the club when it suits them, mainly as a marketing tool. They need to embrace the philosophy that founded the football club, which is about the working class founding a football club for its own community. Hibs have moved away from that and putting excerpts on the website or occasionally referring to the history of the club obliquely as a marketing tool is not what is required.

Relegation from the SPL was a wake-up call for Hibs fans in terms of acknowledging the changing nature of Scottish football and the fact that it has not been able to avoid the ongoing process of gentrification. This has had a huge impact on the business model that Scottish football has been pursuing via TV deals and other commercial ambitions. It was an opportunity for Hibs fans to recognise the change in circumstances and embrace the prospect of returning Hibs back to the community. The club came up with their own model via the Hibernian Supporters Limited scheme, but this initiative is not about community ownership. It is essentially about supporters paying towards the running of the football club, while not getting anything back. I think there is still an opportunity for Hibs and for Tom Farmer to do what he said he was going to do at the very beginning – to save Hibs for the community and return Hibs to the community. Unfortunately it doesn't look like the present ownership will truly embrace the philosophy that Hibs were built on. We need to be back at the centre of the community where we belong. We will never match the wealth of the English Premiership, so it must be an opportunity for the Scottish League to go in a different direction. The SPL and SFA essentially try to mimic what is happening in England and it has failed – it does not work. Scottish football must develop a distinct model which is not based on TV money but on getting football fans back through the turnstiles.

Hibs may have a lovely stadium and training ground but the stadium is half-empty for most games. Many of the people who go to games now are not the same people that would have been there ten or 15 years ago. This has highlighted the process of gentrification, because while we do have this great stadium, we need to get it filled with the some of the same types of people who used to go to the football 20 years ago. The first thing we would want to do is democratise the running of the football club. Obviously there would still be professional people running the club on a day-to-day basis – nobody is suggesting that fans should be doing that. In terms of key decisions they should be made within a democratic framework. The stadium and the training centre should be opened up and used for the benefit of the whole community. At the moment we look like a huge city football club, but in fact the club is a shell. We should be owned and controlled by the community and all the facilities should be available to them. The community foundation is great in that it is doing charitable work but they are doing the work that should be essentially done by the football club. They are the vehicle for the work that is being done in the community so why is the football club not doing that? Every club in Scotland should follow this model, I believe. There should be a new strategy that suits Hibs. At the moment we are drifting along and there is no strategy. We recognise that this a process and it isn't going to happen overnight. There are clubs in England and in Wales run along these lines. We should look around us and pick a model that specifically suits Hibernian. While it is not a case of copying another club or picking a business model off the shelf, we need to look at some of the innovative models being used. We should devise a strategy for the next ten or 15 years. This is exactly what the board are not doing at the moment.

The Mercer takeover bid seemed to me like an attack on the whole Hibernian family. I saw it as an attempt to kill the club. There were Hearts fans who were against it too (though I myself didn't meet any who sympathised), but I do remember fans of other clubs being a bit disgusted by it. The animosity between Hearts and Hibs was always there – it has been there since I was a kid and it probably intensified at that time. That was certainly the experience of my generation. I don't think anyone's going to forget it very quickly.

Hibs supporters don't expect to win every game – that's what separates us from Old Firm fans, they expect to win every game no matter what. But we do expect to see a certain style of football and we want a club that's going to bring young players through. The most important thing is that you can still support your team and see a style of football which is entertaining, played the Hibs way. The friends I go to the football with all have different views and opinions. That is one of the things that I enjoy about being with them,å but we all come together as Hibs fans, we go to the games together and we all want to see Hibs win.

Dick Gaughan
Musician, born 1948.

' I naturally shot into the air, roaring with joy, when slowly it dawned on me that I was standing in the middle of several thousand growling Huns. '

I GREW UP in Graham Street, North Leith and my first attendance at Easter Road was when I was about three years old in approximately 1951. My grandfather, who was from County Mayo in Ireland, used to take me to all the home games which means I was there in the great season of 1951–52. Being so young, I don't remember a thing about it apart from standing outside the pub proudly wearing my Hibs scarf and eating an ice-cream cone my grandfather bought me before he nipped in for a quick pint before the game. When I got to school age, most of the boys in Graham Street used to go to home games at Easter Road. The Famous Five were all still there and they were our heroes. We had no money but that was never a problem, it was in the days before high walls and fences and there was always a willing adult who would give you a lift over into the ground. We used to always sit on the low wall at the edge of the park, near the halfway line.

It would be accurate to say I've been a passionate Hibbie all my life. Being a Hibs supporter was a vital part of our Leith identity. It wasn't a conscious thing; it was just the way it was. Yes, there was a sectarian element to the Hibs–Hearts rivalry, mainly in central and west Edinburgh, but it wasn't really noticeable in Leith. Of all the families in Graham Street, only two of us were of Irish origin and went to Catholic school, but most were just Hibs supporters. Support for Hibs was a Leith thing and not sectarian. Any Leither who didn't support Hibs was considered very odd, and if they supported Hearts that was akin to treason. As a kid I developed my pet theory, to annoy Hearts supporters, that everything west of Haymarket is Glasgow, which meant that Heart of Midlothian is actually a Weegie club. But one of the good things I've witnessed in my life is that a lot of the bitter hostility, sectarian or territorial, has gone out of the

Hibs–Hearts rivalry and been replaced by something a bit more good-natured. I do believe Wallace Mercer's ridiculous merger proposal played a part in that by uniting Hibs and Hearts supporters in determined opposition. I know several quite fanatical Hearts supporters who were solidly behind Hands off Hibs as they understood the vital need for the two clubs to continue to exist.

Due to a combination of circumstances, I didn't get to many games during my late teens but after 1969, I was able to get back. I rarely missed a match during the decade of Stanton, Higgins, Blackley and Duncan but, like every Hibbie of my age, the game etched indelibly on my memory is the 1973 drubbing of Hearts at Tynecastle. I think most of us were drunk for a week after that one!

My favourite spot was always about a third of the way up the terrace above the halfway line. I can only remember one occasion when I stood elsewhere. It was when I took a friend who was visiting from Newcastle to a match. I forget the exact season but we were playing Rangers and for some reason, probably excessive indulgence in refreshments, didn't pay enough attention to what gate we went into and ended up being shunted down among all the Gers supporters. I remember that we scored first and I naturally shot into the air, roaring with joy, then slowly it dawned on me that I was standing in the middle of several thousand growling Huns. I was the only one with a green scarf in a sea of, by now, very disgruntled blue, and they were looking at me as a suitable target for their wrath. As it turned out, Rangers equalised almost immediately and in their own celebrations, they forgot about me and my Geordie pal and we slunk off out of hostile territory. I can look after myself OK but I didn't fancy my chances with those odds!

During the '70s, my regular company at games was Owen Hand (also a singer) and another mate known by the abbreviated form of his name, 'Andy Scap', as his surname was a long unspellable Italian name – 'Scappaticci' I think. Andy was great at terrace banter. I only saw him meet his match once, and that was at a Partick Thistle game. At one point Andy roared, 'C'moan Hibs, get

‘During the '70s, my regular company at games was Owen Hand... ’

intae this shite!' to be answered immediately by a Glasgow voice from behind shouting, 'C'moan the shite!' I used to love games against the Jags, for the wit and friendliness of their supporters.

One other memory which leaps out at me is the season George Best was at Easter Road. He was out of condition, overweight and slow – and he was still better than the other 21 players on the park combined. On top form, he was up there with Pele and Maradonna, and although in that season we only got flashes of his real genius, watching him was still well worth the price of the ticket. Looking back at all the players I've seen wear the green shirt, I suppose my all-time favourite would still have to be the great Lawrie Reilly. I was still just a kid when he was playing and my memories of him have probably improved with age, but he is the one who stands out from the crowd.

So far as games I'd like to erase from memory go, I've already erased most of them. Definitely several from the late '70s and early '80s, and more than a few in recent times!

I was never a great one for singing at games because I go to games to enjoy myself. Regardless of all the other reasons why I sing, singing is actually my job and, like any job, I have to get away from it now and again. I've not yet made any direct references to football in any songs I've written, although I often mention it in between songs to spark a bit of banter with audiences, particularly in Glasgow and Liverpool. But if it was appropriate to the song though, then I certainly would.

As soon as my son was old enough, I started taking him to reserve games for a couple of seasons, then to all the games. Although for most of his life we've had to live outside Leith, or as I say when asked, 'in exile in Central Edinburgh'. His passion and loyalty to Hibs equals my own. What is special about Hibs? The supporters… Why? If pushed, I think I'd have to say loyalty and resilience. Watching great, talented players being developed by Hibs only to be scooped up by bigger clubs has always been part of the mixed joy and anguish of Hibs,

Owen Hand's career in music was a brief one in recording terms – only two complete albums, but through that small recorded output he became a much-loved figure on the Scottish and English folk scenes.

Hand contributed strongly to the Scottish folk revival of the '60s. His life outside music was as varied as it was interesting. He began his working life by taking a job as a miner at the age of 15; later he worked on whaling ships and lumberjacked in Canada. His passion for sport was not confined to football – he enjoyed some success as an amateur boxer.

Owen Hand's musical influence was considerable and his legacy remains alive. Folk luminary Bert Jansch still performs 'My Donal' as part of his repertory.

certainly ever since Pat Stanton took the road west. This causes an inevitable lack of depth in the squad available which means that the second half of any season can often be painful. But we keep going, we keep supporting. Hibs is part of our identity and part of our culture, particularly to Leithers. Our loyalty comes from the fact that, while players, managers and directors come and go, we're still there, victory or defeat. Hibs is our club and the supporters are the club. Without us there would be no Hibernian Football Club.

Andy Blance

Hooliologist, born 1965.

‘ To me there would be no choice. As much as I am proud to be Scottish, it is always Hibs first. ’

I WAS PROBABLY about four or five when I first went to football games. There is every chance it was even earlier than that. Because my dad was on his own with us kids, we would go and visit my aunty at Harrison Gardens and, whatever team was at home that week, we would go to the Hibs game or the Scum game. My dad and my uncle would take us to different games, my dad being a Hibbie and my uncle a Scumbo. To be honest I can't remember affiliating myself with either team at that point in time but I do remember asking my dad, 'What one do you like out of the two of them?' and he said 'Hibs', so that was it for me. I think it was purely my father's influence because if he had said he was a Scumbo then I probably wouldn't have made the right choice. The funny thing is that I didn't know, until we were making my book, that my dad was from a Scumbo family. My publisher was speaking to my dad and asked him the same question: 'How did you end up being a Hibbie?' He told him that his own dad was a Scumbo and that he'd rebelled against it and had decided to choose his own team.

All the way through primary school and high school Hibs would mostly beat the Scum. In that era we were very rarely beaten by them, then everything came full circle and they went 21 games unbeaten by us. John Robertson had a lot to do with that – I would have stopped going if Hibs had ever made him manager! When I started going to high school my dad let me start going to away games with a couple of older guys from Fife. Monday to Friday I would be out washing folks' cars and windows, doing paper rounds and milk rounds, just to make money to go and see the Hibs game on the Saturday. That's all I wanted my money for. I would go to the old Hibs shop on Easter Road till I had everything they sold in the shop. I had piggy banks, loads of different pennants, badges –

the lot! One of my friends was exactly the same. I've been pals with him since I was 12 or 13 years old. He'd go to the football, kind of the same as me with his Dr Martens on, showing one green lace and one white lace. He would carry a big Hibs teddy bear with him to games. We both had huge scarves, with all the Hibs badges sewn onto them. I still have that scarf back in the house.

I remember going to Tynie at a point when I didn't really know many Hibbies, other than folk from Inverkeithing that I was at school with. I couldn't get a ticket for the game and one of my pals said that he had a ticket for the Hibs end. It turned out that the ticket was for the Scum end and I put my scarf in my inside pocket. Of course, we ended up scoring. I found it really hard not to celebrate and some folk I knew were trying to get my scarf out of my jacket in the middle of the Scum end. That was a lesson learnt and I never went back again until years later when the Hibs boys made a deliberate decision to 'visit' their end.

After my choice had become clear I would go to the big terracing and would stand under the TV gantry. You might think, 'How could you enjoy going to a football match with folk pissing down your leg?' People would just start pissing where they stood. And they would be drinking, so the next thing you knew, someone would launch a beer can and you always ran the risk of it hitting off your head. There were so many things going back and forward from the home end to the away end that you risked losing an eye. Although I loved it, it was certainly a more dangerous place to be back then than it was when we were all creating havoc up and down the country with the casuals. I would still stand at the football if I could because it made for a better atmosphere when you had the sways and all that, so I do miss those days and meeting old and new friends on the terraces.

The Gorgie Aggro were pretty renowned in Edinburgh. I knew who they were but you felt that you would have to hide your scarf when you visited Gorgie. I think I might have stuck to being a punk or skinhead had it not been for the amount of hassle that I got from the police. So maybe I wouldn't have been a casual had I not got roped into it by the police. I think that the Gorgie Aggro might have had a similar thinking like: No! We're the Gorgie Aggro and we're no gonna be casuals, that lot are just stupid wee boys! They were right in a way, because we were essentially just a bunch of wee lads that all came together with a common cause and it's actually unbelievable that the whole of Edinburgh were scared of us. Hibs fans before that were sometimes scared to wear their colours but everything went full circle and ended up in reverse. That's really why I called my book *Hibs Boy*, because if people were in a pub and in a difficult situation they would say 'Eh… I'm a Hibs Boy' and it suddenly took on this new dimension. I wonder how many Scumbos or normal guys that got themselves into a scrape said, 'I'm a Hibs boy and I know such and such,' to avoid a real kicking.

I was quite distinguishable before I became a casual and I kind of got hounded out of Fife, if you like, by the police. Although my own actions had a big part to play I still didn't want to go back there. After a short while I found it was happening across here, which I know was self-inflicted. So I thought, 'Nah I'll need tae dae something about this.' Around that time I ended up having a fight with a rival fan, I can't remember who, but the following week after the fight me and my mate Girvan were going through to Glasgow and we got on the train at Haymarket. There was a couple of guys leaning out of the window looking to see who was getting on and shouting, 'Come with us, come with us!' That was the first time I had seen guys dressed smartly, and calling themselves casuals, but they probably said that because we looked like we could cause chaos, so we were like, 'Fuck it, aye all right.' So that was the beginning of becoming a casual. It was kind of hard to give up being a skinhead. I ended up years later getting ready for the football and listening to 'Anarchy in the UK', 'Holidays in the Sun' and songs like that, sort of missing that identity.

I think what they are finding now in Poland and places like that is that it is basically lawless and they don't have any idea how to control things. In England they had the big problem initially and I think it was because the money that people had meant that they could afford to travel abroad. Other countries saw for themselves what 'typical fans' did and so it became perceived as an English disease more than a British disease. Maggie Thatcher was in power at the time and she just didn't like football fans undermining her 'good doings' that she had just done against the miners. She basically brought in people like the Minister for Sport who implemented laws on crowd fencing and that kind of thing.

I think the Scumbos were one of the first to have those kind of controls. With the casual scene there are some that are not interested in football and are only interested in the trouble, but contrary to what the press would lead you to believe, those people are in the minority. The vast majority of them are actually interested in the football. You don't get many guys that are just interested in trouble and think, 'I'll go to the Hibs games for some bother.' You've got to have another purpose to go there in the first place, to know about the team and get involved with them, and so they'll be accepted by other fans on that basis. The main motivation for them is fighting for Hibs! I think that they can criticise casuals as much as they like but at the end of the day, people in all sorts of walks of life are doing it and they don't get the same kind of criticism. Humans, like lions and tigers, defend their area whether it's for money, for notoriety or just for fun. It happens under different guises. I would never ever say that it's right because obviously it is wrong, especially when people get caught up in it. The casual thing is so over-hyped by the authorities, there are far bigger problems than that in society. We have been to pre-season friendlies abroad or when the Inter-Toto Cup was played and Lothian and Borders undercover police would be there. You would ask them, 'What the fuck are you doing here?' and they would say, 'We're paid for it, it's just part of the job,' but in reality it was a decent wee jolly for them and I always thought, 'Surely you guys have some real crimes to solve?' I remember the CS gas incident against Celtic and I was more concerned with telling people to put their scarves over their noses and telling them not to rub their eyes. After it happened we tried to get on the pitch into their end. I also remember the day that Raymond Morrell was battered and we got chased all the way down Easter Road, you were basically running in fear for your life! I can remember pre-casual days going down to places like Ayr and Kilmarnock as well. You would be standing behind one goal because Hibs would be shooting that way but in the second half you would be shooting down the other way and thinking, 'Fuck it, we're going to that end, or maybe in line with the 18-yard box.' Obviously the home fans would do the same thing and you would end up clashing at the halfway line and having a right barney. I remember going up to Dundee with about 50 of us and we got kicked about the place, fighting like fuck but basically getting beat up! A couple of weeks later we were playing the other Dundee team so everybody went up and we were like, 'Fuck you! Somebody did that to us when there were only 50 of us up here last time...' The best of it was that there was maybe 350 of us there for that second game but in reality, it was probably the same 50 guys that were fighting as the first time around. It was really just the same core element doing the fighting and fighting for the common cause.

There's extremes that you go to in any walk of life and within that walk of life you've got Hibs fans and within those Hibs fans you have another walk of life. You've got people who you don't associate with too much during the week but on a Saturday you want to phone them to see where they are. If I get information that Hibs are playing such and such in a pre-season friendly or when we find out who we have in Europe, for example, then I know that I don't even need to phone them and say, 'Right, are you going?' because I instantly know they are.

When it comes down to it, there is probably not a lot of difference between Hibs and the Scum. I daresay that there are guys who support the Scum and hate Hibs as much as we hate them. I think that Rangers and Celtic fans are just a bunch of tossers that fucking hang on to something because they've not got much else going on in their lives. How many people did you know at school who were Rangers and Celtic fans? Where are they now? I know plenty who were Rangers and Celtic fans because they just hated being slagged on a Monday

The Skol Cup won by Hibs in season 1991–92.

6 The time we went through to the Dunfermline Skol Cup Final we had over 40,000 at that, and for the Livingston CIS Cup Final as well. 9

morning. Invariably if you are not Rangers and Celtic you do get a slagging. There's quite a few of those same people now that will go to see Raith Rovers, Dunfermline, Cowdenbeath, the Scum or whoever. I think that the majority of the Scumbos are genuine supporters of their team just like we are, whereas Rangers and Celtic 'fans' aren't. They did a 'real fans' survey in England a good few years ago and they chose Newcastle v Arsenal as a case study. They thought, right, Newcastle is a one-team town, and the nearest you would get to that in Scotland would be Aberdeen. There must still be a lot of Huns and Tims in Aberdeen, but in Newcastle I doubt you will get many Man Utd fans. With real Arsenal fans, if they are that far up north supporting Arsenal, then they are proper fans and to me the majority of Scottish fans are like that. For example, if somebody stays in Aberdeen and supports Hibs then there has to be a good reason for it. In that respect you can see for yourself most of the average crowds, which will maybe fluctuate a wee bit, and on the whole you have the Old Firm then Aberdeen, Hibs and the Scum. There's not much difference between those teams and Hibs have shown that they can match any support outside of the Old Firm. The time we went through to the Dunfermline League Cup Final we had over 40,000 at that, and for the Livingston CIS Cup Final as well. Where are all these people now though? It's alright talking about Rangers and Celtic having glory hunters but for the finals, Hibs have been the exact same. When I go on Facebook there will be folk crowing about Celtic or Rangers and they wouldn't even know how to get to the fucking ground.

I think it's good that Hibs have the harp on the club badge showing their Irish heritage and roots but if they want to proclaim they are an Irish club then go and play in Ireland. It's a Scottish club! I do know some that are into all that, but very few. I think the Scum are worse for bigotry, even a lot of Celtic fans will say that they are worse than Rangers. To me, the Scum don't ever seem to play much good football – it's more just thunder and guts.

In the last couple of decades Tony Mowbray has been the best manager we

Hibs fans have always approached cup finals with a sense of trepidation. The club have never enjoyed the tag of favourites and in the 1958 Scottish Cup Final they lost 1-0 to Clyde, after beating Rangers in the semi. Hibs had been trounced 6-1 by Celtic in the Scottish Cup Final of 1972 but just seven months later they celebrated a 2-1 win against Celtic in the League Cup Final. However, when Hibs have collected silverware it has been more than enjoyed by its fans. Against Dunfermline in the 1991 Skol Cup Final, Hibs won 2-0 – a remarkable feat given the fact that they were lucky to be alive after the previous year's takeover attempt. Against Livingston in 2004, expectations were crushed as Hibs went down to a CIS Cup Final defeat. In 2007, another generation of fans saw the club lift the League Cup, scoring five goals against Kilmarnock in probably one of the best atmospheres of recent times at a cup final in Scotland.

have had and I think if Celtic had been patient enough they would have found that out as well. The one failing he had was that he insisted on playing all the young guys. The best results we had was playing guys like big Mixu, Sauzee, Matty Jack, all these solid guys. Ironically the Scum have also always had that big centre half type of player. One of my pals who is really good friends with 'Elvis' said that it wouldn't matter whether he'd had a good game or a bad game, he knew he'd always have a tough time against Mixu. He wouldn't get a minute's peace and although he was fair he knew he'd be going home with a few bruises. He didn't say that Mixu was a dirty player, he just said that he was really tough to play against. At Easter Road once, when we were 1-0 up, Mixu got taken off. Elvis apparently said that it gave them a huge lift because they knew he was getting taken off. It was like them having 12 men after Mixu got subbed that day and Pressley said that he couldn't have paid enough compliments to Mixu. The Scum went on and won 2-1.

I don't know if you can label football as a sport anymore because when you look at the English Premiership or even La Liga with Barca and Real Madrid, it's a fucking business! You're not going to tell me that it's primarily football because to me it's primarily business. For example, Alan Smith at Newcastle was supposedly on over £60,000 a week for a Championship club and Michael Owen was apparently on £125,000 a week, and for what? If somebody is going to offer you £50,000 a week for kicking about a football then you are obviously going to take it. It's no slight on Alan Smith, for example, but was he worth that money when guys were out in Afghanistan fighting for £700 a week or something like that? Equally, you can't knock the individual for taking what is offered to them. I think with the modern game, and all the massive wages, most ex-Hibs players get booed when they come to Easter Road because they've gone to a bigger club like Rangers or Celtic. I think Scott Brown's one of the exceptions but if you're a joiner getting £500 a week and somebody says to you, 'I know you've been with that boy a few years but if you leave him and come work with me I'll give you one and a half grand a week,' you're not going to turn round and say no!

As a kid I can remember watching the news one time, Alan Gordon had been transferred and I was sitting in my living room crying! I went to the Scottish Cup Finals against Rangers in 1979 and Arthur Duncan, who was one of the best servants from that era, scored an own goal to give them the cup, and I broke down then as well. I can remember Eric Schaedler chasing John McDonald as he took a dive for Rangers to give them a penalty to win 2-1. At the point when we won the League Cup against Dunfermline I'd started going to every single game and had been for a few years. I never saw them win anything at that point and then I got five years in the jail and within two months they'd won the cup! I remember I was in D Hall at Glenochil and I was sitting there watching the game. I can't remember if it was McIntyre's penalty, or Keith Wright with the second one, but for one of the goals I jumped up and picked up a chair and there was another guy sitting beside me who didn't know what I was going to do with it... but I was just joyous! After my ecstatic celebrations, I sheepishly returned the chair back to its original position and sat back down, still buzzing with the excitement of lifting the cup.

When we won the CIS Cup Final a few years ago, I cried. My girlfriend at the time phoned me and said, 'John Collins is on the telly crying,' and I said, 'So the fuck am I!' Non-Hibees have said to me that that was the best atmosphere they've ever experienced at Hampden.

The best atmosphere I can remember in a good while was the second leg of the game against AEK Athens. I went to the first leg in Athens, it was when the twin towers got bombed. I took my two sons along and I was also sponsoring a player, so I spent a shit-load of money and when the match got cancelled and re-arranged, I couldn't afford to take the boys back. It was good but we were American in the eyes of the Athens fans – we were in a square and a load of them were giving us shite for being American, and we got on the buses with a huge escort from the police. We had to go through this wee channel to the ground and they were all throwing stuff at us. We were led from there to a wood and as we were going through it everyone went really quiet with apprehension. There were shadows running about through the trees and all you could hear was crackling. When we eventually got to the stadium, we got searched by the police and they took everything off us, like cameras, spare change, anything you had, before you went in the ground. The next thing we knew was that they scored and pelted us with everything they could – even though it was them who scored! They were climbing up the huge fence between us, draping banners over it and burning things, and they also had two ends that would chant things at each other and so one end would chant and then the other would reply – almost like two separate factions. It was a uniquely hostile atmosphere.

We make a point of saying we are Scottish when we are in Europe but essentially we are English as far as the police and the authorities are concerned. With the Tartan Army, what a load of bollocks it is saying that they are the best supporters in the world. They go on these pre-match marches, get pissed and urinate in people's gardens. I don't think that qualifies them to be the best in my book... They also can't understand that, for example, if Scotland were in the World Cup and they said to me, 'You've got one wish and you only have two options – for Scotland to win the World Cup, or for Hibs to win the Scottish Cup?' To me there would be no choice. Much as I am proud to be Scottish, it is always Hibs first.

Not long after the first edition of this book I was banned from attending Hibs game for three and a half years. Saturday past was the first game I have been to since the ban was lifted. I had retired from the casual scene long before the incident in Glasgow when I got arrested. We had got off a train from Ayr into Glasgow Queen Street when we were attacked by rival fans. For us it was a social day out because we had not played Ayr United in the Scottish cup for a long time. We were not looking for any kind of trouble and we were not walking together in some kind of organised group. It was simply a case of having to defend ourselves. I think that this fact was accepted in court or perhaps some people would actually have received prison sentences.

Before that day I never used to miss a game no matter where I was in the world. I would be at every game including the pre-season friendlies. I think to have been away for so long has changed things a wee bit. I don't have the same appetite at the moment but that may come back to me and I certainly wouldn't dream of supporting any other team.

I took my wee boy to his first game on Saturday as well so he will have to go through the same punishment as I did. He was born exactly a month after the 'unmentionable' cup final so it was a good thing for me in my life at that point. Before I got banned everything revolved around Hibs games and I wouldn't contemplate booking a holiday during the football season for example. Nowadays if we were invited to a wedding on a Saturday or during the season I would probably just say, 'Yeah, that's fine'. I thought I would be really excited and restless before returning to watch Hibs but it didn't really pan out that way. The cup final defeat to the Scumbos really knocked the stuffing out of me and I was pretty depressed for a long time after that. I didn't want anything to do with football and I know it is a few years ago now, but I think it will take a long time to repair the damage that was done that day. My mate Bongo used to go to every game as well but he hasn't been back since. We got into another cup final after that as well but he didn't go to that one either. I sometimes wonder whether we will ever be able to get our bragging rights back.

One of the Scumbos that I know contemplated never going back to watch his team for the reverse reason. He wasn't being flippant when he said 'I'm no being funny but when will I ever see a performance or occasion that will better that?' He had watched his team beat their closest rivals 5.1 in a Scottish cup final so how could it get better for him? The flipside is, when will we ever play them in a final again to get the chance of revenge and if we did would we get revenge anyway? I wonder how many fans we have lost because of that game. You also have to remember that if a kid chooses to support an Edinburgh team, how many would opt for Hibs and how many have changed their allegiance? Going to school as a Hibee on a Monday morning these days cannot be an easy task.

Part of the reason I don't plan to be at so many games is being forced to visit places like Ibrox. We are treated like utter scum in that ground and I'm not talking about myself, who is well known because of my past, but the people who maybe take their kids and family along.

I'm not anti Rod Petrie but I think we essentially still have the same regime running the club even with Dempster's appointment. We could do with a change but by the same token Petrie is not the worst chairman in the world. He has done all of the right things in keeping the club afloat but I cannot see them attracting some billionaire type to invest in us.

I do not have any expectations now as a Hibs fan but some fans think we are still one of the top four or five team in Scotland. We may be in terms of the size of the club but in footballing terms we certainly are not. But we can only hope that things will improve one day and I will always support Hibernian through all the hard times.

Don Morrison

Publishers' Sales Agent, born 1960.

'I would never have gone to that place in my life had it not been for Hibernian.'

MY FATHER AND his father came from Crown Street in Leith and they were very much Hibs people. I suppose if I'd come from Gorgie then I would have been a Hearts fan. Thankfully my dad was a big Hibs man. I always used to phone him after each game to give him a match report and he always said, 'Thanks son – the radio never said that.'

I was maybe about five or six years old when my dad took me to a game for the first time – I think it was against Morton. My uncle Steve, who has passed away now, was a big Hibs fan, so it really was a Hibs family. Most of my mates played amateur football on the Saturday and I never did, because I just wanted to watch Hibs. To make up for that, though, I did play on a Sunday in the church or amateur leagues.

I used to go to all the home games and then eventually to the away games as well. Even now, I rarely miss one. My mates all now take their kids and on Saturday past we had three full cars going through to the game. It's really good, it gets kids out with their dads and grandads so football is important for that reason alone. It's more than just watching the football because it's a social thing as well.

I used to go to the shed behind the goals, 'The Cowshed' as it was known back then. Before that, when I went with my dad, we went to the enclosure underneath the old stand. I remember the huge stadium with the crowds swelling and surging forward and I remember the European nights against teams like Sporting Lisbon, they really were fantastic nights. I can't believe the size of the crowds back then. I vividly remember the smell of cigar and cigarette smoke in the old north stand, from that part of the ground you would always hear the chants of 'HIBEES, HIBEES' with people's feet stamping on the old wooden boards. It was just benches you sat on back then, not the proper seats that you have now. That old stand was where I bought my first season ticket many years ago.

Later on I worked at the ground. My dad didn't go to away matches, so I would be at the reserve matches as a ball boy. That job was fantastic because you had the benefit of being behind the goals with four or five of your mates. A guy called Roddy Mackenzie, who was the Hibs goalkeeper at the time, would chat away to you, as would the likes of Arthur Duncan and others who were maybe not quite fit and so would be playing in the reserves as well. The second job I had was working on the old scoreboard which was located in the corner of the East Terrace. One day – I must have been in my teens – I was asked, 'Do you want to do the scoreboard? You'll get into the game for free and you'll get a programme and you can have a pie at half time.' Someone would come along with a bit of paper at half time and say, 'Right, that's the results so put them up on the scoreboard.' My third and final job was selling match programmes and again it was great, because you got into the game for nothing! If you sold a hundred programmes you'd get £2. But eventually I moved on from that and got myself a season ticket instead. There were some characters around the place like Old Jackie who was the kit and laundry man – he was a feisty guy. He would always wave the team bus away on a Saturday afternoon and, if they won, would welcome them back with his fist in the air before making the players a cup of tea.

I was at the famous 7-0 game, I was about 13. I remember coming home and thinking to myself, 'Was that really 7-0? How good were they?' It was strange, because Hearts had a great chance early on in the game through Donald Park to make it 1-0 but they somehow missed it. The other weird thing I remember about that game was that the Hari Krishnas were around for the first time. I remember walking down Princes Street on the way back with my dad and seeing group of them singing 'Hari Krishna, Hari, Hari.' I watched the game later that night on TV, still not able to believe just how good Hibs were that day!

My dad never saw Hibs win the Scottish Cup. He passed away on 28 February 2015 but I'm sure he will be looking down on us and willing us to win it again. At the end of his life he didn't make it along to the games but he watched them on television. The final against Kilmarnock in 2007 was the last game he went to with my mum. That game was brilliant and the added story of John Collins losing his father the week before made it even more special. A lot of the players at that time didn't like John Collins and thought he was 'up his own arse', but you will never know the full story behind that because that's the way the club are, they keep things pretty secretive. For example, you will never know Hibs have signed a player until it's officially been announced. In a way, you have to admire them for that.

I still clearly remember the League Cup final against Celtic in 1972, which we won 2-1. We left from the Elwyn Hotel, and went through to the game. We had to come back on the bus with the windows smashed in by some Celtic fan but most importantly we won the cup, so it didn't seem to matter too much. I do also remember getting beaten 6-1 by Celtic in the 1972 Scottish Cup final. The score was 1-1 when Alan Gordon scored for us. After his goal we got absolutely cuffed because Celtic had Jimmy Johnston, Kenny Dalglish and all these other fantastic players. I reckon if Celtic weren't as good a team at that time, Hibs would have won a lot more because we also had a fantastic team. Turnbull was a great coach and I think he said that he wasn't a big fan of Jock Stein's, so, typically, he went through some tough times after that.

When Hibs won the cup against Killie a lot of my friends said that if Mowbray had been in charge we wouldn't have won that game. Mowbray's mantra was always 'Pass the ball, pass the ball', but Collins was just the same. I'd sit about ten rows behind the benches and you would always hear them shouting, 'Pass! Pass!' when Collins was in charge. In that cup final win against Kilmarnock, we were four up and then five up but at the same time I'm still thinking, 'Surely we can't lose this now?' There was still something at the back of my mind doubting we could actually win it. The final against Killie was a great experience. Even beating Gretna by six goals was great. But the main thing was the way we played football back then, it was magnificent! Hopefully my best game is still to come. I think the thing that makes Hibs different from any other team in Scotland is that they try to play football. They might not win every game but it's the way that they try to play.

John Blackley was a hero of mine in the 1970s with the Turnbull's Tornadoes team, as were Peter Cormack and Alex Cropley. Blackley was a great player, although later as a coach he didn't really match up to his playing days. Pat Stanton is a great guy and had the opportunity to go to Man Utd to be number two with Sir Alex, but instead he went to be the coach at Dunfermline. He didn't take the offer up at Man Utd so we will never know where it might have taken him if he had worked with Ferguson at that time.

Through my work as a publishers' sales agent, we sold Andy Goram's book. Andy Goram is a fantastic guy and if he walked into the room right now he'd come over and buy you a beer. He was some character, I would say he was one of the best, if not the best ever Hibs goalkeeper, in my time anyway. Even in comparison to Jim Leighton I would rate him as better. I've been at Tynecastle where some of the Hearts fans actually applauded him off the park at half time! He made a fantastic save off someone like Wayne Foster, god knows how he got to it. Granted, his lifestyle was maybe a bit shambolic, but that doesn't make him a bad person. When he first came to Hibs, and I maybe shouldn't be saying this, I had to get him out of his bed in the Kings Manor Hotel for training.

There was a lot written about him that really wasn't true or was certainly much exaggerated. For example, I was at his house over Christmas a number of years ago and he got me tickets for the game. These two guys in the seats behind me said, 'Did you hear about Goram? He was up town on the piss last night.' So I turned round and said, 'No he wasn't, he was with me and he had a glass of champagne and then he went to his bed.' That was the kind of thing he had to contend with.

As manager, Alex McLeish made some great signings like Russell Latapy.

That was at a time when Hibs had some money. Russell was magnificent and they bought Franck Sauzee as well – there was more TV money kicking about back then. It was a fantastic time for Hibs and I saw Latapy play down at Ayr United in his first game for Hibs in a 3-3 draw. Unfortunately, he famously let himself down before the cup final against Celtic when his pal Dwight Yorke came up to Edinburgh for a few bevvies. He ended up drinking not that far away from his house. I always wondered why he took his car – if you are going to have a cheeky wee drink, then surely you don't make yourself obvious? McLeish just said to him, 'That's it, your tea's oot, mate...' and off he went. That was a real shame, because we got easily beaten in the final – mind you, we had the excuse that it was a very hot day!

I went across to Trinidad and Tobago in 2000 to see Hibs play in a mini-tour when Latapy was still with us. We stayed at a hotel on Turtle Beach, owned by an Irish guy. After about a day and a half we had literally drunk it dry. The hotel had run out of lager and had to wait a couple of days to get another delivery in. Irvine Welsh took us under his wing one evening and we took a taxi ride to a local pub on Tobago. It was a great night and a great laugh. The trip was amazing but tragedy struck when one of the Hibs fans, Alex Urquhart, died in the water during the holiday.

After McLeish it was Williamson – what a waste of time he was! I mean, a man who said, 'If you want entertainment then go to the pictures.' Who the hell says that kind of thing? In my opinion he had no commitment to Hibernian. He never lived in Edinburgh, he lived through in the west and just kept driving through. He was the guy rumoured to try to sell Whittaker and O'Connor to Inverness. It might not be true but I wouldn't put it past him!

Alex Miller perhaps stayed too long, I think, but as a coach he was highly regarded. He had a great sense of humour. I met him socially a few times and he was really quite a funny guy, though you wouldn't think that because his body language during interviews usually told you something different. He did

' He went to Petrie and said, "I don't want to jump in a minibus and drive to Portobello beach, I want a facility!" **'**

win the League Cup for us in 1991, which was great. Miller was very close to the chairman, Dougie Cromb, and he did have some good players like Murdo McLeod, Jim Leighton, Darren Jackson and Keith Wright. Actually, around that time, when Miller was manager, I became good friends with Stuart Collie, the club physio whom we nicknamed 'the bag man'. Me and a group of friends decided to sponsor the Man of the Match award but the game was so incredibly bad that we decided to nominate the award to Stuart. It was funny, because he had to get up and receive his award in front of the players!

One of my favourite managers was Tony Mowbray. He was the man that got the training ground built; you can believe what you want to, but he was the guy that told Petrie we needed one. He went to Petrie and said, 'I don't want to jump in a minibus and drive to Portobello beach, I want a facility!' and so Petrie put it in place. Mowbray also brought through all those young players, although Donald Park was the main guy behind the introduction of Riordan, O'Connor and players like that. When big Mixu became manager the fans loved him. I was actually quite surprised when he was appointed. When he left, the fans found it hard to criticise him directly because of what he had done in his playing career for Hibs. Our present manager Alan Stubbs has been doing a good job under the circumstances. I think his man-management is much better than Butcher his predecessor. I thought Butcher, was hopeless and at least the style of football has improved since his departure. The standard of player that Stubbs is bringing in seems to be the young and hungry type with no shortage of ability. I think Stubbs will eventually be successful at Hibs, though maybe I shouldn't say that in case he is not.

I think Graeme Souness's tackle on George McCluskey in 1986 was the most horrific thing I remember at Easter Road. He went right down McCluskey's leg and after being sent off went in to the dressing room and kicked the door in. The old kit man apparently went mental at him for that. He was supposed to be some kind of 'hard man' after that tackle, but Souness said he was embarrassed

Hibernian was one of the first clubs in Scotland to recognise the importance of owning a state-of-the-art training facility. Situated near Tranent, East Lothian, the East Mains project cost around £5 million and was opened by Sir Tom Farmer in 2007. It is considered by many to be the finest facility of its kind in Scotland.

The Hibs manager at the time, John Collins, said, 'I played at Monaco, Everton and Fulham and I can honestly say that the Hibernian Training Centre is an improvement on the centres used by these clubs.'

An expression of commitment to investing in youth development, it continues the Hibernian tradition of being one of Scotland's most innovative clubs.

because his dad was watching from the stand. That's probably the worst tackle I've ever seen in the game, although I do remember Joe Tortolano being sent off in a match against Man Utd for a really bad challenge on Gordon Strachan about ten minutes into the game. I think he put Strachan about ten feet in the air even though it was just a friendly.

I recall going to watch Hibs against AEK Athens in September 2001. When we got to the first game it was postponed because of the 9/11 tragedy. That was it, so we said, 'Right we've got to stay here in Athens for three days then...' and then thought, 'Who's gonna come back for the next one?' Hibs probably had about 1,500 fans at the first game and by the time the second game came around there were probably only about 500. For the second game we flew out and came back the same day, which was horrendous, I would never do that again. We got back about four in the morning.

I have to say I didn't particularly like Athens as a city. When we arrived at the ground we got searched by these kind of riot police guys and they were saying, 'Give us your money,' so you had to give up everything you had in your pockets. Once you got into the ground it was also pretty horrendous – they were chucking coins at us and generally abusing us all through the game. It wasn't a great experience. And to make matters worse, we lost 2-0. Hibs had a great chance to make it 2-1 and somebody missed it. In contrast, the return leg was probably the best atmosphere I've ever experienced in a European game. You could actually feel the hairs on the back of your neck standing up. And the tension in the air, you could really feel it. There was continual singing for the whole game and it was just a fantastic match. It was all about the occasion – the packed stadium and the great European night under the floodlights, that's what made it so special. A player called Paco Luna had just signed and late in the game missed a great chance. My dad was sitting right behind the same goal as me and he said, 'He's got to score! How the hell did he miss it?' It was fantastic performance but I still think about that chance from Luna, all he had to do was head it in from eight yards. But that's football...

I was also in Dnipro for the game against them. I was there for four days, it was a beautiful place with beautiful women and a beautiful culture. The people were very polite and they went out of their way to help you, so it was just fantastic. They had a very work-orientated society and it was interesting because they almost had too many staff for certain jobs, kind of like how you imagine the old Soviet way to be. We were in a bar before the game and the next thing we knew, one of those smoke canisters came through the door, then all these Ukranian thugs stormed in and me and my mate, Graham Jameson, hid in the kitchen with all the pub staff, who barricaded the doors. We waited nervously until they left. After all that, we eventually got to the stadium, sat down and Dnipro scored straight away. We lost by a lot of goals. I remember Tony Mowbray coming across at the end of the game and applauding us, even though we got hammered.

After the game we went into town and were again treated like lords. Anyone you met was really inquisitive, asking what Edinburgh was like and just generally asking you questions. I took a bad turn, mind you, when we were coming back on the bus. I keeled over and the boys were shouting, 'Get up Morrison, you're nothing but a wimp!' Apparently my eyes were rolling in the back of my head and one of the Ukrainian guys came over and said, 'No, no, no... you're not well!' The next thing we knew, this ambulance came along with the siren flashing, it stopped and a guy stepped out wearing a big white coat. I'm thinking to myself, 'You dinnae want to get in there!' It was almost like a scene from *The Cannonball Run* with that scary Dr Van Helsing character lurking in the back of the ambulance. They started taking my blood pressure and doing checks on me but I kept saying, 'Look, I'm fine.' They were so keen to help. I would never have gone to that place in my life had it not been for Hibernian.

I think football is also very important to the wider community. Some of the pub owners have said to me, 'If we didn't have football we'd be closed.' So it keeps people in jobs and it keeps businesses like the local bakery shop or pub turning over. These type of businesses want Hibs to do well because then they will be busy and their business will survive as a result. Maybe all sport is important in that regard – it's all about the community.

I know a few guys who believe Hibs' Irish roots are important to them. For me, it's the fact that they are from Leith that's important. Dalmeny Street was where I was brought up so they were my local team. If you go to Burnley, for example, everyone's got a Burnley top on – they don't wear Newcastle or Man Utd tops, because they are Burnley supporters. What annoys me about walking into pubs in Edinburgh nowadays is when you have Rangers and Celtic supporters sitting watching a game. I mean, guys who live in Glasgow and support them, then fantastic, but when they come over in ferries from Ireland it really pisses me off! Tell me why a guy that's born in Craigmillar supports Celtic? I don't understand that. And with some Celtic fans, it really is a case of, 'If you're going to support Ireland so much then why not live there?' When we go to Parkhead they hold a half-time raffle and the prizewinners always seem to be from Cork or Dublin... so what's wrong with watching Cork City? For that reason, one of my favourite clubs is Partick Thistle. I love Firrhill, a lot of guys from the universities watch Partick, and I like them because they are a traditional club and they also have to fight against all that Glasgow sectarian rubbish. I hate when people start singing 'What a shitey home support' at places like Motherwell, Dumbarton or Raith Rovers. I mean, that's their supporters who pay their money and bother to turn up and watch them every week! When we played Montrose in the Cup, and we beat them by five goals, their fans were at least still there supporting their club; they could easily go and support Rangers or Celtic. You also get these people who say, 'I used to support Hearts, I used to support Chelsea.' What's that all about? When I go down south you get others who say 'I support Arsenal, I support Man Utd,' and they will follow that up by saying, 'Oh no, I don't go to the games.' Edinburgh teams could easily be getting attendances of 35,000 each but we don't because of the position of football in Scotland. It's like a goldfish bowl. Maybe the west coast media are to blame – it really is true that they only care about Rangers and Celtic. I think the media bias has got worse in the time I have supported Hibs, although I think that bias has always been there. The boards behind both Old Firm clubs seem to be constantly harping on about joining the English League. I wonder whether they would be accepted in England given their general behaviour? Why would fans of Nottingham Forest or Bolton, for example, want these people in their city? They constantly undermine the Scottish League with their desire to leave, so I say, just let them go!

There used to be a guy in the old North Stand who would get awfully excited, I mean really ridiculously excited and I used to think, 'You should take a pill because you're gonna have a heart attack.' These guys are normal guys during the day, working in an office for example, but on a Saturday they release all their tensions and that's a big part of what football is all about. I am a member of the Hibs 50 Club that used to have a club room under the old Main Stand. There were some great characters that went there. One guy, Ramsey Dalgety, a great Hibs man, he was a judge,. A glass of brandy in hand, he used to say, 'Any of those Hearts bastards come in front of me and they'll get the jail!' Allegedly he would say in court, 'Are you from Tynecastle? You are? You must be a Hearts fan! I sentence you to eight years...', which I'm sure was an exaggeration for our benefit. It was still very funny though.

I always go to Tamson's Bar before or after the game. It's a small bar where they always welcome you with open arms. The regulars affectionately call it Tamson's Disco Bar but it's not a disco! A group of pals from down south got in a taxi once and asked for 'Tamsons Disco Bar, please?' and the taxi driver apparently almost crashed the cab after saying, 'That's no' a disco bar!' It may be because a guy called Willie Murray still brings in his old '60s and '70s vinyl collection every month and DJ's some old tracks for the regulars. I've got a group of pals that have been going there for 20 or 30 years. That's what it's all about... I would love to think that I could be at Tamsons Bar after we win the Scottish Cup again. That would be some party!

All that matters to Hibs fans is success on the park. The club sometimes talk about community spirit and that is fantastic but I would like to see this translate to the park. Success for Hibs should be getting back into the premiership, being in the top four and also getting into cup finals regularly. For a club like Hibernian that is where we should be.

Lord Martin O'Neill

Politician, born 1945.

❛ There was this sense of
these little rivulets joining
the Amazon and flowing into
Albion Road. ❜

I SUSPECT BEING a Hibs fan is an almost pre-natal condition for me. If you're interested in football, you come from Edinburgh and your name is O'Neill, then I don't think there is very much you could do about not being a Hibbie.

My family were Irish immigrants. My father had renounced his Catholicism but had retained a blind faith in Hibs, which I'm sure he could not justify any more than his previous religious affiliations. My mother's family were not Catholics and had no Irish connections, but were also Hibs supporters. I was born in 1945 and so I was brought up in the glory years of the Famous Five. There was a very popular song at that time, 'A Gordon for Me', and of course we always made the link with Gordon Smith. I was brought up in an atmosphere that was largely concerned with football or politics.

From the age of about five or six I was taken to the game by my dad. What struck me most was the crowd, 40–50,000 people in a massive bowl of a stadium. And of course I remember things like changing ends at half time and the absence of segregation. The bits and pieces I recall about these early games are probably received memory though.

I didn't have any brothers or sisters but my dad had this large extended Irish-Catholic family and we all went to the matches together. People were so hard up that they didn't necessarily meet in the pub. In fact my old man used to work on a Saturday morning – he worked in Ferranti's as an engineer and my mother worked in a baker's shop. I would maybe be playing football and I would come home, we would have lunch and then we'd go to the game, the first team and the reserves on alternate weeks. Unless you were a travelling member of the supporters club, which meant that you paid a wee bit towards it every week, you tended not to go away games. My dad actually was a member of the supporters club so he went to some away matches, but not that many because if you were working on a Saturday morning the chance of overtime was always a very attractive thing. The reserve games could be rather boring it has to be said, but on the other hand, to see Gordon Smith coming back after breaking his leg in 1954 or 1955, there were 17,000 people present, just to see him in a reserve match!

It was the days before replica kits and little boys weren't given Hibs baby warmers or things like that. You maybe had a green scarf if your mother thought about knitting one. Nobody really bothered about that in the 1950s. If you went in to Thornton's, the big sports shop on Princes Street, to look at the football boots, getting a Hibs strip wasn't something you even thought about. It would have almost been seen as a bit 'presumptuous' to be wearing something that other people deserved to wear.

When I was about nine or ten I often went to the matches with my dad and once we were inside the ground I'd leave him to go meet my pals from school. We'd collect beer bottles to take to the pub and get the money back on them.

My route home to Canonmills was up Easter Road and along London Road, or along McDonald Road through to where the Powderhall dump is now. We tended to walk because bus fares cost money. We weren't really poor though, because my mum and dad both worked, but we were still a working-class family and you didn't have the money to spend on that kind of thing. You might buy a programme, and I think it was about fourpence in old money to get in at the children's gate. There were far more children at games back then because we were the baby boom generation. You would walk down all the little streets that were feeding into Easter Road, mainly from Leith Walk but also from different angles, and converge – there was this sense of these little rivulets joining the Amazon and flowing into Albion Road.

It was amazing how people seemed to be able to gauge their arrival. The fact that there might be 45,000 or 50,000 there and most people still managed to get in on time was incredible. The old Easter Road stadium had a number of aisles down it and my dad always went to aisle number nine at the Dunbar End, always about a third of the way down. It meant that in mother's mind, although she never really went to matches, she could be sure that I could go and find him if there was a problem. In those days there wasn't any concept that allowing a young kid to wander off was neglect and I never got any hassle.

I was parked at my granny's in Broughton Road when my mother was working and it's fair to say that it was a split area. There were Hibs supporters and Hearts supporters but you all played together and there was no kind of sectarianism at Wardie Primary School or Trinity Academy, but naturally there was banter and what have you. Throughout my life, until the segregation of the crowd came about, I would occasionally go with Hearts supporters to Tynecastle and they would come to Easter Road for the Hibs v Hearts games. Edinburgh didn't have that hard-edged aspect.

When Hearts won the League Cup I was really sick because the streets were lined with people. In those days I don't think we worried quite so much about not winning a cup. I do remember listening to the Coronation Cup Final in 1953 when my dad went through to the game, I think it as on a Wednesday night. He must have got off his work early to get through to it and I remember the bitter disappointment of failing to win it. In some ways it was far more prestigious than the Scottish Cup because in effect it was a British Cup. Hibs had done the business in the prior rounds and were going to play a Celtic team that were no great shakes. I think it was probably the first exposure I had as a football supporter to failure.

My dad had a virtually photographic memory. If you went to football matches with him you didn't have a conversation because he just stood there and concentrated. The pain was obvious sometimes, but after the game, if you asked him about a move he would recount virtually the whole thing – it was amazing! He died about 11 years ago. In the last conversation I had with him, I asked him how he was doing. He replied, 'Not that great son.' We chatted away and then he said, 'Well, a draw yesterday. No' good enough, we'll have to win the replay.' Those were his last words to me. He was 90 and he'd gone pretty much blind but he still had all his marbles. He had listened to the 1998 World Cup in its entirety on the radio and he would always say to my son, 'What happened at the game? I want to be told. Your father never pays enough attention!' which was true enough.

About four or five friends go the games together sometimes. If you are at the match and you are catching up about your work, their work and talking about your families, then it's more than just the game. For my old man that would have been irrelevant though, as he would always say, 'There's 90 minutes for watching and ten minutes for pleasantries at half time.' He had a whole fund of stories I think that tended to reinforce the Hibs tradition for me. Although he was just a metal worker and fitter, he had also been a clever boy at school. His parents both died early and he was never able to go to university, which as a working-class guy would have been very difficult, although I think his mother would certainly have fought for him to do so. He was always very articulate. I remember him saying: 'In the early 1920s, when Hibs were playing rubbish and were near relegation, it was great because when you walked up from the match you'd be dying on someone asking you for the score so you could tell them you won.' He would also tell you about players and the circumstances back then, little things, like how The Albion Bar used to be owned by the man who owned Hibs and the kick-off was always delayed until 3.15pm because the pub shut at 3pm and he needed time to get round for the game.

Dad's experience of the improvement of the side in the war years was also interesting. He was fortunate that he wasn't away fighting as he was based at home or in Grangemouth and he got to see most of the games. He was at the 8-1 game against Rangers, which in some ways, until 1973, amongst the *cognoscenti* was of far more significance than any defeat of the Hearts. Whenever I see a book about Rangers' history, I always try and see if there's any reference to that 8-1 game, which is pure 'badness' you might say. Once, through in the west, we were standing in a station with Hibs supporters and some Celtic supporters had come back from a game. 'You're not fit to wear the green,' they were shouting. My old man went through this guy like a hot knife through butter. 'We were the first team and if it wasnae for your publicans and your bent lawyers then you wouldn't have stolen our half back line and destroyed the club for five years!' Boom! And it was perfectly true.

I was lucky that I had this working-class intellectual of a father who was well read, politically active and clear-minded, able to articulate things and perhaps offer a balance. But he wasn't interested in the economics of the game as a lot of people now have to be because these factors determine things. You were expected to talk intelligently about the game afterwards so that questions like 'What did you think?', 'Why did that happen?', 'Shouldn't we not be doing this?'. It took up a lot of the conversational space and of course the electronic media was virtually non-existent.

Football was a central part of the whole business of growing up for me. After the dip in the early '60s, from when I started work in 1963 things begun to improve a wee bit and you could see light at the end of the tunnel. From then until the mid-'70s it was a pretty good period to be a Hibs supporter.

Football was a somewhat mercurial process and teams could rise and fall. Celtic were well supported, but not fantastically well until Jock Stein came along. I would really like to know why Hibs went from 1954 to 1963 in almost constant decline apart from little rises like the Barcelona game and getting to a cup final. Why was there this inconsistency and how was it allowed to drift?

Rangers just marched on continuously and until 1954 Hibs and Rangers were on a par for a number of seasons, and yet it seemed as if there was a certain 'softness' about the Edinburgh support. Admittedly the Hearts had a purple patch to which even they were entitled, I say grudgingly. But you just wonder why that Hibs decline took place because the Celtic renaissance was down exclusively to the Stein influence. I read somewhere recently that Falkirk beat Celtic 5-1 two years before Stein arrived, and of that 'Lisbon Lions' team there were about seven or eight surviving that were beaten so heavily. That is something that fascinates me almost as much as anything else in football. Stein showed that you could enthuse a team and you could direct them. I have just started reading Lawrie Reilly's autobiography and I wonder, what was the turning point? I mean, Hugh Shaw was the trainer along with Sammy Keane, who had played for Hibs. McCartney died in 1948 and yet the Hibs carried on for another six years. You could probably date the demise of Hibs with the departure of Bobby Johnstone. When players return they are older, and in his case they were fatter, but he was certainly very, very clever and in the shape of Harry Swan, the Hibs chairman, they acquired this farsighted maverick called Joe Baker. Swan didn't have a lot of money and he didn't suffer fools gladly, but he had ideas about wages, which in some respects almost replicate what is happening now.

For me as a youngster, the peaks were enough. I remember going to watch the reserves with MacLeod and Baker playing in them and they were both fantastic! On average, at reserves game back then, you would get maybe 6–8,000; they would sometimes open the terraces but most of the time it was just the enclosure and the stand. There may have been the odd interesting cup tie but there was a second 11 structure which meant that there was an element of competition in it. There were sometimes clubs that weren't doing so well in the First Division but in the Reserve League they were doing well, so you would think, 'Well, why are they not doing well in the main league?' There was also this sense in which the dedicated football supporters wanted to see who was coming through. Joe Baker didn't spend much time in the reserves and I suppose really that in the post-Famous Five period Eddie Turnbull was never given the credit that he was due. Willie Ormond was a dazzling player and a superb left-footer but his other foot was for standing on.

Sometimes I find it difficult to separate the legend from the reality but I remember this guy maybe 5ft 8 or 9, slim, athletic and immaculate, who would run around the pitch playing keepy-uppy. This was Gordon Smith, a real professional. He enjoyed quite a reputation outside of Scotland, although there was always this suggestion that Willie Waddell and the Rangers influence in the SFA prevented him from getting the number of caps he should have had. Having said that, he was the captain of the Scottish team in 1955 when they had a very successful central European tour and it was shortly after that his ankle was injured again and his career went into decline. What can never be taken away from him is that here was a man who won three league medals with different clubs and who, in his youth, was both a goalscorer and a goalmaker. I remember talking to some of his contemporaries and not one seemed to have a bad word for him. They said he was really a nice guy, he was very caring, he took his job as captain very seriously and he provided them with opportunities to go and play golf. He was also accepted within the pantheon of great sportsmen of his day. Tom Finney was also on that list.

At home it was still almost 'Fortress Easter Road', there was always the emphasis on attack more than defence. I remember Reilly scoring a goal, which for a man of his size was remarkable. Turnbull took a corner, he hit it hard, and Reilly ran from outside the 18-yard box and rose dramatically to head it in. It was obviously on the understanding that Turnbull knew what he needed to do and Reilly was going to have a bloody good try at doing it. I saw more of Reilly as his career petered out. He played against Rangers on the Wednesday before the cup final and that was his last game, but by that time Joe Baker was taking over. Baker was probably the hero of my early adolescence and it was great meeting him in later years. I remember talking to him after he had heart trouble. 'How are you doing Joe? All right for the game tonight?' And he said, 'My boots are clean, Martin, give me 15 minutes and I'll give you a goal!' In fact I went to see him playing for England at Hampden and I didn't know what team to support. I have earned my living through defeating Scottish Nationalists but going to see Joe Baker was like going to see my hero and I wanted so much for him to do well! Of course there are all the stories about him speaking with a Scots accent and being asked, 'How can you play for England?'

When Stein came in it seemed Hibernian had gone into terminal decline.

Walter Galbraith, a manager whose job it was to dig clubs out of holes, was there but half the time he would take clubs halfway out and then leave again without taking them much further. Stein came in with one or two judicious acquisitions and he also inherited a number of young players like Stanton, Cormack, O'Rourke and other good professionals, guys who had that wee bit more. After the stumbling in the early to mid-'60s, you had Stein and you also had Shankly, who won the league. He was the best manager in Scotland after Stein and there was a great frustration because we felt that Hibs were really on the crest of a big wave. It was not insignificant that Stein was signed as the Celtic manager after Hibs had beaten Rangers three times in the one season. You had intermittent bits of glory like a Summer Cup victory, albeit a bit of a 'no-no' in terms of glamour, and there were games where they really were quite outstanding. Hibs were never far away from their past glories but instead just tantalisingly close…

I went to see Hibs playing East Fife in a rubbish game and they won 1-0, but at the expense of John Brownlie's leg and Alex Edward's sixth booking of the year. Edwards then got 'put away' for about two months, which was horrendous punishment, and it meant that for Turnbull's team two of the most critical players were denied them and so the season died after that. Turnbull brought in Alan Gordon, who was regarded as such a great player. The truth was that he was slow, but brilliant in the air. Put the ball at his feet and he could do it, but he was ageing. As Arsène Wenger always says, 'Twenty-nine, and you sell them. Keep half backs until they are 34 or 35.' So it's true to say that Alan Gordon was running out of steam although he had had a good career. Of course they brought in wee Joe Harper but Joe just never clicked with the fans and when he came to Easter Road he was fat!

Hibs never seemed to give sufficient attention to replacing players, perhaps because there was a steady stream of talent coming through, but I think that was one of the biggest frustrations for me. They didn't get rid of an awful lot,

The Hibs team arriving back from Barcelona, 1961.

'Even though Hibs went into decline from 1954 onwards they had intermittent high spots like the Barcelona game.'

so after the mid-'70s it became very disappointing. As I got a wee bit older, I started to ask, 'Why do we support Hibs?' And my father would say, 'Well, the Irish ghetto was down in Holyrood Road where trades and professions were closed to Catholics and the church was the focal point of a lot of people's lives.' He told me how the young men who lived in the area formed a football club and organised themselves into a team. It has become clear that the role of the priests was less important than originally thought. I wasn't really aware of the extent of the anti-Catholic prejudice which would appear to have been prevalent back then. But I don't think that Hearts sought to prevent Hibs because they were rivals. It was because Hibs were Catholic and Hearts were more middle-class. I think history shows that Hearts weren't really sectarian, they just reflected the general prejudices of the time. I would find it surprising though if there are many people with Irish backgrounds supporting Hearts. I mean, there are Catholics who support Hearts but I'm not sure if there are so many O'Neills, Murphys or names like that. But let's face it, neither club has adopted a sectarian employment policy.

In the '70s I taught at a school where most of the boys in the Standard Grade class were Jambo fanatics and one day when I went into the classroom these guys were sitting there singing '1902! 1902!' That was the first time I had heard that reference. I think I even hit one of them with a jotter! I suppose the point was that the Hearts supporters had to find something against the 7-0 win. I do remember Hibs getting beaten by Hearts 6-1 on the first game of the season and a drunken guy saying, 'C'mon Hibs, beaten but not defeated.' That was a good line. I suspect that's one of the things that keeps you going: Hibs can be beaten but not ultimately wiped out.

Going to Tynecastle was something I might do once a season. But when Hearts were in the European Cup I never thought about going to see them because I'm not a Hearts supporter. Some people say that what they like is a good game of football but what I like is a Hibs victory. Some might say that a

In February 1961 Hibs and Barcelona faced each other in the return leg of the European Fairs Cup. Having thrown away a 4-2 lead (drawing 4-4) in the first leg at the Nou Camp, Hibs were considered to be a shadow of the Famous Five side that had so dramatically lit up the 1950s. Barcelona, in comparison, were everybody's favourite, having ousted Real Madrid from the European Cup.

Joe Baker was the shining light in both legs but it was John McLeod who won a penalty with just minutes remaining on the clock. Bobby Kinloch duly converted as all hell broke loose inside Easter Road. Barca players chased officials and police were involved on the pitch.

Hibs won 3-2 to record an incredible victory!

draw is a fair result but a draw is never a fair result! A friend of mine recently said to me, 'If I go to the match and we dinnae win I'm sick until Wednesday, but it's better by Thursday because Saturday is coming!' I'm at the stage now that I kind of masochistically read the newspaper reports just in case there's been any fallout from yesterday's game or in case there are players going to be signed. There are those for whom football is a substitute for religion.

I think that nowadays there's a degree of 'link' between the club and the management that never existed before. Previously the manager was seen as a rather austere figure and the owners were the men who sat in the box. In Sir Tom Farmer we have someone who is committed to Hibs emotionally – and in a way he wasn't at first. But he can't get too emotional because this is a business and it should be run as a business. He has imposed disciplines which his sergeant major Petrie carries out. The board will formulate a business plan, by and large adhering to what Tom would probably want to do, and then he looks at it, his people crunch the numbers and with certain adjustments it will go back again. Provided that is adhered to he is happy. The board appoint the manager and the manager is given a budget, and within that budget they have a lot of discretion. Sometimes there have been issues about whether players should have their contracts extended and the potential knock-on effects on other players, and Rod Petrie might intervene, probably second-guessing what Tom Farmer would do.

I found it illuminating to be on the board. It made me realise the constraints within which well-run clubs have to operate. Hibs have got the best of difficult worlds in that they have a guy who foregoes profit in order that the ground becomes properly established and the training facility gets built. In my view they have a facility that is as good as any club's, and at a far lower price. It's easy to spill away the money from the sale of players by paying inflated salaries. When Scott Brown left Hibs he was on under £4,000 a week and at Parkhead he got at least £27,000 – I say 'at least', because there would have been added bonuses. The problem is that you have to speculate to accumulate and that is probably where Hibs have been a wee bit less adventurous than they might have been. Again you come back to the point where we should only be spending around about 50 per cent of the gate money on wages. So how do you increase the gate money without having the players? Chickens and eggs...

If a manager makes the wrong choices that's just part of the luck of the game. When I was on the board, the manager would come in and give an overview of the last two or three games at the monthly meeting. He would indicate that there are players who have got injuries that might well take longer to repair than had been hoped and equally if there were players who are coming back. (I remember once when Scott Brown broke a bone in his foot, he got the plaster off and said to Tony Mowbray, 'I've just got the plaster off now boss so I can start playing again.' (He was about 18 at the time and keen as mustard. He was in the gym every day doing lifting when he couldn't do any running.)

The manager might say, 'There's a player we need to try and get and we've made initial noises, Rod knows about it so I'm just keeping you informed. We think we can get him for this wage bracket and X will be going out to make the space for Y.' Board members were kept abreast. We didn't meet on a Thursday night to pick the team, as they might have done in the past. Basically our job was to make sure that somebody was answerable for the expenditures. We would sometimes try to identify solutions to problems and it's fair to say that with projects like the training facility we agonised over whether to have a one- or two-tier East Stand. Essentially it came down to money: a million pounds. It's a bit like the argument for filling in the gaps right round so that you would have a bowl shape, but to do that would probably cost as much as the East Stand and you would only be getting a handful of extra seats. To build the shop we had to borrow from the bank because we didn't want to use money that we would use for players. We set ourselves a target that it would pay for itself in two years, and it did. We chose to centralise the retail facilities at Easter Road although it might have been nice to have a shop tucked away in one of the shopping centres. The idea of using a bit of the money to improve the capital of the club is one thing but whether or not we could have used more of the money to bring in better replacements is open to question.

When John Park was at Easter Road you had this guy who was out every day of the week looking for players. As Tony Mowbray said: 'There are players who are good and whom a manager coming into the club doesn't recognise. There are players who are good but get injured and by the time they are fit they get replaced by someone better. There are players who are just pissed off and then there are players, for personal reasons, whose career has just nose-dived. The secret is trying to identify which of these might be good enough to come to a club like Hibernian.' I think that's something people don't always appreciate but a good manager should always be looking at. The problem is that when you buy players in the January window, they tend to be distressed purchases. Because you're toiling, you're thinking, 'We need to get a player, we've got to do something.' It's a difficult call. That's why I think there will be always be pressure on managers. But they are ultimately professionals, who understand the realities, whereas the public don't. If journalists were more prepared to get away from the simple hype then you might get a more intelligent football support.

I remember going to Ibrox to see Rangers playing Alloa Athletic because as a Member of Parliament I used to go and see them occasionally. Looking round at the adverts and seeing the number of businesses that wish to be associated with Rangers FC, I realised we don't have that kind of business backing on either side of Edinburgh.

Football is still predominantly working-class while rugby is more middle-class. That might be why none of the financial giants support us. In Edinburgh the people that make the decisions would rather pour money into the rugby internationals and I think that type of thing goes back to the city's private school set-up. But also, we at Hibs have never really 'attacked' the universities and there are four of them in Edinburgh now, with 30,000 plus students. I remember in the late 1960s and '70s tons of students were coming to Easter

Road because it was a great team and it was good to watch. We started a thing at Freshers' Week to get folk along. We are doing something similar in the schools and a surprising number of youngsters get into Easter Road for nothing, and they're not reflected in the attendance figures. An interesting thing is that Hibs, when stating attendances, only give the season ticket holders who come through the turnstile, whereas Hearts give every season ticket holder, as they are assumed to attend every match.

In terms of helping the community, to be philanthropic we need to get businesses to recognise that we have a quality facility at Easter Road. This would mean Murrayfield and Easter Road were in competition, and Hearts will come into the game before too long in a serious way.

In the main you don't get many clever, capable, articulate people representing Scottish football and the ones who do are so few that they tend to get overexposed. I'm not sure a football academy is the best solution. I know the French have done it but France has a population of 65 million and we've got five million. John Collins was very keen on it, but I don't think he considered the social consequences in a relatively small country. How many clubs could do it? What happens if a club gets relegated, then the whole thing goes to hell? Again it might be a case of trying to impose models that are not relevant to Scottish clubs. It's a very costly business.

When I was the Labour Shadow Defence Secretary I was on a visit to Washington when I got a message to phone *The Sun* in Glasgow. I was in meetings but as soon as I got back to my hotel I called home and my wife said, 'Oh, it might be about the Hibs,' and she got our son, Michael, who must have been about 10 or 11 at the time, and he gave me the verbatim from the Teletext page about the Mercer takeover. In the end I never got back to *The Sun*. The next morning I picked up a copy of the *Financial Times* and there was the story, so I kind of saw it from afar. I could see the sense of what Mercer was doing but it was exactly the wrong way to do it. A friend of mine summed it up when he said, 'I think we should have one Edinburgh team called Heart of Hibernian.'

It was all a bit brutal but I think it exposed Hibs' weakness and enabled Tom Farmer to be brought into the club. Dougie Cromb and one or two others deserve an awful lot of credit for the way that they restored the credibility of the club. I was not one of those that bought shares in it, and I wasn't at that stage of wanting to get involved with the running of the club. What the attempted takeover brought home was that there needed to be a degree of reality. Fortunately it happened in the close season so the players weren't exposed to it all. In my opinion Alex Miller handled that period extremely well. He's sometimes regarded as being a rather boring manager but he brought in some good players and he also won a cup. I think that he deserves credit that he has never received.

When Tom Farmer took over there remained people who felt that they could have been part of something but weren't. The thing with a lot of football clubs is that there are always people who would like to have part of the action but don't have enough money. The ones that do have enough money usually have more sense than to get involved. Initially Tom Farmer came in as a guarantor but he has since become more involved. It's no secret that the money that he lends, he lends with a view to getting paid back. In large measure it has been paid back and the asset that is now Easter Road and Ormiston is far greater than what he took over. As I understand it, he wouldn't sell it to anyone that couldn't show that they could make a go of it. It would take maybe 20 million pounds to acquire the assets and a fair bit more 'ballast', as it were.

The Hibs–Hearts banter has become more bitter but I don't necessarily think that's to do with the Mercer takeover. Hearts have had more problems in respect to ownership. There's a joke that goes round: 'Hearts are the only team that can have a different 'Manager of the Month' every month.' But both clubs have had experience of a bit of that. The city isn't two divided armed camps but simply two different clubs.

You can't measure the attitude of a whole club by the nutters. They tend to be vociferous and are the prey of easy journalism – and journalists have to make bricks with the straw that is available, and sometimes they make bricks without straw.

Part of the passion of football, is that you are always hoping for the giant-killing. Next Saturday we play Celtic – and we are going to win!

Irvine Welsh

Writer, born 1958.

❛ You had the illusion that the Highlands were just there beside you and that you could escape into this green kind of grandeur. ❜

MY OLD MAN was a Hibs supporter but he came from a Hearts family, his brothers were all Hearts supporters and his old man was a Hearts supporter. He became a Hibs supporter just to be awkward really and thank fuck he did! He and his brothers were that last generation of supporters who used to go to Hibs one week and then Hearts the next. I got taken along to Easter Road and Tynecastle as a kid but was never pushed in any one direction. I hated Tynecastle and I hated that horrible strip and the smell of the brewery and distillery, it made me fucking boak! I really did hate being crammed into that dirty wee space in Gorgie. Paradoxically, I used to love going to Easter Road because I liked the Dunbar End and the great view of Arthur's Seat. You had the illusion that the Highlands were just there beside you and that you could escape into this green kind of grandeur, it had a scenic kind of openness about it. I liked the strip, the sharp contrast of the green and the white sleeves. It just felt much more like a home for me.

The first game I went to I was maybe about five or six but at that age you're not really that aware of things and you were probably running up and down the terraces, bored. I'm pretty sure it was Hibs v Motherwell and I think we won 2-1, I remember being happy we won but I don't remember too much about the game. The first game I ever took a real interest in was in 1968 when I went along to see Hibs and Kilmarnock. It was a 3-3 draw. Colin Stein scored a hat-trick for Hibs and I think it was Tommy McLean, Eddie Morrison and Gerry McQueen who scored for Kilmarnock. It was one of these end-to-end, pulsating kind of games that could have gone either way. Both teams went right at each other and it was really exciting with loads of chances missed. I imagined it was going to be like that every week and I thought, this is fucking great, this is what it's all about! If anyone asked what team I supported I would always say, 'Hibs, but that game made me properly become a Hibs supporter,. As a young kid you would argue with cousins and family members who were Hearts supporters, getting really vitriolic – 'Hearts are shite!', 'Hibs are fucking great!' and all that. It just seemed to be some kind of tribal reference that I had embraced for some reason and I didn't really know why at the time, because my old man was from a Hearts family. I was never brought up to hate Jambos or anything like that and I was not so much anti-Hearts, just pro-Hibs.

Before they put seats in 'The Cave' – the old shed behind the goal – I remember a European game against Malmö that Hibs won 6-0. It was pissing down and there were maybe 10,000 people all trying to get under cover in The Shed. We were right at the front getting crushed and it just kept pissing with rain. Every time Hibs scored there was a huge surge and the next again day all my ribs were bruised from being pushed against the wall. I think I actually went on the pitch a few times just to get away from the crush.

If the weather was good we always used to go to the floodlight nearest The Cave. I was kind of besotted by this bird that used to stand there as well so that's why I used to always stand in the same place. When we changed ends I used to go by the scoreboard at the corner of the Dunbar End. I never did find out who that bird was, I tried to chat her up a few times with no success whatsoever.

For a couple of seasons I went to every single game, home and away, in the league and the cup. From about 14 to 17 years of age I got kind of crazy about it, just totally absorbed by it. A bunch of us used to go, sometimes we'd go on the bus from St Andrew's Square but usually we'd go on the train.

You go through different periods of being really obsessed. When I'm back in Edinburgh I always go to games but I've lived out of the country so much that it's curtailed the amount of games I can go to. There's no real logic to it. Sometimes there's been periods where I've not gone to matches but ironically during those periods I get even more passionate about the club than ever. I'd read the reports on a game and get much more upset if we lost than if I actually witnessed it. You kind of become more mellow and zen about it as you get older but if Hibs lost when I was younger I would go into a depression about it and it wouldn't be over until about the Wednesday after the game. By that time of the week you would think, come on Hibs, we've got a chance to make good on Saturday. To this day if we lose the derby I just want to get home and watch crap on the TV or stick a DVD on, I want to blank it out and all that. I don't even want to look at it in the newspaper, the internet forums or anything like that. It's not until about Thursday or Friday that feeling goes away.

Going to the game is a big social thing for me because it's a way of keeping in touch with people. The crowd of guys that I go with come from all different backgrounds – underemployed 'duckers and divers', schoolteachers, computer programmers and builders. There's nothing else to tie them together, they would never have been pals but they have been big mates now for about 30-odd years by going to the football together. Football and music are the only two ways to meet people, aside maybe from working with them. Everybody I know I've met through football, and not just Hibs. I lived in London for a while so I went to football there with a guy who's a big West Ham fan and he drums in a band as well, so in that case it's a combination of the two things.

I remember our three League Cup wins. There was the 2-1 game against Celtic in 1972 which I thought we would lose. I was so used to seeing Hibs lose in finals back then, I couldn't actually quite believe we had won the League Cup! The final against Dunfermline in '91 was a great game because, again, I thought we'd kind of blow it at the last minute. We'd been through so much with the Mercer takeover and I was at the game with this guy who was just bursting into tears and I'd never seen him do that before, and will probably never see it again – everything just came to a head with thinking about the whole takeover business. It felt like much more than a cup win, it was almost like a fucking spiritual experience! In contrast to the crowd at the other two cup finals – the Kilmarnock and Celtic games – where everyone was jumping around and singing, everybody walked out that ground like they had just seen the Second Coming. It was quiet on the bus going back and it was only when we got to Harthill that it all started to sink in and we went mental again.

For the 5-1 Kilmarnock League Cup Final, in 2007, I flew over from Miami. It was absolutely fucking baking with heat when I left and it was snowing when I got to Glasgow. So I was dressed somewhat inappropriately at Hampden – I had a Hawaiian shirt on and a pair of white chinos or something like that. I'd flown to London and then straight to Glasgow so I was jet-lagged to fuck by the time I met anybody – I was all over the place! I thought to myself beforehand, 'I'm going to fall asleep at the game here,' but thankfully it just kept on snowing so it kept me awake. After the game I went back to Leith where they had the big party, it was a crazy night, but eventually I thought, 'I've got to opt out of this now, it's two in the morning.' I had to get back the next again day to Glasgow Airport and then a flight to London so I tried to think: 'Waverley Station will be shut so I'll just try and find the timetable so I can get the early morning train

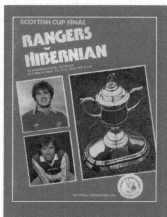

‘ The other big disappointment I recall was the Rangers Scottish Cup Final game in 1979. We should have won the cup then, we really got close to it!’

to Glasgow, or maybe I could get a taxi so I could kip in the airport.' My heid was wasted! So I met these two guys who were electricians and were working in the station. One of them was a Rangers supporter and the other was a Celtic fan. They were Glasgow guys and they were driving back there so they gave me a lift through, dropped me off, and I got a cab to the airport. I flew to London and then straight to Miami with the newspapers. My mate Kenny, who does club promotions, was in Miami for a dance music festival so he hadn't been able to get over for the game. So he said, 'Give us a paper,' and because of the time difference it was bizarre, almost like almost going back in time – here we were sitting with the Sunday papers on Miami Beach, Monday morning, reading about the game in the *Sunday Mail* and *Scotland on Sunday*. I never slept for a couple of days after that, I was just in a bubble.

It's weird because the League Cup tournament has been really devalued since the Dunfermline League Cup Final game. Now there is no European place for winning it, although it never feels that way when you're in the final because the final is something in itself, it's something to be enjoyed and celebrated. There's the times when we didn't win at all and I felt bad, for example, at the 6-1 Celtic Scottish Cup Final, in 1972, I was convinced we were going to win that one but the team just kind of fell apart on the big day. We were good for a part of it though. Hibs have got to go down all guns blazing, as opposed to that Jambo shite of grinding it out, it bores me to death...

The other big disappointment I recall was the Rangers Scottish Cup final game in 1979. We should have won the cup then, we really got close to it! I was living in London and I hitchhiked up. The guy I travelled up with was from Manchester and he was a big Man Utd supporter. Man Utd were playing Arsenal in the cup final at Wembley but he couldn't get a ticket so he was determined he was going watch it up in Manchester. So we hitched up to Doncaster and decided we would split up, he'd go west and I'd go north. However, he found this stash of acid, we took the acid and we were fucking out our trees! We're

In the 1979 Premier League season Hibs finished in fifth place but only 11 points behind champions Celtic. Arthur Duncan, the speed merchant of 'greyhound' athleticism, was still very much at work. The team that battled with Rangers for almost five and a half hours over three games perhaps lacked the pizzazz that Turnbull's Tornadoes had given the Hibs support in previous years.

After battling past Aberdeen, in the semi at Hampden, Hibs survived a fearful last 20 minutes to clinch their place in the Scottish Cup Final, running out 2-1 winners. The omens even then were not particularly good – seven years previously they had reached a Scottish Cup Final and were trounced 6-1 by a rampant Celtic team. Rangers ran out 3-2 winners in an unforgettable second final replay. Hibs' Scottish Cup hoodoo continued for another year, and once more against a Glasgow team Hibs were left feeling a bitter sense of injustice.

kind of walking around on the A1 with cars shooting past us and the next thing I know we're waking up in a jail in Grantham – with a charge sheet. I didn't realise what had happened, I thought we had been arrested somewhere on the road. I literally had all this egg down my face and apparently what had happened was that he was dancing on the tables in a café when the police arrived and I had fallen face down into someone's egg and chips. It was a total fucking drama and I had to get out of there – the game was on at 3pm, I couldn't get back to Edinburgh first so I had to try and get from Grantham to Glasgow, hitchhiking. It was a mad experience, covered in egg and still off my tree, but I managed to get there and it was a 0-0 draw. I had to go back down to London and then come back up again for the final replay – that 3-2 game.

I went to the big event against the Mercer takeover in the Usher Hall and everyone was moaning like fuck about 'toon prices'. At the one last month, to mark the 20th anniversary, it was the same lot moaning about prices again. It's amazing you get people that just go to their local boozer and never come in to the centre of town. I vividly remember the vitriolic hatred that everyone felt for Wallace Mercer, I remember the graffiti on the big tent in Princes Street Gardens with 'CCS Mercer must die' scrawled on it. There was a sense of sheer injustice at how somebody like that, and everything about him with his background in politics and general attitude, could destroy Hibs. But in a perverse kind of way, I think it has saved Hibs. He drew our attention to the mess that the club was in. You will see it with many clubs that are going to go the wall over the next five years, not managing to stop the spending that will destroy them. We got into the mindset that so many clubs need to get in to, but we did it earlier and we've not really relinquished that yet. We did get our fingers burnt financially, a wee bit, in the McLeish era but since then we've not really been coming out with these kind of grandiose declarations about what we're going to do.

The takeover bid definitely upped the ante in terms of the dislike that the two sets of supporters feel for one another, I mean, there's always been an element of Hibs and Hearts supporters who just don't like each other, they just don't. The rivalry, with all that historic credence, served to make the mainstream supporters really dislike each other as well. The atmosphere in general at derbies now is so much more poisonous, there was always that aggro and trouble in the Wheatfield or The Shed, coming out the ground etc, but amongst the rank and file supporters there is also now an atmosphere of poison.

In every city you get your cavaliers and your roundheads. In a very generalised sense, you might get one club who will maybe hold right-wing politics and then you get the other club that's more traditionally the underdog of the city. The underdog also maybe holds more of an appeal to the intelligentsia and the romantic. Roughly I think that does hold true. As far as the roots of the club on a personal level are concerned, I lived in Ireland for five years but I don't really know my family history. I don't think I have much Irish blood, if any, in me but I do feel quite proud that Hibs have that kind of connection because it gives us something unique. It was a harder thing to live with in the '70s and '80s when it was 'The Troubles' but Ireland has moved on and I think it's actually something that people can be proud of rather than slightly embarrassed by. A lot of the flag waving in the 1980s was an excuse to wind people up, I don't think that the people doing it took their Irish politics too seriously. Hibs have lost a bit of touch with those charitable roots and I'd like to see them get back to them and be more involved in the community. I know it's a business and it's got to be concerned with the bottom line but the more they invest in the community, the more the community will give back to Hibs. The Dnipro Hibs charity is great, there are still Hibs fans out there doing things, but I would like to see the club itself do more.

I remember big Jimmy, who is sadly no longer with us, he worked on the rigs so he kind of moved around a lot… we were at the Videoton game and there was basically nothing to see or do in the town, so we bought these bottles of wine and took a walk up beside a lake. We're all sitting there and Jimmy's absolutely fucking steaming by this point. He was lying beside this lake with his bottle of wine and so eventually we said, 'Come on Jimmy we're going tae the game!' He replied, 'Fuck aff!' and then promptly fell asleep. He just wouldn't wake up so we said, 'Just leave him, he's guttered anyway and he wouldnae see much of the game in that state.' So we walked down into the ground and saw the game – and incidentally, it was one of the best performances by Hibs on European soil. Afterwards we were sitting having a drink and someone said, 'Where the fuck has he gone, where is he?' We got talking to some locals and explained we had lost our mate and one of them told us, 'It's not a lake it's a reservoir, it fills up at night and the water level rises.' So we quickly got ourselves together and ran up to the lake. Jimmy was still lying there, the water up to his neck and the same bottle of wine sticking out of the water. Here he was, basically sleeping in the fucking water and we asked each other, 'How are we gonna wake him without him panicking?' We were chucking these stones in to the reservoir and the water's splashing all over him and when he came to he thought we had somehow put him in this reservoir. It was like the closing credits of the Benny Hill Show as he chased us back into town. Eventually he calmed down and saw the funny side of it!

Irene and David Birrell

Irene Birrell, born 1939.
David Birrell, born 1935.

‘ It's because you don't know what the end result is going to be, it's the unpredictability of it all that you don't get with cinema or theatre. ’

DAVID   When I first moved here from Fife I stayed in digs. Strangely enough, if I went to the football at all, I went to Tynecastle. As a boy my team was East Fife and then when I came to Edinburgh I mainly followed Hearts because they were the nearest team to where I lived and I had a school friend, Andy Bowman, who played for them at the time. But I had no strong feelings for them in the way that I did for East Fife – I could rattle off the names of the East Fife team back in the '50s. It was when I met Irene and her family that I became a Hibs supporter – it wasn't a condition of marrying Irene! And ever since then I've been hooked on the Hibs.

IRENE   My family originally came from Dumfriesshire. My father moved to Edinburgh to work and my mother followed him. We lived opposite the old picture house on Junction Street, right in the middle of Leith. I was about ten when I went to my first football game, it was my aunt and uncle who eventually took me because I went on, and on, and on about wanting to go. That first game was against Motherwell – I think they beat us. What I remember most was that Hibs, in the green and white, just looked so lovely compared to Motherwell, they looked so clean and fresh. I was taken to the Main Stand because my aunt and uncle had plenty of money. That was when we had the Famous Five playing so it was easy to get hooked.

When I was about 13 or 14 I would go to matches every other Saturday with three of four other girls in my class at school. It wasn't as common as it is now but there were still girls that went along to see Hibs. I never went to the pub before games because girls just didn't do that kind of thing when I was young. When I left school I went to work in an office and made a friend there who was as mad about Hibs as I was. The two of us went to games together for years. We would go to what was called the enclosure, which wasn't seated; it was below the old Main Stand. Valerie and I always stood just at the player's tunnel, I suppose because you were only 16 and you fancied the players. At that same time my father would go along with his friends and we would argue when we got back home from the game. He never seemed to see the same match that I saw.

DAVID When we started going to Easter Road together, we always stood at the opposite side from the Main Stand in the East terrace. At New Year's Day games you would get a bit intoxicated, as there was alcohol allowed in the ground, but I was never aware of any real crowd problems even though people were probably drinking too much. In those days the reason that you didn't attend away games was because you couldn't afford to. I think that was an issue for most people back then. People would go to Easter Road one week and then Tynecastle the next Saturday mainly because you couldn't afford to travel. The first game I remember was a New Year's day game against Hearts. There was maybe eight or nine of us, made up of half Hibs and half Hearts supporters. It was really just on the derby days that you tended to hate each other a wee bit, at other times we were quite friendly.

IRENE The conditions in the stadium have changed tremendously. It's clean now and comfortable. It certainly wasn't clean before! You have to have segregation now for some reason, whereas when there was none there used to be a certain amount of banter between the opposing fans, although I never saw any real fights. Now you would get trouble if the fans were together because they actually do hate each other. They even have songs about hating each other, which to me is stupid and ridiculous, but back then people had a superb sense of humour and the things they would shout were funny. OK, you did get bad language but not as bad as the language that you get now. I remember once at a Rangers match there was a Glasgow guy that shouted, with about two minutes to go, as Rangers were getting beaten, 'Hey, Waddell! The game has started!'
    My granny lived in Dumfries and we were there for a holiday once when Hibs were playing Queen of the South, so I went along to the game with my dad. It was a really hot August day and Hibs were toiling – they always seemed to toil to beat Queen of the South. It was a wee pitch at Palmerston Park and my dad shouted at Eddie Turnbull, 'Come on Eddie, get a move on!' and Eddie turned around and shouted back, 'If you can bloody do any better then get out here.' That was quite embarrassing, as you can imagine!

DAVID You still do get funny comments nowadays. I remember a guy shouting at Samaras, who played for Celtic, 'Samaras – you need a red handbag to match your red boots!'

IRENE After we started a family I lapsed as a Hibs fan. I still read about them but I didn't go to a game for years. And then almost ten years ago, my daughter was going on holiday and she said, 'Would you like our season tickets while we are away?' My initial response was to say, 'No, I don't think I'd like to go back after all these years,' but she left the tickets anyway, in case we changed our mind. And we did. Later that week we thought we might as well go along. The minute we entered the ground I felt like I was 16 again... I loved it! I don't think we've missed a game at Easter Road since. My sister had never ever gone to Hibs games before that but she decided to come as well and she became more hooked than us. Now she travels away to places like Carlisle to watch Hibs in the close season, it was a revelation for her! The first year we just paid for our tickets to each game and then we bought season tickets, so now that's what we do every year and we love it. I quite like having a season ticket because it's the same people that are there every week and I think it's become a social outing for us now, there's definitely that side to it.

DAVID I think it's much better now the ground's seated, it's a definite improvement. The toilet situation used to be pretty primitive and the catering side of things was dire as well.

IRENE There were times you got crowds of almost 70,000 at Easter Road and now you get a maximum of 20,000. I can remember people fainting, it was so packed. The men used to wave their white hankies in the air to alert the first aiders to run over and help the person that had collapsed.

DAVID Back then it was only the Main Stand that was seated. The rest of the ground was open but now you get a volume of noise that maybe got lost in the old open air stadium. The game that sticks out in my mind was the New Year's Day game at Tynecastle when Hibs won 7-0. Obviously the Hearts fans weren't best pleased – we had Hearts supporter friends with us at the game who were very disappointed.

‘ The bravest one rang the bell and Gordon Smith's sister came to the door. ’

IRENE One of my own worst disappointments was in the 1950s. Hibs were in the Scottish Cup and they got Rangers in the semi-final and drew. Then there was a replay and we beat them! I was at both games, they were both held at Hampden. And after we won that second game we got Clyde in the final. I would have been about 17 and I thought, 'This is it, we'll definitely win this game!' But Clyde were quite a good team in those days, they were certainly no mugs, and they beat us. What's new – that's the story of Hibs.

Whatever happens you still go back for more and each season you hope it's going to be our year. Hibs have always played a good style of football. They have had the odd manager that's changed it a bit, but they've always been good to watch. All my friends wonder why I go along and I say, in humour, 'Look, I'm not a hooligan, I've got lung problems and I don't even shout or anything like that.' I still get excited when they come onto the pitch, there's just something about it, it's special! Hibernian goes way back in my memories and I will go to watch them for as long as I am physically able to go. Hearts have had good teams as well but, as Hibs fans, you don't tend not to like Hearts and you always want to beat them. Hearts are sometimes higher up the league than us but on the whole we play better, free-flowing football than them.

DAVID Apart from the style of football, I don't think there's a lot of difference between us and them, to be honest.

IRENE Hibs were formed by poor Irish immigrants, but that was in the 19th century. I don't see why religion should come into football at all – this religious thing really does bug me. I mean, what has that got to do with nowadays? I didn't know about the real historical roots of the club when I was young but when I got older I read *The Making of Hibernian* and it was really only then that I started to learn about the history of the club. Ironically, my father would

Gordon Smith is one of Scottish football's most unusual treasures because he is the only Scottish footballer to have won league championships medals with three different clubs, none of which included either of the Old Firm. He entranced, hypnotised and dazzled defenders with his remarkable movement and skill.

On many occasions fans bore witness to his displays of keepy-uppys on the right wing, seemingly five steps ahead of any opposition defender.

Hibernian were unconvinced that he could shrug off a recurring injury and so Smith paid for an operation on the offending ankle himself, and promptly signed for Hearts.

Gordon Smith is most remembered for his part in the Famous Five forward line of the 1950s.

never have been a Hibs supporter if he had thought they were a Catholic club. I think who you support tends to depend on what side of the city you come from, but not necessarily in all cases. My grandson is a Hearts supporter and I can't convert him. I've offered to pay for a Hibs season ticket for him but I think it's a lost cause!

DAVID On the subject of religion in football, when we first started going it was never an issue and neither was it for Hearts supporters. And I mean, we're Protestants ourselves.

IRENE You do hear some sectarian stuff at the games but it's nothing like Rangers or Celtic, God forbid we ever become like them. I get annoyed with Hearts supporters calling Hibs 'the wee team'. It's not true, really not true! Maybe at the end of the day they have a bigger support than us, I don't know. I wouldn't like it if Hearts weren't around though.

DAVID When Mercer tried to amalgamate the two teams he met so much opposition from both sets of supporters, I'd say the two teams definitely need each other.

IRENE OK, it makes financial sense having one Edinburgh team that could probably take on Rangers and Celtic, but we need two teams in this city.

DAVID What you don't get to the same extent now, maybe because we're older, was at the derby games when the likes of Bauld, Wardhaugh and Conn got the ball your heart was in your mouth because you knew there was a real danger there.
    When I was young, I would meet my friends before the game. We wouldn't go to what you might call a Hibs pub, it was usually just to pubs in the Junction Street area near where we stayed – Berry's and The Hawthorn. When I walk into the Hibs ground now I still feel a certain anticipation, hoping that it's going to be a good game. I go there wanting to win. Nowadays I tend to be a bit more philosophical about things. Hibs were the first British team to enter a European competition and make the semi-final, so you can't help hoping that they somehow get back to those levels again.

IRENE Hibs have always brought through great players. You always hope that they keep them but instead we always seem to sell them. We had a budgie once that my brother trained to say 'Give us a goal Baker.' So you would always hear this bloody bird repeating that same line in the background. It was funny though! Gordon Smith was another Hibs great. I remember when he broke his leg and one Sunday three or four of us went for a walk down Willowbrae Road because Gordon Smith had a grocer's shop there and he lived above it. There used to be a pub nearby called after his position on the park: 'The Right Wing'. When we got to his shop one of us said, 'Do you think we should ring the doorbell and ask how he is?' Someone else said, 'Oh no, I don't think so.' But after much deliberation we decided, 'Och yes, why not.' The bravest one rang the bell and Gordon Smith's sister came to the door and so we asked, 'How is Gordon?' She said, 'He's doing fine. Would you like to come in and see him?' We were like 'Oh yes! That would be nice!' We were invited into his sitting room and there he was with his leg in plaster up on a stool. He was really very nice and I got his autograph – incidentally, I was looking for it recently and I can't find it! That would have been around 1951 when I got his signature.

DAVID When you think about it, in the days of the Famous Five it was a different wage structure to what there is now. You could keep the same team together for a few years whereas nowadays you will sometimes get a player for only a season. It must be very difficult for a manager to build a team on that basis.

IRENE Joe Baker always stands out in my mind because when he got the ball you just knew that he was going to get a goal with it. He was definitely the best striker that Hibs have ever had. He was quick and he was very, very accurate. He could get round defenders and get that ball in the back of the net. He was just wonderful! He left the club as well, they all get sold eventually. In the last decade Derek Riordan was one of our best players. He can be a bad boy outside of football but he most definitely has a football brain.

I would say that people take their family along more these days that they used to but sometimes they take children who are far too young to be at a game. Maybe their mother is working and it's the only way their father can get to the football.

DAVID For me it's very much a social outing on a Saturday afternoon.

IRENE I go because I want to, because I enjoy it, and because I get a thrill out of it! It makes me feel young. I get excited and I lose my breath, I get annoyed and I get frustrated. You get an adrenaline rush and there's a certain feeling, when I see the team come out, that it almost take me back in time. I would rather go there than to the theatre or the cinema, that's for sure.

DAVID It's because you don't know what the end result is going to be, it's the unpredictability of it all that you don't get with cinema or theatre.

IRENE Yes, like when we were beating Motherwell 6-2, only Hibs could end up drawing that game 6-6!

Grant Stott

Presenter, born 1967.

‘ My brother appeared on
Blue Peter wearing a Hands
Off Hibs T-shirt. He had to
fight to get that on television. ’

IN THE HISTORIC sense of following a football club, family and location made
me a Hibs fan. It goes all the way back to my grandad, Jackie Stott (his real
name was actually John Stott but everybody called him Jackie). He grew up
in Bothwell Street, just off Easter Road, and went to school at the old Leith
Academy, close to the stadium. He moved to Dalry when he got married and
that's where my dad was born.

My dad, Les, was brought up in deepest, darkest Dalry, surrounded by Hearts
fans, but because my grandad was a Hibs fan he took him to Easter Road to
support Hibs. We've always been a Hibs family and that tradition continues
with my brother John and me; there's never been any waifs or strays that have
gone in any other direction, it's been Hibs back to the early 1900s.

I remember the subject of Hibs always being round the house. My dad is the
biggest Hibs fan I know. Hibs are part of his daily routine in some shape or
form, be it looking at the paper or the internet, or just thinking about the game
at the weekend. He's lived his life like that all his days. He even skived school to
go and see Hibs play Clyde at Hampden in the 1950s. He still doesn't remember
how he managed to get there, but get there he did!

I grew up in the 1970s. I was well aware of Turnbull's Tornadoes because my
brother had the single and that iconic *Evening News* poster for the 1972 League
Cup which Hibs won against Celtic. John had all the pictures and the football
cards. He was in the school football team and he went to Hibs matches with
my dad. There's only two years between us and like a lot of brothers I rebelled
against everything that he did and he rebelled against everything that I did. So I
wasn't a football fan back then, although I knew what Hibs were all about. My
passion was pop music and buying records.

I do remember the famous cup final replay in 1979, I kind of got swept along with it, but I still didn't go to the match, I stayed in and I taped it off the radio for my dad. I remember there was the first cup final, and then the second, and then the third when Arthur Duncan scored the own goal. So football's been a massive part of my upbringing, even though I wasn't actively going to the games and supporting them.

It wasn't until the early '90s that I started going to the games and supporting Hibs. Through the whole of the '80s I was away DJ-ing and I lived in the Borders for a couple of years. To be honest, it maybe wasn't a bad thing to be away from Hibs, because that was a pretty turgid time for them. When I started working at Radio Forth, we used to get some complimentary seats at Easter Road. John had moved to London and my dad was going to games on his own. I had been watching football on television, all the Scotland and World Cup games, and enjoying it, so I said to my dad, 'Why don't we go to the games together?' Within one or two games at Easter Road I was hooked. It was as quick as that. That was it for me, there was never a question of supporting any other team. This would have been just after the Mercer takeover bid, when Miller was in charge. Keith Wright signed and very shortly after that we won the cup, so it was an interesting time to get into Hibs.

In June 1990, when all that kicked off, my dad had gone into hospital to get two new knees put in. I remember I was driving down the High Street and I noticed an *Evening News* billboard outside a newsagent opposite the World's End pub, saying: 'Mercer to Take Over Hibs'. I slammed on the brakes and went over to buy the newspaper, then I drove straight up to the hospital to show it to my dad. He went bananas – there he was, confined to his bed, unable to walk, and all this drama was going on at his club. It was massively frustrating for him – and you have to remember, this was 20 years ago, before the age of 24-hour news.

At Radio Forth our head of news, David Johnston, programmed an emergency live phone-in about the takeover. He got footballers and pundits round the microphones and opened the phone lines up for a two-hour broadcast. It was really exciting, back then it was a big story and the station reacted to it. So my dad was constantly asking, 'What is going on?' and saying, 'This is the worst thing possible!'

Shortly after it all got concluded, my dad was released from hospital and the first thing he did was ask my mum to drive him past Easter Road, just to make sure it was still there! He didn't want to go home, he didn't want to see his two boys, he just wanted to go and see that Easter Road still existed. That's all he wanted to know. He didn't want to get out the car, he just needed to get that reassurance. My dad is still along sitting among the fans on match days and still moaning about them as much as ever. He says stuff like, 'You should have seen the game it was bloody awful,' and I say, 'But we won and we're still in the cup so what do you want?' He wouldn't be the same without having a good moan about the Hibs.

My brother appeared on *Blue Peter* wearing a Hands Off Hibs T-shirt. He had to fight to get that on television. I remember us talking about it beforehand and John saying, 'I've got to do something, I've got to do something!' He thought this would be a great way to make his stand, because it was a network TV show that went out right across the country. Most people down south perhaps wouldn't have known anything about Scottish football, let alone Edinburgh football, let alone Hibs. So he went to the bosses and told them, 'Look, I really want to do this.' He took his Hibs shirt and got the wardrobe department at the BBC to cut out the Hand Off Hibs lettering. At the end of the programme he took his shirt off and said, 'I've just got to do this to show my support for my club, because they are in deep trouble at the moment.' The takeover was a massive issue for us.

When I started going to Easter Road, it was always to the Main Stand until they knocked it down a few years later. Everyone gets romantic thinking back to the old ground and what it was like to be there. My abiding memory of that old stand is the fact it was where I was for the 6-2 game. I was also there when Foster scored that late goal for Hearts in the 1994 Scottish Cup tie. I had my highs and lows in there. But we are in a modern age now and we've got a stadium suited to it. It's a much more pleasurable experience going to the football, without pillars in the way and with decent toilets and that kind of thing. My dad must have covered every inch of the old stadium over his years as a fan.

I am the Match Day Host, which came about through my role at Radio Forth. The station used to have a box in the old corporate section of the main stand that was moved to the Famous Five Stand, so they had a corporate box at every match. If there were seats available, myself and Bill Barclay from Radio Forth would get invited and I was always allowed to bring my dad along. One day at the start of the season when she had just started in the job, Amanda, who runs the corporate hospitality, got up on the microphone and she was trying to get everyone to sit down so that she could welcome them all on behalf of Hibernian Football club: 'Welcome to Easter Road, please take your seats, the meal will be served shortly,' that sort of thing. She came over to our table and she was shaking. She said, 'I just hate getting up in front of people and getting on a microphone. Do you know anyone that would like to do this instead of me?' I nearly choked on my food. 'Yes! I think I could handle that, I'm sure I could manage it,' I replied very quickly. So that was that.

Over the years I've been doing it, I became very good friends with the other hosts there – Joe Baker, Lawrie Reilly and Pat Stanton. It's the most fabulous thing that's happened in my connection with Hibs. The fact that my dad sat beside Pat and Lawrie, and got to be friends with Joe Baker, Dad's idol before he died, is the greatest thing I have ever been able to do for him. I like to think that this is my way of carrying him over the turnstile. I don't think there's anything that could have topped that.

My dad used to collect all the Hibs programmes so these names were very familiar to me when I was young and to get to meet them later in life was amazing. Pat Stanton even asked me to write the Foreword for his book, and that was a real jaw-dropping moment for me! And Lawrie Reilly gave me a wee mention in his book. You can't put a price on how big a deal these little accolades are for me and my family to have. It's great, great, great and I think any Hibs fan would bite their hand off to have those kind of things. One of the most special things about supporting Hibs is having friendships with these guys. We have lost Lawrie Reilly since my original interview for this book and that was a big shock. I really miss my wee buddy who sat beside me every second Saturday. I was honoured when Iris asked me to speak at his funeral and it was very emotional. There was so much love for him – he is so badly missed. For the season that followed, me and my dad always kept Lawrie's seat empty – we felt that he was still kind of with us.

Even though I have watched Hibs for the past 25 years or so, I still feel like I have to justify it. Some people will actually say, 'You never really supported them when you were a kid, so are you really a Hibs fan?' Sometimes there is a sense of shame that I can't say I followed them when I was at school, because I didn't, or that I followed them through the '80s, because I didn't. I think that I have given full support to the club, but some people will always believe you have to have followed Hibs from when you were first able to speak. It's almost like I haven't quite served my apprenticeship, despite the fact that it's been 25 years now that I have offered my faithful and undying support for the club. I've been home and away, and yes, I have combined work with pleasure, but I would still be at the games even if I wasn't working at them.

The players that stand out in my memories of the '90s are Keith Wright, Darren Jackson, Mickey Weir, Pat McGinlay and Kevin McAllister, one of my favourite Hibs players – I was just completely transfixed by him! The latter part of the '90s, when Sauzee came in, was just fantastic. I think if I was to pick one player, and it's tricky, but I have always, always said that David Murphy was a great player to have in a Hibs shirt. He would score some goals, not many, but when he did score them they were either vital or it was an absolute peach or a raker. He was a great passer of the ball and sometimes you would think, 'Oh my god, what's going to happen? So and so is on the attack.' But Murphy was always there. He had this cool stance when he was on the ball, his hands would go slightly limp and his legs would be doing all the work. He would place that ball to whoever was in a good position on the park. So he has to be a favourite. If I was that way inclined, I would ask him to marry me!

Through the club's different eras we've had some cracking players from the youngsters to the sort of mature heads like Sauzee, Jackson and Wright. We've had some great goal scorers mixed with guys like Matty Jack in defence – and how we could do with him right now. We have also had some real personalities, like Jimmy Boco and De La Cruz. I remember just having taking my seat in the derby and 'ping', De La Cruz put the ball away in seconds. He wasn't the greatest player we ever had, but he did give us a couple of great moments. John Burridge – what a fantastic character! God, we could do with these big, strong individuals who were in it for the game of football. OK, John Burridge had no previous association with the club but after he signed for Hibs he became passionate about it. Sauzee was just the same. These guys really cared about the club and I'm not a hundred per cent sure there's the same feeling among players now. I don't think that's just to do with Hibs, I think it's a modern footballing fact that players aren't necessarily as passionate for the clubs as they once were.

The CIS Cup final in 2007 was very emotional for me. I do get emotional at the football and there are times when I well up and have to stop myself. It's just incredible that it has that kind of effect on people. That 'Sunshine on Leith' moment at the cup final will live with me forever. I couldn't sing the words, especially when it got to that big moment in the chorus. I was miming because I was welling up so much. It was that sense of belonging, and the fact that we were there, and how much it meant to us winning the cup. I knew how big a deal it was to every single person present and it was like, 'Christ we've done it, we've fucking done it!' I was there with my dad and my brother and because it's such a family thing and it meant so much to my dad, that got me choked as well.

On the day of the Scottish Cup final against Celtic in 2001, I was on air in the morning and my mate Willie Docherty was on Forth 2, so we got a limo organised. It was the first time we had ever done that 'limo' thing through to Hampden. We picked up my dad and my brother and we had a great journey and then on our way back to Edinburgh, 'Sunshine on Leith' came on the radio. The driver was taking us through Glasgow to get back on the M8, and there was just a silence in the car. We were absolutely gutted. I couldn't speak, I was looking out the window with tears in my eyes, thinking about how we had got so close to winning the cup that day. Before you knew it we were on the M8 and we're cracking open the beers, 'bang!', and we started singing the Hibs songs again and getting back into a happier spirit.

The club is really pushing this family idea now. It's not unique to Hibs, but it's something that I do feel proud to be part of. The club and the fans are a lot closer, given the digital age we live in. I think a very important part of any football club is having close links with the fans and being able to listen to

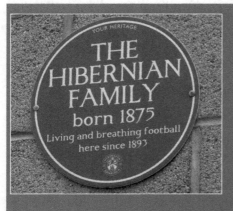

'I think a very important part of any football club now is having close links with the fans and being able to listen to and communicate with them. '

and communicate with them. The days of clubs being aloof and standoffish with the fans has gone. Board members will come and go but the fans are the one constant in any football club. I'm working in panto at the moment with people from down south who don't understand football and certainly don't understand Hibs. They say, 'Why do you put yourself through this?' I reply, 'You just do... it's your club!' Your club is your club and just because it's really shite at the moment doesn't mean to say that you think, 'I'm not gonna support you anymore.' You hope, with a sense of romantic optimism, that it will all turn good. That's what football is really... romance!

I've been involved with the club's Historic Trust on a number of different projects, speaking at dinners, helping put together videos and launching the Hall of Fame. It's an interesting story how Hibs came about, and there's the story of Celtic starting in 1888 and stealing the hoops that Hibs were wearing, as well as stealing half of our decent players. Surprise, surprise! Some things never change.

The Irish tricolour was banned from Easter Road in the 1980s and I remember all the hoo-ha that went with that. There is obviously an unpleasant side of Irish politics and the danger that, if we are associated with it then we are going to get dragged down that 'dirty road'. I think Hibs have done a great job of embracing their Irish roots and heritage without going down that horrible path you get in the west of Scotland. It's a very difficult thing to do. The club has managed it, gently and slowly, over the years. I probably know more about the history of the club than my dad did when he was my age, because we research and archive better now. The Historical Trust has taken a very active role in that.

In Edinburgh we had a massive influx of Irish people, we now have a big influx of Polish people; we've become a multicultural society, so Hibs should reflect that as well. When we were planning the 20-year event we did at the Usher Hall, we talked about how we were going to stage it and I said, 'You know what, let's make it a wee history lesson because there are fans now who

Sir Tom Farmer, major shareholder of Hibernian FC, has deep family ties to the club: 'I grew up, the youngest of seven children, in Union Street at the foot of Leith Walk. My memories are of a great feeling of security and a genuine community spirit.

In the 1880s, just after it was formed, the club got into some difficulties. So in 1891 my grandfather and his brother, along with a group of other men, met in a hotel on the High Street. They decided to set up a fund to "resuscitate" the club and all put in about five pounds each to get the ball rolling. As a positive expression of its present-day social responsibility, the club established the Hibernian Community Foundation in 2008 and created a new Learning Centre in Easter Road Stadium to deliver educational initiatives. It's all part of making people proud of what Hibernian FC represents.'

weren't around when the Mercer takeover came along.' So we went into great detail on the night as to what actually happened. We spoke to Sir Tom, we spoke to Petrie, we spoke to Margo MacDonald and all of these people who were actually involved. I think it's very important that as we progress as a club and as a support, we know exactly what happened. It wasn't just a case of Mercer trying to take over but also that we almost went bust twice at that point.

We came out of the situation for the better. It's a hard time for the fans at the moment and they are spouting off left, right and centre, but without what Sir Tom Farmer did, this club would be gone. Who else would have come in and saved it? I think he knew that he would be spending money that he would never see again. And he also worked well with Rod Petrie. Without these guys, where would we be? Naturally we're not all going to agree with everything done in the running of the club. The only part that is letting us down today is the product on the park.

There are similarities and differences to what McCann did at Celtic. McCann was very clear. He said, 'I'm coming in for five years, I'm going to sort out your mess and I'm going to walk away with a big wad of cash.' Sir Tom Farmer said, 'I'm going to get you sorted out, I'm going to balance the books and save the club, but I'm not walking away and I'm not going to take a wad of cash.' Both were very clear from the outset about what they were going to do. Sir Tom, I think, is there for the long haul; Fergus McCann came in to fix things over a period of years, which he did. His promise was that he'd go away minted, and you know what, I think most of the Celtic fans applauded that. Sir Tom is not ploughing money in hand over fist, but he provides backbone for the club, which we need. That night at the Usher Hall it would have been easy to just have a massive rally for the fans and sing Hibs songs but we were very keen to get the story across to all the folk there so that they'd know how we were hours away from extinction, hours away from just being nothing – you just wanted to go and remind yourself that Easter Road was still there, like my dad did. That's how scary it was.

Hibs and Hearts are fundamentally the same. We're all from Edinburgh, we support our team, and that's it! However, I have always said that Hibs fans are the more realistic of the two city teams. We know what we are, we know who we are, we know what our abilities and our capabilities are, and we know that we can be fantastic on our day. But we never get carried away and never spout off that we are going to do this that and the next thing or say, 'This is our season! We're gonna win this cup!' Certain other fans have done that and been bitten on the bum for their efforts. Hibs fans, on the whole, are more realistic and more grounded, probably because we have had so many massive disappointments.

When you think of football fans, you think of the characters. I've got to know the likes of Frank Dougan who was the treasurer for many years at the supporters club, a big Hibs fan through and through – and a big character, in both senses of the word. He's become a pal. He has great pictures of visiting Trinidad and Tobago with Russell Latapy. Frank will follow Hibs until he

shuffles off his mortal coil. Maud McFarlane, she was another big character.
I wasn't one of these fans who was on her bus but I know that she was a
formidable character that you didn't mess with. Her passion for Hibs was just
remarkable! Very close to her passing away she was still getting brought into
the club and taken up to her seat. She was well looked after by Willie McEwan,
Billy McLennan and a lot of other individuals who knew how important it was
for her.

In terms of players, I liked Gordon Hunter who scored a great goal to break
that horrible run of defeats against Hearts in the '80s. Gordon Hunter wasn't
the most vocal of individuals but he was a nice guy and a good lad. I also got to
know Darren Jackson and Scott Brown over the last ten years through my job
as Match Day Host. He was a complete bam at times, but he was a guy that I
really liked and I had some really interesting post-match interviews with him
when he was Man of the Match. The first time he wasn't 18 yet, so instead of
being presented with a bottle of champagne I had to give him a can of Irn-Bru.
I remember once asking him:

'You had an interesting showdown with so and so, what started that?'

'Well, I was just in the middle of the park doing my thing and then this big
cunt came from behind and took me oot!' is what he came back with.

So there we were in the middle of the corporate hospitality suite, with
families listening to every word. But it was so funny – he certainly shot from
the hip. There was speculation about him and Kevin Thomson signing for the
Old Firm as a double package. When I interviewed Thomson, I asked, 'You're
both meant to be going to Rangers?' He replied, 'Well, if Scott goes to Rangers
he'll be delighted because Broony's a big blue nose.' And there was this kind of
'tumbleweed' moment in the room – as Scott Brown had just been pretty much
'outed' as a blue nose. Lo and behold, he later signed for Celtic, which made it
even more interesting!

If you think of the personalities at the club I have probably interviewed them
all at some point. A real stand-out would be Lee Griffiths, he was buzzing to
play for the club. The best post-match interviews are when you have someone
who is so happy to play for Hibs. Jason Cummings is another good guy to
interview. You just don't know what he is going to say and what little nugget he
is going to give you. He has a unique style of repartee. I remember having a bit
of fun with Alan Gow because he decided to wear his 'street clobber', including
a baseball cap on back to front. So when I introduced him I started doing a bit
of beat box down the microphone. The rest of the players really appreciated
that because Gow's dress sense was one of a kind. He was obviously trying to
get down with the kids.

As Match Host you never want to introduce a player by the wrong name.
You have to quickly recognise the players, especially when new faces appear.
I've had a great run in getting to know the club behind the scenes even if it's
not been so enjoyable on the park – it's a great insight into how a football club
is run.

We have not had a great amount of success with managers of late. Up until

Terry Butcher arrived and ultimately got us relegated, I don't remember anyone saying, 'This is a dreadful appointment.' I remember there being a great deal of excitement at Butcher's arrival and I reckon the vast majority of Hibs fans wanted him to be our manager. It turned out be absolutely disastrous. You can blame whoever you like for making that decision, but it wasn't made against the will of the fans. It worked pretty well up until Christmas, then we went into free-fall. It was more to do with management style and the way that he handled the players. They didn't react well to it.

On the flipside, we have had a very positive turnaround behind the scenes with Leeann Dempster coming in as Chief Executive. I have never felt as low as when we got relegated in May 2014. After that, I would have never imagined we would be in the very positive position of finishing second in the 2014–15 Championship. The transformation within the club has been great. Leeann has stripped the club back and revamped the personnel structure. Some decisions have been popular, others not. She knows what she wants.

At the training centre, the club now have individuals working under their own contracts, which means that new managers can't bring in a full group of their own backroom staff at the expense of others working at the club. And when a manager moves on, it will not upset the whole apple cart. That's just one example of something that has changed for the better.

I cannot speak highly enough of Leeann. I conducted the first interview with her when she arrived at Hibs. When the club asked me to do the interview, I insisted I would have to ask my own questions and not show them to Leeann in advance. I also insisted that nothing should be edited out. My insistence on this was partly influenced by the way my role at the club was being perceived by some fans. The YouTube footage that came out after we got relegated had a lot to do with this. Because I was wearing the club tie, some of the fans identified me with the management and started having a go at me. As a fan I was hurting as much as them.

Going back to the interview, Leeann was fine with my conditions. She openly answered every single question, so from that moment I felt were going in the right direction.

There is not going to be a quick fix at Hibs with so many years of problems behind the scenes. The last piece of the jigsaw will be seeing it all click on the pitch. I was a wee bit bemused by the fan protests against board – I believed that everybody wanted a change. That includes Sir Tom Farmer and Rod Petrie.

Football fans will never dictate to the club owners. At the end of the day it is Sir Tom's business, whether you like that or not. He is not a multi-millionaire by default or good luck. He knows that this business has been in trouble and, yes, he has put money in and, yes, he will take money out. I still think we are in better shape having had his support than we would have been without it.

There is still a lot of bitterness and division within Scottish football. This was highlighted when I presented *Scotsport* a number of years ago. I mentioned upfront that I was a Hibs fan, in my naivety thinking that would be OK. I had worked in TV and radio and loads of other different bits and bobs, and it had always been a very positive and pleasant experience for me. I then stepped into the world of footballing broadcast! I very quickly learned all about putting your head above the parapet. I now know the reason why so many pundits, commentators and sports presenters don't tell you what football team they support because as soon as you declare your footballing loyalties you make yourself a hate figure for the fans of all of these other clubs. I was thinking, I'm just gonna come in as 'Mr Nice Guy' because I'm not an ex-player, I'm not a journalist, I'm a football fan who can present live TV programmes, so let's sit and have a bit of a gas about the weekend's football. 'Come on let's have a bit of fun guys!' But 'Oh no... No!'

There seems to be very little room for a bit of fun. The sort of banter that goes on in programmes like *Football Focus* was what I was aiming for really. When I went for the interview to get the job I said, 'Don't ask me about the science behind 4-4-2 and tactics, I ain't got a clue!' That's why they brought in Andy Walker. Andy's got the brain and he's got the knowledge of the game and he's got that dry sense of humour as well. But I soon found out that there are certain roads that you cannot go down with certain pundits and ex-players. The mood was one of 'this is fitba, this is no funny, dinnae try and crack a gag'. It was a real surprise. The one big positive that did come out of it was my friendship with Andy. We were literally thrown together – the first time I met him was on the photoshoot to promote the new series. My first year as the presenter of *Scotsport* was a bit of a blur, but as we were getting into the second season it was really coming together and I knew in my head how it could work if we went down this path – and that I was going to have to convince people to change their approach. It was quite heavily scripted and a lot of the links were on autocue. I wanted to make it a lot more relaxed, like it is on radio. By all means, make your notes for your analysis but let's just go with the flow a little bit more. Unfortunately STV's contract with the SPL ran out and they didn't renew it, so that was that – and just when Andy and I were really beginning to get into a bit of a groove.

Maybe I was naive in playing the Hibs card, but I wanted everybody to know that I'm not an Old Firm fan. But on Rangers fan sites the assumption was that if I supported Hibs I must be a Celtic supporter. Mix that with the fact that I was paired with Andy Walker. It was really frustrating to read some of things being said on the forums. By all means have a pop at me if I didn't introduce a game nicely enough for you or if I asked a shite question, but don't start making things up about me and don't start accusing me of this, that and the next thing, just because I support Hibs! Some of these faceless wonders behind their keyboards posted horrible stuff because I was honest enough to go on and say 'My name is Grant Stott and I support Hibs.' They can quite easily say, 'I support such and such a team' but you won't know who they are because they do it anonymously. It's the same when I write for the *Evening News*. But that's the nature of the world we live in and you've got to take on the chin. I loved my time on *Scotsport*, Andy is still a big pal. I just wish we'd had a chance to get to where we wanted with the programme...

Most football fans go the game hoping that it will end in victory. You believe that your team's going to do the right thing and that you will get a little 'kiss on the cheek' every time they score a goal. For example, we could be going out to play Celtic on Saturday with not a hope in hell, and you know what? I still believe that we could get a 3-2 win. You believe these things, that's what sees football fans through the dark times. We all still think that our club's best best days are yet to come.

Scale model of the old Easter Road stadium, on view in the exhibit room at Hibernian FC.

Easter Road Stadium viewed from London Road, 2011.

TO THE MEMORY OF JAMES CONNOLLY
BORN 6TH JUNE 1868 AT 107 COWGATE
RENOWNED INTERNATIONAL TRADE UNION
AND WORKING CLASS LEADER
FOUNDER OF IRISH SOCIALIST REPUBLICAN PARTY
MEMBER OF PROVISIONAL GOVERNMENT
OF IRISH REPUBLIC
EXECUTED 12TH MAY 1916 AT KILMAINHAM JAIL DUBLIN

Above: Plaque commemorating James Connolly (Hibs fan) in the Grassmarket, Edinburgh.

Right: The first strip to be worn by Hibernian FC, on display in the club exhibit room.

St Mary's Street, the location of the CYMS meeting to form Hibernian in 1875.

The Cowgate, nicknamed 'Little Ireland' in the 19th century, the community that gave birth to Hibernian FC.

Ian St John's Football School, 1984. Back row (from second left) brownlie, O'Rourke, Hunter, Hearts Coach, Bert Slater, Ian St John, Jimmy Kane, Jim McQueen. Andy MacVannan second row, third from left.

The East Terracing, photographed by Stephen Young on the day he met Paul Kane painting the railings (1980s).

Andy Blance wearing his famous scarf.

Hibs fans in Trinidad and Tobago (left to right) Don Morrison, Alex Balloch, John Green.

The now defunct Albion Bar in 2011.

Inside the Four In Hand pub on Easter Road, 2011.

Exhibits from the Hands Off Hibs campaign.

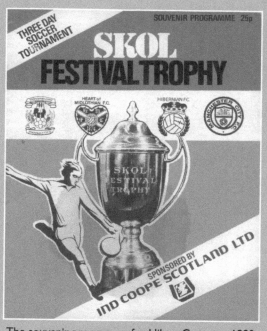

The souvenir programme for Hibs v Coventry, 1980, the first game attended by Andy MacVannan.

I Love Leith banner featuring The Famous Five, Leith Walk, 2011.

The Harp & Castle (formerly the Tommy Younger Bar) 2011.

Staying On At Easter Road campaign, 2004. Gordon Munro second from left and Lord Martin O'Neill centre.

The back of the Famous Five Stand.

The East Stand shortly after construction, 2010.

Tamson's Bar, Easter Road.

Artefacts found in 2010 during the
demolition of the old East Stand.

Right: The back of the East Stand.

Below: Park View Hotel 1990. Pat Stanton (with mic) and Ger Freedman at the Hands Off Hibs victory party.

Club historian Tom Wright at his beloved Easter Road ground, 2015.

Jim Hendren Hayes

Retired Civil Engineer, born 1942.

' If the Hibs had got beat you were drowning your sorrows, if they'd won it was brilliant – it was a win-win situation really. '

I WAS ABOUT seven or eight when I first went along to watch Hibs and I remember them playing against all the teams in the First Division as it was known back then. When I was very young I stayed in St Clair Place, a wee cul-de-sac within earshot and eyesight of the Hibs ground. On the days of the football matches supporters would bring their cars in and out of our street and they would be parked up both sides of the street with a row down the middle. Some of the guys had the really old cars and as you can imagine, because we're talking about the 1940s, some of the car doors didn't actually lock. We used to have rare fun when all the men left their cars while they went to the game and some would say, 'Here's a shilling son so look after our car while we go and watch the match.' We'd be inside the cars pretending we were driving all over the world and then these guys would come back after the game to pick them up. We'd always say, 'Aye, we looked after your car, mister,' but little did they know we'd done about 10,000 miles in our own imaginations! There wasn't nearly as many cars back then but they could get a lot closer to the ground, to the top of St Clair Road at the Cemetery End, and then into Easter Road and Dalmeny Street. I don't think there was a Hibs car park then, but they did build one eventually, where the Hibs Club used to be.

Coming from Easter Road you instantly had a connection with the team, so there was never any doubt you would be a Hibs fan. You were just naturally a Hibs supporter because you lived almost right beside the ground, and from our window you could even see the stadium, although you couldn't see the actual pitch – you could see the terracing where the Famous Five Stand has now been built. My dad was a Hibs fan, and his father before him. Eventually they took me to my first match and when I was about eight or nine years old I started going to the matches regularly with my mates. Sometimes if it was Rangers or Celtic our mums wouldn't let us go. That was in the days of the Famous Five and 40,000 supporters could be in the ground – my, how things have changed!

The love of the team and club is kind of inbuilt into your brain. Even if you don't go to all the matches, it's always the Hibs result that you look for first. They have always built you up to let you down but I think that's part of being a Hibs supporter. I think it's the green, with the white sleeves, that make Hibs different to any other team in the world and it was magic when they came on to the park, although there was always the fear that by the end of the game you'd be shouting at them. When they came running down that tunnel the whole ground would just erupt.

I always went to the Cemetery End, where the Famous Five Stand is now, because that was where all the guys that I knew went and you could all gather together and shout the odds. It was a case of 'safety in numbers' and that part of the ground was usually the Hibs end. You could move about so if Hibs were attacking one end you would go there and if they were having a good game you could go round to the other end at half time. You would pass the other team's fans on the way round. In the normal games it was OK, supporters were mostly well behaved towards each other.

When there was a shot at goal the whole crowd at the Cemetery End would surge forward all the way down, and then back up again. The Hibs would play down towards the goal, have a shot, and 'whoosh', it might not have been a goal but you would all have to climb back up the steps to your original position regardless. You didn't realise at the time but it was quite dangerous, even though they had the crush barriers for safety. We used to go up to the ground, up the Saint Clair Road, and head round towards Hawkhill where the turnstiles were on the other side of the road. The police would keep you on one side and then let a few people across at a time. When we were little we used to just stand at the turnstiles saying, 'Will you lift me over, mister?' And they might say, 'Cannae, son' or 'No the day, son'. You would just keep at it until someone said, 'Aye, c'mon.' When they lifted you over the turnstiles that was you in. At other times we would go up about 25 minutes into the second half when the gates had opened to allow disgruntled supporters to leave, so we used to get in for free.

After I left school, I always went to stand on the 'new' terracing away up the back where all the ex Holy Cross School guys used to congregate. My sister and brother now have season tickets for the East Stand and they've gradually got to know the people that sit beside them at the games but back then we always had a good time, win, lose or draw.

It's much more civilised now going to watch a game and of course it's much more expensive. From the spectators' comfort point of view it's probably better but the atmosphere in the 'good old days' was absolutely magic! You did get trouble back then, I remember it happening when you walked up Easter Road after the game. It usually involved Celtic and Rangers. I do remember bottles getting chucked – I have to add it wasn't coins back then because you couldn't afford it! The police were always on top of things, as of course they still are.

It was nothing to be standing and then hear the noise of someone having a pee behind you. Sometimes they would pee into a bottle, and sometimes they wouldn't, which of course you wouldn't get nowadays because it's obviously a bit more civilised with proper toilets and all that.

The local pubs would always do good business on match days. They'd be absolutely chock-a-block and then they'd all start emptying at half past two. Folk had a fair bit to drink and you could also sneak drink into the ground. After the match you would see guys going round picking up the empty screw-top bottles and putting them in a sack. They took them down to the local pub where they'd get one old penny per bottle. That was how some guys made their beer money. Willy Wishart's, which my dad frequented, was on the corner of St Clair's Road but when we moved to St Clair Avenue it was Binnie's, now The Cooper's Rest, on the corner of Lorne Street and Easter Road. As a kid you were never allowed in the pub.

On match days, after I got married and moved away from home, we would be let into St Clair Avenue to park by the police because my mum and dad still stayed there. We'd go to see them and we'd watch all the crowds going up to the ground, looking for someone we knew to go up to the match with. The house would always be full after the match, especially at New Year – we had some rare parties! If the Hibs had got beat you were drowning your sorrows, if they'd won it was brilliant – it was a win-win situation really.

As far as away games go, I went to Tynecastle and Hampden but that was about it. I think I was once over at Raith Rovers. Not as many people travelled to away games, money was tighter. Some of the supporters clubs would put on buses but not to the extent that they do now.

I didn't particularly dislike Hearts, I just know that I liked us to beat them. There are bad Hibs fans and bad Hearts fans, but the trouble ultimately comes when these two factions come up against each other. I do remember coming out of Easter Road with all the Hearts fans standing throwing bottles at Hibs fans coming down the steps but that sort of thing didn't happen very often. There were undertones of the Irish connection at Hibs but not as far as me and my friends were concerned. In fact, in the '60s people stopped going because of that carry on.

I always remember a guy beside us in the terracing who shouted the same thing every week. Everything to him was a 'pentley'. He would shout, 'C'mon ref, that's a pentley, a staring pentley.' We always used to get a laugh at that. I remember being in the Centre Stand years later with my wife Grace and her dad, a season ticket holder, when the BBC commentator Archie McPherson walked in with a woman and two kids. You could see the kids were from some kind of posh school by their school uniform and there was a lad up behind us who shouted, 'Hello there, Archie, is that you out with the wife and bairns an that?' Archie just nodded wryly without saying anything.

The game that sticks out in my mind is the New Year's Day game at Tynecastle when Hibs beat Hearts 7-0. I was there with my mate, who was a Hearts supporter. There was always a fear that some trouble could blow up but I think they were so well trounced that it didn't happen on that day. It wasn't like they had been beaten by a fluky or a disputed goal, that's usually where trouble starts, if there's a bad decision. The Hearts supporters were absolutely dejected, as you can imagine, but for me it was brilliant – any day that the Hibs beat the Hearts is brilliant for me, but I'd imagine it's the same, vice versa, if you're a Hearts fan. The other games I particularly remember involved Joe Baker when he played for Hibs. I was a teenager then – those were magic days! Pat Stanton and Jimmy O'Rourke were at school with me and when they started playing it was an added incentive to go to matches because I knew them. Joe Baker was wonderful. 'Gie the ball to Baker!' they used to shout. When Baker went to Italy that was a real disappointment to me. He did come back latterly but he wasn't the player that he had been. Interestingly, he had actually played for England a few times. Another thing I'll not forget was Alex Cropley's goal in 13 seconds or something like that. I can't remember who it was we were playing against but there were about three people who touched the ball from the kick-off and suddenly it was in the back of the net. He was brilliant. And then, like Baker, he moved to an English First Division team.

We stood at the back of the goals in the days of Tommy Younger, the legendary Hibs goalie. He may have been in his latter playing days but he was still the best goalie in Scotland. You could honestly feel the ground shake when he dived for the ball and hit the ground – he was a big, solid guy, what a man he was! My hero was Gordon Smith, there was a great following just for him. People would come to see him from all over the country. I remember him running down that wing like a gazelle, and his incredible hairstyle. I was very, very disappointed when he got a free transfer after a bad injury. He was out for a while and the next thing we knew, he was transferred to Hearts and won the league before going on to Dundee where he won the league again! One of the worst things I remember was John Brownlie getting his leg broken. Again I was with Grace's dad in the Main Stand and everybody heard the crack and thought, 'Oh god, his

Eastern Cemetery, resting place of Jimmy Hendren.

' My grandfather, Jimmy Hendren, played in the forward line for Hibs from 1912. '

leg's broken.' He was out the game for a while after that and when he did come back he was never quite the same. Eventually he ended up at Newcastle United.

Nowadays they've got all these third-rate foreigners playing in Scotland but when I was young the Hibs players were mostly local lads who loved to play for their local team. The fans used to actually know players like Smith, Johnstone, Riley, Turnbull and Ormond. You knew the pubs and shops they owned and if you were walking past you would go and buy something in the hope that one of your heroes would serve you. You felt part of the team in those days simply because you knew where the players came from. I think the money that players receive now is just obscene. What I would like to see is Scottish players playing for the Scottish clubs. I would like to see the attitude that the people playing for the clubs would die for their clubs, not a case of it being about how much money they make and the next transfer they get. Nowadays you go to Easter Road and see 11 players playing and I reckon you could go along to the pitches at Saughton Park and pick 11 players that are every bit as good if not better. They used to have the scouts going round these places and picking the cream of the players they spotted. The best went on to play for professional clubs though of course they didn't get anything like the money they do now.

My uncle Stanley played for St Mirren. He wore those old-style boots. When they were new, he'd put them on and immerse his feet in a bath of water, he'd be in there for hours and they would soften, shrink and mould to the shape of his feet. These guys would jump to head the ball and in those days it would almost knock your head off! The old players were tough. My grandfather, Jimmy Hendren, played in the forward line for Hibs from 1912 until his untimely death on 19 June 1915. He was married to Annie Gordon and they had two children – Jimmy and my mother, Annie (known to her friends as Nancy). Annie was born in March 1915 so she was only three months old when her dad died and therefore she has no recollection of him. She could only tell us what her mum had told her about what happened. It seems that Jimmy was

Jimmy Hendren was signed by Hibs from Cowdenbeath in 1911 and played four full seasons. He became the club's top league goalscorer in the last three and overall top goalscorer in two.

Prior to his arrival at Hibs, Hendren had played for Kilmarnock during his time as a coal miner in Ayrshire and then emigrated to America in search of greater opportunity. It was on his return to Scotland that he joined Hibs.

He was described as a tough and physical player and was fondly thought of by the club and its fans.

He is buried in the Eastern Cemetery, behind the current Famous Five Stand. He died of influenza just 12 weeks after the birth of his second child. The club's floral tribute was a broken harp. Despite their dwindling finances, they managed to donate some money to his wife Annie. As an uncle of Pat Stanton's mother, Jimmy Hendren has a notable family connection to the club.

suffering from influenza and, in spite of this, he was asked to play for Hibs on the Saturday. He played and his condition worsened, so much so, that he had to be rushed into the Edinburgh Royal Infirmary where he died very soon after. My granny, who had been left with two young children to bring up, remarried a few years later to Tom McMichael, one of the sons of Dan McMichael the then manager of the Hibs Football Club. She had two sons from that marriage – Tommy and Stanley. In the study at my granny's house there was a big marble mantelpiece and on top of it there was a clock shaped like a Grecian temple with the inscription 'Presented to Jimmy Hendren by Hibernian Football Club 1912–1913.' I always remember it sitting there, just above the fire. After my granny died, my step-grandfather lived alone for a while. He went a bit senile and started to think the house was full of fleas. We had moved to St Clair Avenue, which was the next street down. My mother got a phone call one day from one of the neighbours that stayed opposite my grandma's house. She said, 'Nancy, you better come up the road because faither (as he used to be called) is emptying out your mum's hoose.' A character with a van had showed up and he took all the furniture, including that old Hibs clock. 'Faither' had given him the lot! My mother ran up to the house and met the guy coming down the stairs and she said, 'You better stop because that's my mother's stuff.' Then she ran into the house. Her stepfather said, 'No, no, it's all going because the house is full of fleas!' There wasn't a shred of furniture left. We had to buy a bed and a couple of chairs so he had something to sit on and sleep in.

Somebody, somewhere, must have that old clock with that memorable plaque on it. I was really, really sad not to see it again.

Grandfather Jimmy Hendren had a sister who married Johnnie Gordon of Craigmillar and they had four daughters – Mary, Bee, Helen and Margaret. Bee Gordon married a Michael Stanton and they had a son called Pat. So my mum and Pat's mum were first cousins. Pat and I went to the same school and we were altar boys at the wedding of his Aunty Margaret at Craigmillar Church. Pat was born and brought up in Craigmillar and he was a dyed-in-the-wool Hibbie from the start. He was one of the first Hibs players to be poached by Jock Stein, who took him away to Celtic.

I remember meeting Pat in the street one day when he was playing for Celtic and I said to him, 'How are you finding it through in the west and what do you think about the Hibs at the moment?' He said, 'Well, the first thing I look at in the *Pink* (the Saturday *Edinburgh Evening News* sports section, which was printed on pink paper) is to see the Hibs result. And do you know what the second thing is?' I said, 'The Hibs reserves?' Pat said, 'No, I look to see if the Hearts have got beat!' In those days, if you were playing for Celtic or Rangers you were halfway to being in the Scottish national team, so nothing changes really. Pat played many games for the Scottish team before hanging up his boots and going into management. These were the good old days of Scottish football. Nowadays there's far too much money tied up in the game and too much play-acting. That's progress?

Tom Wright

Club Historian, born 1947.

' I had to sleep with his five
league medals under my pillow
for five nights. That really was
a thrill! '

THE HISTORICAL TRUST is essentially a supporters-led initiative that is fully backed
by the club. We're a registered charity. The club handed over everything they
had collected throughout the years and it was actually a considerable amount.
Our remit is to promote and preserve the history of the club. Where we might be
short in silverware, we've got a magnificent and rich tapestry of history.

I am the curator – I handle and prepare the exhibits. The club gave us a store
room and installed a lot of the cabinets and such like. We get exhibits donated
to us and some of them are quite valuable. We also raise funds and buy exhibits.
For instance, we bought George Stewart's Scotland cap from 1904 and an inter-
league jersey worn by Davie Shaw, the Hibs captain in 1949–50. We decorate
the stadium with exhibits and try to put on an exhibition every year. These have
included *The Life of Gordon Smith*, *50 Years of Hibs in Europe* and *Hibs and
Internationalists*. Another really interesting exhibition called *Home* charted the
changing face of Easter Road from day one of the original stadium right up to
the present day. It takes weeks to prepare exhibitions because we all do it part-
time and for the love of the club's history.

The club doesn't want a permanent museum at the moment. We did suggest
it to them and it's something that we'd like to push for again at some point
but they thought it might become a bit static, that having seen it once people
wouldn't come back, so it would just lie empty. They recommended that we use
three or four different locations in the stadium for displays. We have a lot of
artefacts and archive material so I think that with a purpose-built museum there
would be no problem refreshing displays.

As a youngster, I was always really interested in the past and I would ask
people about the club's history, but they didn't know. So I would like to think

that when we go we are leaving something behind for the youngsters coming after us. Can you imagine how good it would have been if they had kept the jerseys, the balls and the boots from pre-war or the turn of the last century? So that's what we are trying to do now.

I think that every period of the club's history is important. The great period for me is 1946 to 1956, which I missed because I didn't start going until 1957. When the Historical Trust got Gordon Smith's jersey it was great for me. We put on the *Life of Gordon Smith* exhibition shortly after he died and at the time we were waiting for a safe to get installed, so I had to sleep with his five league medals under my pillow for five nights. That really was a thrill!

As a small child I lived in Greenside, not far from Easter Road. I had a lot of uncles and some were Hearts fans and some were Hibs fans. Even when I didn't really know what football clubs were, I just used to think the name Hibernian was great. One of my closest uncles took me to Easter Road one day, and that was it. If one of them had taken me to Tynecastle then it's likely I would have been a Hearts supporter. When you are young you don't know about any political or religious background – you just go to the game. Within months it became a major part of my life. I don't think I even checked to see who Hibs were playing, I just went along at 3pm every Saturday. It was the big team one week and the reserves the next. Unfortunately that pattern's continued to this day – hence my white hair!

At the old Dunbar End, there used to be a path right up the back. We went up there for my first game and I always remember just before I turned the corner, I could hear this roar and I was excited, wondering what I was going to see, not realising it was going to change my life. When they were knocking that end down I got a friend to take a photograph of me standing on that same spot which for me it was so evocative.

That first game was a friendly against Leicester City. I was instantly captured by the atmosphere and have been ever since. I was only nine and I didn't know

Joe Baker.

"It was a guy called Joe Baker, and it turns out he was everybody's hero because he really had it all."

who the players were or anything like that. The only memory I've got of the actual game itself, and it's a stupid thing, was that Leicester City had a guy called Hogg playing for them on the left wing. He had a bald head and I still have a mental picture of him – don't ask me why, it's just something that has stuck in my mind. I went to buy a '50s team card of Leicester City a number of years ago and this same guy was on it, exactly the same as I remember him. An intriguing thing I learnt later about that day was that there were three former Hibs players on the team – Pat Ward, John Ogilvie and Tommy McDonald.

My uncle took me to my first game. My family had moved to Hillside Crescent and because I lived so near to the ground I was allowed to go down to Easter Road myself. It became a religion from that point on. I wasn't allowed to go to the Hearts, Rangers or Celtic games though. In 1957 it wasn't a great time to be a Hibs supporter. Hearts were in the middle of winning some cups and I remember on Mondays at school I used to get taunted by two Hearts supporters. It was something I didn't look forward to because Hibs really weren't great at that time. Turnbull, Reilly and Ormond were still there, and Smith, though I didn't see Smith for a while because he had an injury. Bobby Johnstone had moved on but of course he came back a couple of years later.

I didn't have a favourite player until later, but suddenly this one guy really, really, really excited me and I didn't know why. It was a guy called Joe Baker, and it turns out he was everybody's hero because he really had it all. He had speed, he was hard in the tackle, he could head the ball and shoot with both feet – he was just exciting! When he came back to Hibs for a second time he had those white boots and I don't think anyone else had white boots back then, they played in the old leather studded boots. Joe Baker was my only favourite at that point.

I remember when Bobby Johnstone came back in 1959 and because I had missed the Famous Five playing as a unit I was desperate to see him. I used to go into the ground through the boys' gate but they didn't have a boys' gate for

Joe Baker was, on paper, most notable for scoring 100 goals in both the English and the Scottish leagues. Perhaps even more unusual was the fact that he was the first player fully capped for England having never played for an English club side at that point in his career.

Baker was born in Liverpool, to Scottish parents, and moved to Scotland as a young child where he was brought up. Baker scored a club record 42 goals in 33 league games during the 1959–60 season, and 102 goals in only 117 league games for Hibs. Tragedy struck in 1961 after he was transferred to Torino and was involved in a serious car crash. Very close to death, he recovered and left Italy to join Arsenal, achieving top scorer status for three out of four seasons. Baker rejoined his beloved Hibernian in 1971 but his remarkable abilities had somewhat diminished, despite a very respectable 12 goals that season.

the enclosure and I wanted to be in there so that I could touch his jersey as he ran down the tunnel. I pleaded with my dad to give me the money to pay the full price to get in and although I didn't manage to touch Bobby Johnstone, I got to see him close up. That was the magic of football. You lose that magic as you get older. You become more involved and more interested, but that childish magic and naivety goes away.

When I first started going to matches there was no segregation. There might have been mild arguments and occasional punch-ups but there were never any serious incidents. In the '60s it was a traditional thing at most grounds to change ends, and so supporters would pass each other. There may have been occasional punches thrown but I think it was mainly a case of glowering at each other as they were passing. Match day hospitality has changed – in those days a guy would come round with a cinema usherette type box and the choice was a pie, an orange, or a Duncan's hazelnut chocolate bar. If you ordered a pie they would just hand you it, there were no napkins or anything like that. One of the good things about non-segregation was that unlike nowadays when you can be stuck beside a guy you don't like in the seats, in those days you could walk about and meet people that you knew or if it was freezing cold you could walk about and keep warm, so it has changed in that respect.

When they knocked the old East Terrace down recently it wasn't remotely about bricks and mortar, it was about memories of people that had stood there watching the many great games we have seen over the years. There were some magnificent European games but now they've expanded the number of teams so we're generally playing sides you've never heard of. In those old days we would play teams like Barcelona, Valencia or Napoli and every one of those games had their own sense of magic. One of the great European nights was against Real Madrid – a team past their best but still a bloody good side. It wasn't a great night weather-wise but to beat them was fantastic! I spoke to a customer in my picture-framing shop recently, a Spanish lad, and when I asked him who he supported he said, 'I'm a Madrid fan. And I said, 'Oh, did you know that Hibs once beat Real Madrid?' He said 'Really?' I went and got a photo I have of the players taking a lap of honour round the pitch. Looking bemused, he asked, 'Why were they doing that if it was only a friendly?' From his manner I could tell that he had totally and utterly missed the point that this was a great victory, whether it was a friendly or not.

The Napoli game, if you talk to any Hibs supporter, was just magical because after that first leg we were 4-1 down and it seemed that there was no way that we were going to recover from that. Then there was that early goal from Bobby Duncan. I've checked the papers of the time and he was actually only about 24 yards out. Now people say, 'He was at the foot of Leith Walk when he hit that ball and the goal went in.' Time leads to exaggeration but there really have been so many great European nights.

We are not doing well at the moment but there have been plenty of periods that have been the same over the 50-odd years I've been watching Hibs. For many years as a kid I thought that they were one of the top teams in the country and in Europe. I'd heard about them being the first British team in Europe in 1955 and I believed they were one of the biggest teams in the country. But then you discover that maybe they're not...

From the outset, Hibs was a community club and for some reason Hearts were seen as the establishment team. Hibs were certainly a team for the people and always a great community side. There was no Scottish League until 1890, so apart from national and local cup competitions they just played in friendlies. Many games were played to raise money to help to feed poor people in the local community. The charitable aspect of the club seemed to disappear for a while but the current board have set up the Educational Foundation to help people who have maybe missed a chance at school. So they say, 'Come along in the evening and use the facilities.' We've always been a people's club I think. If we get a good victory we see it as a great victory and enjoy it. In contrast, Hearts' expectation levels are far higher. I know it just comes from my Hearts pals in the pub but if they win two games on the trot they think the league is on. We Hibees don't think we are rubbish, but we have different expectations.

It's always been said that Hibs are the team in Edinburgh that wants to play good football, but whether that's just come from the Famous Five era, when they were magical and special, I don't know. At the end of the day it's a results industry. Nowadays we are much more success-orientated than ever before. Between the wars, for instance, a manager could manage a club for 25 years and as long as they stayed in a safe, mid-table position then the club wouldn't get rid of him. Nowadays they want you sacked if you lose three games on the trot. Money has been important ever since the game went professional but now that's all it seems to be about! Football is secondary. If Rangers and Celtic qualify for Europe it's not a case of 'We can win this cup', it's more like, 'We can get 12 million pounds for doing this.'

Something that has disappointed me in recent years has been the Bosman Ruling; it has not turned out to be very good for the game. They thought it would be wonderful to not have to pay transfer fees. Instead, they just started to give that money to the players and then SKY came in and that provided even more money for the players. So the wages went up and the clubs are still in debt. With the Bosman ruling, player loyalty disappeared; it meant short-term contracts and bringing in foreigners – and how could they be loyal to a team from another country? I mean, Celtic won the European Cup with a team that was born within 30 miles of Glasgow – when will that ever happen again?

We shouldn't bring religion or even nationalism in to Edinburgh football in any way. Hearts, everything being equal, do get bigger crowds but I always put that back to percentages. Hibs were originally an Irish-Catholic team who would probably have been supported by mainly ex-Irish-Catholics, maybe 20 per cent of the population. Now, normally you start going to games through your family so the club's origins do have an effect, but the Hearts just see it as a case of 'our team has won more than you'. The Mercer scenario made things a lot worse. It stoked up the rivalry when perhaps it had been dying away slightly. Incidentally, the Jambos' nickname is resented by a lot of my older

Hearts supporting friends. 'We were never called the Jambos in our time!' they say. 'The Hibees' is just obvious in the sense of being a shortening of the name.

If you go right back to the very beginning, Hibs were almost a sectarian club. They went out of business in 1891, then when they came back in 1893 they had a strict policy of non-sectarianism and that has been carried through to the present day. At the time of the Famous Five there were very few, if any, Catholics in the team. It's never been a big thing for the club and, when I was young it was never a big thing for the supporters. I do remember in the 1960s that they would sing the 'Soldier's Song' and things like that. I should stress that I am a non-religious person but I think that every single one of us is proud of our wonderful history. There was a wee period about ten years ago when you might see a couple of Irish tricolours in the ground. They weren't forced out or told not to do it, it's just not a big part of modern Hibs.

I think everybody has a routine when they go to the game. I don't go for a pint beforehand. Instead I will usually go in to work on the exhibits. We have the first cups that Hibs ever won, including the Edinburgh Cup in 1879, which we got back from from St Patrick's Church after all these years. For 50 years I don't think I've seen a kick-off. I always look away until I hear the ball getting kicked but it's not exactly proved successful, has it? I think it's a superstition that started when I was kid, I took it very, very seriously. Also, I never so much as open up a programme before the game, I will only read it after or at half time. Again, that has not proven too successful! I know it's daft but I'm scared to stop it in case we really get thumped.

There was one trip away when we went to play against Essen for the 50th anniversary of the first European game in Germany. It was about £123 for a flight and there was one guy who said he'd got his for £73! What he didn't realise was that he had booked it for the wrong week, that's why he got it so cheap!

Lots of folk had a favourite place on the terracing so you would pass by the same people all the time. There was a video released a couple of years ago called *Easter Road Parade* that shows the 'one man band' playing on Albion Road and I thought, 'Jesus Christ, I remember him, how old am I?' This guy had cymbals attached to his legs and he had a mouth organ and would be banging a bass drum at the same time. It's daft things you remember. At the matches back then there was sometimes a guy called Paddy, at least that's what we knew him by, because he would wear a green suit and a green and white bowler hat. Once at half time he jumped out of the crowd, placed his bowler hat on the penalty spot, and then ran up and smashed it in to the back of the net. The police came towards him and he jumped back into the crowd again and disappeared. I never witnessed the famous guy who first shouted 'Gie the ball to Reilly!' I always wanted to know who that was. Another wee point of historical interest – I was told that that when they were refitting the shop on the corner of Albion Road, they uncovered and old sign saying 'Hibs Ice Cream Saloon'.

I remember Maud McFarlane who used to handle the membership tickets at the Hibs Supporters Club, among other tasks. She was a permanent fixture.

There were also characters like Wattie Robb who died recently; he missed just one game in 50 years, which is just amazing! I've read up and researched the subject of Hibs and it was always great when Wattie used to come into my shop and talk from pure memory. He could list some of the old teams backwards. The guy was fantastic, he was a right Hibs worthy was Wattie Robb.

With the internet and Hibs interactive it lets people tune in to see the away games. At one time the main form of communication was the match programme but programme sales are dying out. Now the club emails out a newsletter to several thousand supporters. I'm not an avid collector of programmes, but I have them because I was at the game. For me the feeling of having something tangible in your hand is still great.

In terms of the Historical Trust's exhibits, I have a couple of personal favourites. We put together a catalogue of every programme made since the war, which was really interesting. We've also got maybe a hundred jerseys that have all been documented and recorded on computer. There's one exhibit I particularly like. There was a guy called Tommy McIntyre that played for Hibs before the war and in 1938 he went away with a Scotland touring party to Canada and America but it wasn't an international party so he didn't get capped for it. We have his jersey and his shorts from one of the games on that tour. The top is a bog standard Scotland jersey, but he got all the players to sign the shorts as well as all the press and SFA members of the time. His wife then embroidered these signatures. We had the shorts on show at the last exhibition. They're actually quite funny – the elastic has broken, so they are absolutely huge. There are other exhibits which perhaps don't immediately seem exciting. For instance, the east of the stadium was concreted over in 1959/60, but before that it used to be just wooden slats with ash filled in between, and when they were knocking down the terracing they uncovered these big, long wooden runners which would have had an 18-inch metal pin put in at either end. So the trust recovered a bit of that old wood as well as a couple of the pins. They also found an old ginger beer bottle, a Worcester sauce bottle and a jug, fully intact. Some of those items would have been there since 1924 when they built that terracing up and changed the stand to the other side. With those kinds of artifacts you really feel like you are touching the past!

On a different note, but illustrating the same point, when I went to the *Titanic* exhibition in London, they had this big piece of the actual hull made of thick, heavy steel and there was a hole cut in the top with a wee sign: 'Feel free to touch this.' So you could put your fingers through and touch the *Titanic*. Touching and feeling history, we have that with some of our exhibits at Easter Road. A youngster coming to Easter Road in ten years' time will look back and all they will remember will be the new stadium, so it's all relative. When they were building the new West Stand I would go up every couple of days to take photos and as I sat there and I thought how people must have been roughly where I was when they were building the 1924 stand: they must have had the same kind of feeling. I actually now own a turnstile that was originally located in a corner at the away end, they would have been moved from the old stand in

1955. I have that in my garden accompanied by some of the old red brickwork – it's daft really!

For me, the League Cup Final against Celtic in 1972, and winning the first cup in living memory stands out as a magnificent game. We've won two since, which is really not a great reward for going to watch them for 50 years. While the other cup wins were good, they were not nearly as good as that one in 1972 because it was a great side. The first cup final I remember was in 1958 but I wasn't there when we got beaten by Clyde. Then there were the cup finals after that when we got beaten, the 6-1 Scottish Cup, and the 6-2 League Cup before it, but just to go there and win is something I will never forget. I was in the Centre or Wing Stand, I couldn't see the actual cup but I caught a glimpse of the light glinting off it, it was just a very, very moving moment for me. The cup win in the 1990s was special because a year before that the club almost went out of business so that was spectacular. The win against Kilmarnock in 2007 was kind of different. We won 5-1 in the end but, being a Hibs supporter, you kind of hang on until the very end not ever being sure about what's going to happen.

The most memorable thing about that was what happened off the pitch when they played 'Sunshine on Leith'. The hairs were literally standing up on the back of my neck. I remember saying to one of The Proclaimers, 'After writing that song, you must feel so proud. That was one of the most moving moments of my entire life and for you to have heard these people singing your song must have been so heartwarming.'

Talking of cup finals, at the 1991 game when we won 2-0, I was there with my wife and daughter. When Tommy McIntyre came up to take the penalty I had my camera at the ready and got a wonderful shot of it. As I was taking that shot and the ball hit the back of the net, there was a wee kerfuffle right behind my daughter. Tragically, a guy had collapsed and died at the game! I think his wife wrote to the papers saying how fitting it was for it to happen when the Hibs had won a cup at last. I thought of my brother Kenny, who died aged 39, how much he would have loved it if he had been there at the 2007 final. At that game in 1991 there was there was a guy in front of me with two young bairns. It sounds a bit immature but I thought, 'You've just seen Hibs win a cup and I've had to wait all those years!'

The feeling I get from the fans at the moment is, 'what's the point of having this stadium if the team is rubbish?' You've got to give credit to the board for completing the stadium. It would have had to be done at one time or another and I think they thought it was the right time because they got a good financial deal, but unfortunately it's rebounded a bit on them. However, we're going to be here for another hundred years so all the foundations are there and there are no excuses now. What happens on the park is what it's all about really so when good things do come, let's enjoy it.

I can understand why a lot of people were against the televising of football, but I thought it seemed to be handled well initially. You would see the occasional game and it would be really exciting because you would be sitting in the house and suddenly it would be announced, 'There will be an extra 20-minute programme tonight to show you the highlights.' It didn't matter if it was Hibs or not, I would watch it anyway. Nowadays the mass coverage can ultimately do no good for the game apart from the money that it raises. If you are taking a youngster along to Easter Road or Tynecastle for the first time, they are going to be disappointed because they have watched Real Madrid, Barcelona, Manchester United or Arsenal on TV. What's more, the number of Manchester United jerseys you see around the town is worrying. They all know Messi and players like that but they don't know who is playing for Hibs. The only saving grace is that once you do go three or four times it gets under your skin even if you realise that Barcelona are 25 times better than us. Once you have become a Hibs or a Hearts fan you just feel compelled to go.

Nowadays youngsters might have a Hibs jersey, a Scotland jersey and a Man Utd jersey as well, even if their first loyalty is with Hibs. My first Hibs top would have been in 1958 or 1959, I believe there weren't any replica kits before that. In the early days you could buy a Scotland top but it didn't have a badge on it. Now it's 'authentic' replicas and they will have all the advertising logos as well. My mum bought my first strip for me at a sports shop called Neil's at the top of Antigua Street. It was the old-fashioned, collar-type Umbro design with the shorts and the jersey. It had long sleeves with no advertising or anything like that. Hibs never had a badge until Tom Hart's time so that would have been the first time a badge appeared on the replica Hibs strip. I also remember that you didn't get socks with the kit so my mum, not knowing any better, went away and bought a pair of green and white socks for me. She didn't know they were green and white Celtic 'hoops', so I got ribbed by my pals for that. My brother has got an England replica top because our dad is English and I still kind of support them because of Joe Baker – I support Scotland as well, obviously.

To my knowledge, Hibs never ever had a harp on their jersey but in the store room we have a big 8ft by 4ft flag with a harp on it: it's black and gold with the head on it. They reckon that the flag dates back to the 1930s and they used to fly it from the flag pole. Tom Hart introduced the Real Madrid style badge with the crown, the leaves and the ball. Apparently you can't have a crown on anything without permission from the Lord Lyon, which Hibs didn't have. It was just the most wonderful of coincidences that when Duff and Gray decided the club should have another badge, they were alerted by the Lord Lyon to the fact that the club had been breaking the law. Toffs brought out the replica strip, with the harp and they brought out silly things like the HFC badge that they wore in the Scottish Cup Final in 1972, but with a jersey from the 1960s, so it was all kind of mismatched. The great thing about the current badge is that we talk to the youngsters about it on tours of the stadium and it explains the entire history of the club. You might ask the kids where the name of the club comes from and about the Edinburgh reference, which is self-explanatory. What really gets them thinking is when you ask them about the relevance of 1875, or, 'what are the three badges?', 'why have a boat, the castle or the harp?'

They have done the badge really well and they haven't overfeatured any of its components. It's wonderful, it has meaning, and it's a really compact design.

When Fishers were the shirt sponsor the strip was made of a silky material and that might have been the point that it changed colour, if it actually did. I think they have the colour of green that they will stick with from now on. There are bound to have been changes in the colour over time but I don't think it's been a deliberate act.

Hibs run the Community Foundation and part of its remit is education. The club has a programme to bring kids in and spend a day in the classroom. They are getting more schools involved and I have done guided tours with them round the ground. We have a tactile box, which is wonderful for kids and we have several different sets of boots we can show them – from the 1930s until the present day. We also have a big, heavy old jersey, an old ball with the laces and a set of the old-fashioned studs, which have three nails about an inch long coming out of them. They used to hammer them into the boots. The kids sometimes think that the studs went in the other way round, with the nails showing on the outside. It's quite amusing! We are going to try and get some other exhibits from the Hampden Heritage Group, where the clubs go once or twice a year to meet, they have been great at lending us items for the exhibition. One of the things we have is an old football rattle because the kids think its wonderful. Nowadays we encourage them to touch the exhibits, whereas in the past, you would just look at everything through glass. The schools want their visit to be part of their education. It's not a simple case of, 'This is Franck Sauzee's jersey.' We ask, 'Sauzee's from France. What part of France does he come from? What is that region of France famous for?' so it's an educational experience rather than just a football experience.

A couple of years ago, at one of the meetings for the Heritage Group at Hampden a guy called Mike White, who is Falkirk's historian, was telling us that he'd heard that the old Falkirk captain from 1957 was in hospital with Alzheimer's. He'd decided to take some pictures down to show him. Well, when he went in and showed him a picture the guy instantly came alive.

'I remember that day,' he was saying, 'the sun was shining so I decided to kick down the way so that the sun was behind us.'

He literally had a new lease of life. So I thought we could maybe try this with some other guys that I know. The next thing I knew, the Hampden Museum Committee had taken it on board. They got funding from Alzheimer's Scotland and started doing a year-long pilot project. I was asked to cover the east of the country under the auspices of the Hibs Historical Trust. We uploaded about 150 pictures of Hibs, along with old programmes and adverts, onto a website of old photographs. I went round the hospitals and made people aware of the project. The Caledonian University assessed the impact and they concluded that there had been a definite improvement in the Alzheimer's sufferers who had taken part. It just goes to show the healing power of football – it really is magic!

Gordon Munro

Labour Councillor, Leith Ward, born 1958.

'Football takes you away from everything else, no matter what else is going on in your life, you forget about it.'

I'M A THIRD generation born Leither. I never met my grandad. My dad's reluctance to take me to the games when I was younger was based on the fact that at the record crowd game in 1950, my grandad had a brain haemorrhage and passed away while my dad was there with him. He was only 13 when it happened.

We emigrated to Clermiston on the west side of Edinburgh and I remember agitating for months to get to go to Easter Road but my dad wouldn't let me go on my own. Eventually he said he would take me along, so the first game I saw was against Malmö of Sweden. At the stadium my dad gave me a 'lift over', as he knew one of the guys on the gate who was from the Leith Dockers Pipe Band – Jimmy Cleary was his name, and my dad just gave him the nod and that was me over the turnstile. That day, for the first time, I stood on the spot where I would stand for ten years, until I became an adult. It was on the halfway line, facing where the team would come out, so you could see both halves of the pitch. We never, ever moved from that spot, even if the majority of fans changed ends, depending what end you were shooting towards. Sometimes I'd move about a bit more, depending on the guys that I went with. A couple of times we'd go to my uncle's, who stayed on Easter Road, and my dad would sometimes have a tin of beer with him. If they decided to have another one, I would maybe get sent to the ground on my own but on the understanding that we'd meet at the halfway line. I liked to be right down at the front, as close to the action as you could be.

The old ground seemed really big and open to me when I was a kid – the only bit that was covered was the Main Stand. The terraces seemed really high. It was either empty-looking or packed out, depending on the team we were playing. There was a scoreboard at the Dunbar Road End that would show the half-time scores so that people could fill in their football coupons.

The 1972–73 season is the one that stands out in my memory. Some of the European games that we played that season were absolutely stunning. Night games were always special – as darkness enclosed the ground it was revealed in that special glow of the floodlights on the pitch. There seemed to be a different kind of atmosphere at the night games.

There was one midweek Scottish Cup quarter-final against the Huns. My dad was still on the tools so while I was waiting for him coming off his shift I went to my uncle's for my tea. I'd been going to meet my dad at the bottom of the stair but when I went down I got chased back up by some Rangers supporters who had seen a wee bit of my green above the blue parka I was wearing. They shouted, 'You Fenian bastard!' and made a swing at me, punching the door as I went racing back up the stairs. I rapped all the doors as I went up the stairs and everybody came out so they backed off and after that I just waited at my uncle's for my dad. I remember that particular game for the wrong reasons maybe, but that whole season was magnificently memorable for many good reasons as well.

I am still firmly of the belief that if John Brownlie hadn't broken his leg in that game against East Fife, we would have been in contention for winning the league. We were just sweeping all before us, but that was the beginning of the fracturing of that team. There was Pat Stanton, who was absolutely great and John Blackley, whose approach was so cool. Sometimes he was a bit too slack, yet he always seemed to be in control. And the partnership between O'Rourke and Gordon was just great – they just simply understood each other! Alex Edwards was mercurial and some of the football he played was brilliant. He was one of the smallest players on the park, but he had one of the biggest hearts. I can remember him going toe-to-toe with Forsyth of Rangers, who was a beast of a player.

These days there are more women at games than in the 1970s. Back then, when a woman needed the toilet she actually had to get out of the terracing and walk along the ash track round the pitch to get to the Ladies in the Main Stand. Everybody in the ground knew where that woman was going – and she had to come back the same way as well. You can imagine the pelters these women took from the crowd.

In my early years of going to Easter Roa, there was a guy on the terracing who would get out his bugle and start to play a tune and then the fans would take up the chant. You don't get stuff like that now and I miss that. I think the crowd is not as spontaneous as it used to be, although they're still capable, on occasion. The AEK Athens game was evidence of that, whether it was the 'Sunshine on Leith' song or the guys scudding along in front of the Athens fans with their fists up when we scored, knowing that they were going to get lifted.

When they were doing the ground development, I wrote to the club, and the press as well, advocating standing areas. I had just come back from a trip to the Bernabeu Stadium in Madrid, where they still have a section of the ground where there's standing. What they would probably call the Ultras were in that bit, singing and leading the chants. The atmosphere was electric. I think we've missed a trick there. It was Bobby Williamson who said, 'If you want to be entertained then go to the cinema.' Football isn't another form of corporate entertainment, the beauty of it is that it is live there in front of you and just about anything can happen. I think you've got to have a space for that on the terraces as well as on the pitch.

Regarding the roots of the club, as the song says, 'If you know your history, it's enough to make your heart go...' Hibs were founded in response to poverty in the Cowgate and that same poverty is still there in parts of the city. The genesis of the organisation remains pertinent. When the potential was there to move out to Straiton, I was against it. You would not only have taken away the club's identity but also something from the identity of the Cowgate and Leith; you would almost have been excommunicating yourself from these communities. Part of the reason for the club starting was to eradicate the anti-Catholic feeling within Edinburgh and awareness of that sort of prejudice is a good reason for the club to reach out to the people that have come into Leith. Leith has always had that foreign influence throughout its history, partly because it's a port and partly because it's one of the cheapest areas for getting housing in the city. The lure of our club and the history of our club is enough to hook and keep them. Therefore I think it's in the club's interest to do the sort of outreach work they are now starting to do through the Community Foundation.

There's still a wee 'hands off' approach from the Edinburgh bourgeoisie, they don't really support Hibs in the way they support Hearts. That might be faith, tradition or upbringing, but I think that it's also linked to how these clubs started. There are some folk that keep that flame alive in both clubs. Segregation of grounds has actually led to a more frantic atmosphere, a type of atmosphere that doesn't actually need to be as bitter. I can remember going to the 7-0 game with a pal who was a Hearts supporter, it was because my dad was taking us that his dad allowed him to go. He was two years younger than me. Even though he wanted to leave at half time, when it was 5-0, I said, 'No there will be more goals,' and I was right. I also still remember Celtic supporters talking to me when we got beaten 6-1 in that cup final and they said, 'Your turn will come.' It did indeed come later, in the League Cup final. In those days you were able to be in beside opposing supporters at Hampden, Easter Road, or even at Tynecastle. One of the books I have, which I got from a pal of mine who is a Hearts supporter, is of the Gilzean cartoons from the *Pink,* where Eck and Bob take it turn-about to go to Easter Road and Tynecastle. The loss of that mingling with each other has kind of ramped up the atmosphere so you're making them 'the other' without actually knowing them. My brother and I used to meet up with Hearts supporters at the Blue Lagoon – they were called the Lagoon Maroons. You could still go in with your colours on and have a beer with them, they might have booed when The Proclaimers came on the jukebox, but it never got any more towsy than that. The 7-0 game, though, was just unbelievable, it was free-flowing football and everything we did just seemed to go right that day. We could have been 1-0 down in the first five minutes, because

Hearts nearly scored. From then on it just seemed to be all us, the whole team was outstanding. I can remember going home to my gran and grandad's and my grandad saying, 'What was the score today, son?' And I said, 'We won 7-0!' Surprisingly he came back with: 'What? That's buggered up my coupon!'

I've had different match-day routines when I think about it. As I said, when I went with my dad we would go to my uncle's on Easter Road. His stair was right by the old train platform at Albion Road, where the programme seller's stand is nowadays. He had a contact from Rowntrees and we would get these bags of mis-shapen Smarties, Mint Cracknells and Rollos. Most of the time we launched into them quite a bit before the game. So that was a tradition for a while. When I was older, after my dad stopped going and I started going with my pals, we would go to the pub before the game, fulfilling that Hibs' tradition of drinking until ten to three, and then racing down to the ground from The Artisan. Now I go with my daughter and I have actually found myself going to Out of the Blue arts centre in Dalmeny Street. I have a coffee there. It's very rarely that I go for a beer and if I do it's usually somewhere close to the ground like the Four in Hand. I have gone to the Dockers Club a couple of times as well, because a bunch of folk I know from work are in there every Saturday. One of them, Jim Burns, used to do youth coaching with Hibs after he retired as a fire brigade officer. Another one that I see is Dave Scott, he's at Queen Margaret University and still sits somewhere in the West Stand. We kind of drifted apart but will still wave if we see each other.

When you grow up and have kids, that's when the traditions change, and it's also how you renew the club in your mind. In the '80s I went with people I knew from the Labour Party and we had a left-wing enclave. Dick Gaughan the folk singer was there and a pal of his that was an NUM official – I can remember us collecting for the miners' strike outside the ground. At the time of the Mercer takeover I was a full-time carer for our children so I was just one of these people that had the 'Hands Off' stickers and signed the petition and all that. I would speak to people in my circle about it though, it was a case of 'all hands to the pump'. My Labour Party friend Dougie Kerr, he was right involved with the committee and he still has a really sharp memory of how close things did come at that point. It made people realise that this institution that had survived for over a century was in danger of just disappearing and the threat was such that people from all walks of life realised that they had a part to play in saving the club for the community. We are still on the path back from that and I don't think that we are fully through it yet, partly because we have never had a stable team or stable management for the last ten years.

I remember having an autograph book – I have no idea where it went to – and I had all of the autographs of the 1972–73 team. I got them via my uncle's laddie, Ronnie Hunter, who played along with Mervyn Jones who was with Hibs. When you couldn't afford to go to away games, you would go along to the reserve matches and that's how I got Cropley's autograph – he was playing in the reserves while he was recovering from an injury. I was in the stand, they used to just open that section up rather than the rest of the ground for the reserve matches. I still miss that because I still can't really afford the away games and if they still had reserve games on I would go along to see how they were doing. That's something the authorities need to tackle, if they want the game to continue and not just be full of mercenaries looting clubs for their money. It's also a way of seeing the next wave of players coming through.

John Hughes had a strategy worked out but they didn't give him the time unfortunately. Folk in Leith are still passionate for him. I met him at the 30th anniversary of The Citadel youth centre, they were doing awards and he said he would come along to present some. What he didn't know was that The Citadel was giving him an award as well. I was the one that gave him his 'Oscar' to say 'Thanks very much'. When I presented it to him I said, 'I dinnae very often disagree with my own club, but I do disagree with the fact that they didn't give John enough time.' And a roar went up from the whole hall. He understood the link between the club and the community. One of the things he did at The Citadel was passing on tickets for youngsters. That sort of charitable gestures harks back to the beginnings of the club. I can recall a lad who, the first time I met him, was in the homeless hostel on Parliament Street in Leith. It's a turnaround facility where they give people eight weeks to put a bit of stability back into their lives. The next time I met him was at the launch of the Community Foundation at Easter Road. He was learning computer skills from the club. That is the sort of work they do that needs more publicity. I strongly believe that the community gives freely to the club, so the club should give something back to the community.

On the more 'unsavoury' side of things, my first memory of that as a laddie was the big games where folk couldn't be bothered going to the toilet. I would be at the front and the urine would be coming down the steps – you had to make sure that you had a good pair of shoes on so that your feet didn't get wet! Conditions were quite primitive. I remember going to East End Park to see Hibs and thinking, 'How come they've covered three-quarters of their ground and we've still only got that scruffy wee shed at the Albion Road End?' That was where the neds used to go, so they actually used to divide the corner of the East in half and when the fans wanted to battle with each other that was the area they went to, whether it was against Dundee, Rangers or sometimes even Hearts. They would go there to fight each other and the police would keep them in that part of the ground and let it happen.

When we first started going I would have been ten years old, and my dad would pick and chose the games we went to. It would mostly be your St Johnstones and friendlies that he would take me along to. For my birthday in 1970, I asked for tickets to the Scottish Cup final – which turned out to be that 6-1 game against Celtic. I knew it was a 'big ask'. That was reinforced when we got off the train in Glasgow and walked from Queen Street down to Hampden, because we couldn't afford the bus fare.

The only story I remember being passed down through the family was one that my uncle told us. It was about the New Year's Day match when my dad's dad passed away. He said that he could recall trying to draw the attention of the ambulance folk by waving a white handkerchief and some of the crowd being a bit reluctant to part until they realised the severity of the situation. He had to walk round the pitch with his father being carried on a stretcher by the first-aid people. Then he had to go back and tell my granny that Paddy wasn't coming back from the game. I must have heard that story when I was in my mid-teens and that was when my dad's reluctance to take me to the games became understandable, whereas it had been a source of resentment. My grandad's death was seen as an 'act of God' by my granny.

I still get a thrill when I walk into Easter Road. I recognise the portal has changed, but what I am going there for hasn't. Football takes you away from everything else, no matter what else is going on in your life, you forget about it. What I am going there for is essentially my love for the club – come hell or high water, it's my club! My ambition for the club, although I think we have financial stability in terms of the ground that we have now, would be to have a team that can build together. Money does dictate who the winners are in the game nowadays, whereas there used to be more of a level playing field. A lot of the players came from the same background. Alan Gordon was the exception, he was an accountant, but the bulk of the team were working-class laddies. That has changed. They are definitely more pampered and unless you have got a bit of heart for the team that you are playing for, then you might not have that full commitment to the cause. I think the platform is there for the club to get to the next level but it's whether the investment in that potential is there. That has to be balanced by what they can afford. I think that there is a crunch coming for football.

At the core of it is getting a group of players together that are committed to the club. Keeping that together is the hard part. Look at the current Scotland team, some of the players in the first 11 were part of that 'Teenage Kicks' group who won the League Cup for us. If we could have held them together, what could we have done, even just for another two seasons. That's where I tip my

Hibs v Dnipro, 2005, during the reign of Tony Mowbray.

'Look at the current Scotland team, half of the players in the first 11 were part of that "Teenage Kicks" group who won the League Cup for us.'

hat to players like Scott Brown. I said that to him at the civic reception here when we won the cup: 'Fair play to you for staying, because now you've got the medal. Kevin Thomson's got the money but you've got the medal!' Quite a few of the guys donated their signing-on fees with other clubs to the Hibs youth system. I certainly know that O'Connor, Brown and Fletcher did that, and they all stipulated that it went back into the youth structure which I think is the real potential for us. If we can get a cohort that goes through from 13 to 19 years of age and then keep them until about 23, that is where we could do something.

I would like to see the club play an even bigger role in the community People used to have an identity through their work, as a Leith docker or a miner or whatever. There's a loss of that identity now and one of things that will give our community identity is Hibernian Football Club. I really like the redesign of the badge, which emphasises that, by linking the city of Edinburgh, the Port of Leith and the Irish roots of the club. We've still got kids leaving school who aren't literate or numerate. One of the things that would maybe get them interested is if their local football team were promoting classes for them. That's not just a benefit to the individual, it's a benefit to the community and ultimately to the club itself. The commercialisation of football has been such that it has alienated ordinary supporters. The supporters' trusts are one of the things that will see Hibs through this century and beyond that, by giving the fans an active role in the running of their club. There needs to be a two-way communication line between club and supporters. The Historical Trust has some exhibits in the stands, they're doing good work getting people to appreciate our history. There's been a lot of work given freely over the years. So extending the social and educational role would be a recognition of the contribution ordinary fans have made over the years. The club have started to do that but there are still cascaded messages from the management and there isn't parity yet.

In the 1977–78 season I always remember going out on the batter with some of the guys and we went into this newsagent at Easter Road, just at the foot

Tony Mowbray replaced Bobby Williamson as manager of Hibs in 2004. Harnessing and guiding the considerable talents introduced by the previous manager, Mowbray set about building a young team that would shine. Crowds also began to return to Easter Road as the enthusiasm displayed by the likes of Brown, Thompson, O'Connor and Riordan on the pitch was met equally from the stands. Hibs finished in the top four of the SPL during Mowbray's two-season tenure, the only time this had been achieved since the legendary stewardship of Eddie Turnbull in the 1970s. Many of those talented young players were soon to leave the club for considerable transfer fees; many also donated their signing on fees to the future development of young players at the club. These fees helped the club move towards the sound financial footing of the present time.

of the stair where my uncle stayed. We all bought plastic sunglasses for five pence each and ended up doing a pogo on the terracing with our sunglasses on, so I like to think of that as being the genesis of the Hibees Bounce! I can still remember us jumping up and down and folk were just standing staring, there were only about half a dozen of us, we must have looked like we were nuts.

I can still recall Derek Johnston going to throw a punch at George Best because he nutmegged him. Johnston brought him down and Best picked himself up and handed him the ball. Johnston got the ball in his hands and he wasn't sure what to do next. The crowd was just laughing because they knew that Best had just pegged him right there and then with that single, simple act. By the time he came to Hibs Best was chubbier and slower, but in terms of brain and ability he was streets ahead of everyone! It was kind of like when Steve Archibald came back and played for us, he was head and shoulders above everyone else as well. Who would have thought that we would beat Sporting Lisbon 6-1 at Easter Road? Gee whizz, I still can't believe I actually saw that.

There are two stand-out memories, though. One is coming back from the 2-1 League Cup final against Celtic. Our train got delayed, but the team had got delayed at Maybury as well. We actually had just got up the Waverley Steps as the bus came past the North British Hotel (now the Balmoral). We just stood and watched in awe as Pat Stanton held the cup aloft. The other one was the Athens game. I went there with my daughter and at the end of the 90 minutes, during extra time, I recall turning round to her and she was standing on the seat with her scarf up singing 'Sunshine on Leith'. She had never heard that song before then. The bristles on the back of my neck stood up. Another stand-out game, that was just pure luck and chance, was the 2007 Cup Final when the Lord Provost Lesley Hinds held a reception in the City Chambers for the team when they came back. So we managed to get back in time with my brother and he left his car at our house, we nipped back into town on the bus up to the City Chambers. We got to mix and mingle with the players and got a photo of me, my daughter and Rob Jones with the cup. As the players were leaving to go on their open top bus, we got an offer to go down to Easter Road because they said there was a bus that would take us down to the ground. As usual I'd got captured by somebody and was talking away so I said, 'Look, I'd better go!' and someone else said, 'Hurry up, the bus is just about to leave!' So we got on this second open top bus just behind the players' bus. I saw a coach parked over the road with all the players wives, girlfriends and other club officials. I said to my daughter, 'I think we're meant to be on that one but I think we should just stay here,' and she whispered, 'Aye, Dad.' So we went on the whole of the parade back to Easter Road and it was just great. I remember picking up all the Hibs flags and scarves as they were thrown onto the bus and then giving them out to guys I knew. I was trying to tear a flag off the bus because a mate of mine was at the corner of Albion Road shouting, 'Go and geez the flag!' And I was shouting back, 'It won't come off! I'll gie it to you on Saturday,' which is what I did. He was dead chuffed with that. But to see all these fans as you went down The Mound, along Princes Street, down Leith Walk, along Duke Street and up

Easter Road and into the ground was absolutely tremendous.

The final in 1991 is what I remember most though. What my daughter remembers is me taking her up outside The Centurion on Corstorphine Road and holding her on my shoulders to see them going past with the cup. I didn't go to that game, we sat and watched it on TV, so I said to her 'C'mon, we'll go up and see them.' Conversely, I also remember the Skol Cup final in the '80s when John Hewitt crucified us. He just kept charging down that wing and we just didn't have an answer to him.

At one time the fans used to sing songs relating to the conflict in Ireland, that's kind of been ironed out. If I reflect on it now it was probably part of that early '70s boot-boy culture and its identification with what I would call 'the war on Ireland', but the government called it something different. I think it was a reflection of that and seen as a point of clash and conflict, and the tradition of the football taunt had a part to play as well. I think the reasons that people bring along an Irish tricolour, for example, are different now, because fans are now aware that our club came from the Catholic community in the Cowgate. They are also aware that Michael Whelehan, who was one of first captains, was actually a distant relative of Pat Stanton, one of Hibs' most famous captains. So there is that direct lineage all the way through the club and its history. It's probably culturally quite close to the communities of Leith and the Cowgate and that sense of 'we are all in this together'. The past is important for that reason alone.

The first time I really became aware of the roots of the club was when the history of the club's first 100 years was published in 1975. That was the first time I can recall reading something that actually gave you that background. The more that people have gone in to depth about it, the more you find out there was an altruistic edge to the club that meant they did benefits for striking miners in Lanarkshire and they did matches to set up what are now rival clubs. It really does go back to the song lyric, 'If you know your history, it's enough to make your heart go...'

Any form of racism at Easter Road is against our tradition. I'm aware, through others, that the BNP did try to infiltrate the casual element at Easter Road. I was told that it was firmly stamped on. That story came from people who were involved with alternative youth organisations in the areas that the BNP were trying to infiltrate, they were people who were former gang members of the YLT and Lochend Shamrocks. I think to a certain extent that segregation in grounds has helped to exaggerate certain elements of these things so that people can flaunt badges and symbols without maybe being aware of what they truly represent. So whether it's somebody waving the tricolour in our section of supporters, or somebody waving the Red Hand of Ulster in the Hearts or Rangers support, they should really try to understand the history behind those symbols.

The parish priest who was involved in founding the club got transferred and took the team with him to start up this bunch of scruffy individuals that are now known as Celtic. Could that be the first instance of professional management in the Scottish game? Joking aside, ultimately there is an internationalist outlook from both clubs that will hopefully drag some of the more regressive influences into this century. Both Hibs and Celtic have had in common the ability to progress and adapt, not something that every club has.

I think the club are going through a really interesting phase at this moment. It's a period where the club could really build for the future as well. The share ownership scheme is a really controversial topic among the membership but I think it presents a great opportunity for the supporters and I believe it is one that should be grasped. However, I know that this is not necessarily a popular view. The scheme opened up two places on the board for supporters that were not available before. It could give fans a chance to understand the dynamics of running a football club. Also if we get fan ownership to a level of 25 per cent it will ensure that we stay at Easter Road for the long term. I tip my hat to Hearts fans for what they have achieved at Tynecastle. They have dug their club out of the hole that money had put them into, they were effectively dead and buried unless they did what they did. I just wish that Hibs fans would take up the gauntlet and do exactly the same thing.

I've been impressed with Leeann Dempster as she has a can-do approach rather than a 'talk to the hand' approach that we experienced before her arrival. You cannot underestimate the effect that a woman in her position can have in changing the macho atmosphere that surrounds football. It's something that can encourage women to support their club and to also take part in the sport itself. When I first went there were very few women that went to the football. If they did go they normally went into the Main Stand to get away from the fact that terracing was full of urine and foul language. But I think the fans are currently experiencing a greater understanding of the complexities of running a football club in the modern age. I think our strength lies in actually encouraging fans back through the door. If you look at German football, they have one of the strongest national teams and some of the strongest club teams in Europe and the World. But they still have some of the cheapest admission prices in European football. This is a model we can learn from and one that could benefit Scottish Football. The pricing of the game is such that the traditional working-class element can't really afford it now. Me and my daughter get the family season ticket which you can pay up over the months. At other clubs it can be a lot dearer. Some of the kids in Leith and the Cowgate honestly can't afford even the cheaper tickets for a game and that is where the club could devise the modern equivalent of the 'lift-over'.

There was a bunch of people that migrated from our area across to the East Stand when it re-opened, one a guy who is a tax inspector. He stayed on the East Terracing although he could easily have afforded to move to the Centre Stand. I went to the Famous Five Stand when I started going back with my daughter. But now we sit just a couple of rows behind the home dugout and I like it because you are in the mix there, you get to see the manager giving out the instructions, instructions that players sometimes don't obey.

Football is an expression of working-class culture that was self-engendered, and as such it was something that Thatcher had to stamp on. I remember The Clash song 'Groovy Times' about the fencing in of the fans. For me that was highly symbolic of the culture and the way you were thought of, not just by the clubs, but by the folk that actually administered the game as well. They treated you like beasts that had to be caged in and I think it's why some people still like to go to the junior games. One of my friends who is coming on a trip with us to see West Ham also wants to catch a shipyard's team playing. He is one of those guys that's been to see St Pauli as part of the Tartan Army and has that love of the raw edge that can still be found in certain places.

There are some significant anniversaries coming up for our club. It is currently the 140th anniversary and in ten years time it will be 150 years since it started. To come from the humble beginnings of the Irish immigrant community in Edinburgh, to organise that community towards positive behaviour, and to still be here entertaining people, speaks volumes about us. But we need to rock up to the gate and support the team and the club in their endeavours both on and off the park. I think that is the biggest challenge the club faces now is competition with other forms of entertainment. We need to seriously consider the dynamics round attending matches and make it more inclusive and fun to attend. So we need a varied and imaginative response to the needs of the supporter. This is where fan representatives on the board could wire new ideas into the rest of the board's thinking. Our neighbours need to be our supporters and if we aim to be a fan-owned club by 2025 (our 150th anniversary), what an amazing result that would be. Equally, it would be a great legacy to leave for future generations of Hibs fans.

The beauty of watching Hibernian is that even if it is a crap game, something can happen that lifts your whole week out of the mundane. You just don't know what's going to happen and that is what makes it so special.

Stephen Young

Contract manager, born 1963.

❛ He sat us down in his office and the postman was still raging, he had the aura of a "righteous healer" about him. ❜

I WENT TO St Patrick's Primary in the Southside. My mother's family were of Irish origin and came from the Canongate while my father's family were strict Protestants who came from Leith. The one thing that both families had in common was Hibernian, so it was inevitable that I would end up being a Hibs supporter.

I was seven when my dad first said that he would take me to Easter Road and by that time we lived on Easter Road itself, between Iona Street and Dalmeny Street. I didn't know what he meant because as far as I was concerned Easter Road was where we lived. It became apparent that the place he was talking about was just round the corner, yet a thing of mystery to me. One day that all changed. He took me to watch a match against Cowdenbeath, a 2-2 draw. I can't remember anything about the first three goals but I remember the equaliser being scrambled in, it was John Blackley that scored it and he went on to be a hero of mine. But what I recall most was the smell of the Centre Stand. It wasn't a pleasant smell, but it was interesting to a seven-year-old – a mix of cigar, cigarette and pipe smoke, old men and toilets! The old terracing, which was three-quarters empty that day, looked so vast. I'd never seen anything like it. It was very cold, as it invariably does seem to be at Easter Road. From the entrance on Albion Place – the door openings were literally a man wide – that first climb to the top of those wooden steps, 'clank, clank, clank, clank', seemed to take forever. And then the terracing appeared in front of you. It was just a wonderful feeling! The players were like dots far below and I couldn't wait to go back.

After that my dad took me to see Hibs against Leeds United, Juventus and Sporting Lisbon. For that type of game you would see the terracing full under the floodlights on a Wednesday night. He wouldn't take me to Hearts, Rangers or Celtic games because there was sometimes trouble inside and outside the ground. But we went to games against the likes of Cowdenbeath, Airdrie and Clyde, generally on a Saturday afternoon. At reserve games how the big team was getting on would be announced over the tannoy system at half time. By the time I was ten I had become really interested in the concept of football. I couldn't play to any great standard but I read a lot about it. I would try to grab the *Evening News* before anybody else got their hands on it, then start at the back and read it in reverse because I was so obsessed with football. All my birthday presents were football books.

Huge crowds turned out for games against European sides. In the early '70s I went to see Besa at Easter Road and to see Albanians on the pitch playing the Hibs was something incredible to me! The turning point though was probably the Leeds United game and I'll never forget the heartache of getting beaten on penalties against a side that was full of internationals. All the press reports at the time said that Hibs played them off the park so I thought from that moment on that Hibs were going be one of the biggest teams in the world! Unfortunately that hasn't transpired but Hibs were a massive club as far as I was concerned. It was possibly down to the stadium – Easter Road was just an Acropolis of a place. My idea of Hibs when I was young was that they were a right big side that everybody should have heard of, I thought that they were definitely worth supporting and I've never looked back since.

When I was about 11 I started going to Easter Road without my dad. We lived literally a stone's throw away from the stadium and I could see the top quarter of the old terracing through our kitchen window. By the time I was 12, me and my mate Stevie joined Maud's bus – the Hawkhill branch. They took dedicated buses to every away game and you had to sell pontoon tickets to raise money for them. We went every week, with the exception of Parkhead, Ibrox and possibly trips to Aberdeen, when kids weren't welcome on the bus. The Hibs bug had well and truly bitten. Everybody I knew grew up a Hibs fan but they didn't all take it to the level of obsession that I did. A lot of my mates played football on a Saturday but I couldn't see the wisdom of playing when Hibs were there to be watched. Stevie and I were the hardcore fans, we went to every game that we could and we still go to games together. We always used to stand at the split where the top and bottom half of the terracing met as a walkway. It was an ideal spot, as close to the halfway line as you could get. In these days you could just move around the ground. They'd kick down the slope one half and then up the slope for the other. You would just follow whatever way they were kicking.

I remember fans on the pitch at a Hibs and Rangers Dryborough Cup game, it was maybe '73 or '74. I was just dumbstruck at what was unfolding in front of us. People kept spilling on to the pitch. It was exciting but at the same time a wee bit worrying. When I was older the trouble was primarily outside the stadium. I was never a born fighter and to travel to the extent I did to go and see the Hibs, and to think that I could get a pasting on the back of it... At Parkhead,

Tynecastle and Ibrox you pretty much came to expect it but where you didn't was at places like Ayr. I remember going to Somerset Park, I'm talking '77 or '78. A big team coming down to their town seemed to them like an excuse to go mad. Thankfully, it was always outside the ground and I managed to keep out the way of it.

The '80s was a different culture altogether. By then I was drinking and I could look after myself a bit better, knowing where trouble was and wasn't. It just never seemed to come our way. I suppose the casuals had a different agenda, for them it wasn't so much about the football, it was about fighting. It began in the early to mid '70s with the 'boot boys' going to games looking for trouble. These were guys wearing hard hats painted in Hibs colours. If the game wasn't going someone's way there would be bottles flying so I think banning alcohol was probably a good idea.

When they cut down the old terrace I thought they had castrated the place. It just looked like a wee stadium and maybe that's when the 'wee team' mentality started to kick in. I prefer to sit down at the game but it's a totally different atmosphere. And they've made a pig's ear of rebuilding Hampden. We'll never get the atmosphere that the continentals have there. For example, at the Athens game it was electric, if they'd got that third goal the roof would have come off! I went to see the Croatian national side play against Belarus and throughout the whole 90 minutes they were singing in tandem, back and forth, from one end to the other. But when Easter Road is filled to capacity and we're doing well against Celtic, Hearts or Rangers, you can't beat that atmosphere. The 6-2 game sticks in my mind not just because of the enormity of what was happening on the park, but also because of the fact that we never shut up for 90 minutes. The Jambos left in dribs and drabs until it was just green seats left in front of us.

The best atmosphere that I have experienced, outside of a cup final, was at Rugby Park in 2000–01 on our Scottish Cup run when we got beat by Celtic in the final. We beat Kilmarnock in the quarter-final 1-0 and it was probably

' They'd kick down the slope one half and then up the slope for the other. You would just follow whatever way they were kicking. '

The Easter Road slope being levelled in 2000.

the inaugural 'Hibees bounce' – you could feel the foundations of the stand reverberating below you. We got a late goal which meant it was inevitable that we were into the semis and everybody thought that maybe this was our year. The place was going berserk. The two 3-0 games against Rangers at Ibrox were exceptional as well.

I have to say the Aberdeen League Cup Final was lacking in atmosphere for me, which I suppose was because the game was over so quickly, the team physically gave up in front of us. For the second leg of the semi-final at Ibrox, we had that whole end packed and the 1991 semi-final against Rangers when Keith Wright put us through to the final and we went on to win it was equally special. I'd like them to have built on that cup win but they went to sleep for another ten years or so after that. It was unforgivable, we maybe got to Europe twice in the '90s and yet we were in it every other season not long before.

The roots of the club have become less relevant to me the older I've got but when I was about 25 its history was ultra important to me. I'd had that history instilled into me at an early age. As I said, I went to St Pat's and that's where Hibs come from, so the school was full of old Hibs stories, the church was full of old Hibs stories and even the priests at St Pat's had an affinity with Hibs. Blackfriars Street, the Cowgate and the Grassmarket were of interest to me because that's where it all started. I had been born into that and somehow you were continuing to make that pact with the club. It's probably less important to young Hibs supporters nowadays but maybe it's a good idea because I wouldn't want to see them turn into a Celtic. I'm comfortable that there's enough of us out there who are quite happy with the split identity that we've got. There are still people that see themselves as '50–50' – Irish background but Scottish blood, or maybe Irish heart and Scottish blood – whatever it was that Morrissey said about it. For me, that's your typical Hibbie. In the late '60s and early '70s there was still a lot of rebel songs going round Easter Road, old men sang them and young men sang them but they don't now. I have a theory about these

Up until the turn of the new millenium it was said that if you laid your head on the goal line at the Famous Five end of the pitch, you could only just see the crossbar at the Dunbar End. The slope was said to descend around six feet from one end of the pitch to the other.

If Hibs won the toss they would always elect to play down the hill in the second half. Lawrie Reilly was later to compare the boost of shooting downhill to the positive effect that a war cry might have in the heat of battle.

In the year 2000, Hibs fans finally waved goodbye to the old pitch in a game against Aberdeen.

songs maybe not being around prior to that period. In the '50s there would be a crowd of 65,000 at Easter Road for a game against Hearts. Where were all these people ten years later? They disappeared. So I think part of that popularity was Hibs' success and a lot of people must have taken Hibs as their club mainly for that reason. The Troubles in Ireland maybe brought something deep-rooted out in a lot of Hibs supporters. My dad never went on at all about anything remotely religious when we were at the football but my mother's family came from an Irish background and for them Hibs were part of that. It was such a community thing for them. Their fathers and grandfathers remembered the club at its embryonic stages and that connection was passed down through the generations.

If there's two sides to a city, then we are strictly East End and Hearts are strictly West End. We can talk about 'big teams' and 'wee teams' but I think Hibs have always had that wee bit more class, more spirit and wee bit more identity. We weren't called St Andrews and we didn't run about the Meadows in blue – they did! We've always been Hibs and we've always played in green and, for me, that is a big factor in my affection for the club.

I was fortunate enough to be in my mid-teens before I encountered any Hearts fans because of where I came from. At school it was Hibs fans and Celtic fans. At playtime, playing football it was always Hibs versus Celtic, that's the way it worked. At that time Hearts weren't a threat to anything that Hibs were doing because they were miles away from us in terms of football results. But Rangers were the Antichrist as far as I was concerned and they were everybody's pet hate. If you were a Hibbie then Rangers were the team that you hated first and foremost and Hearts were an inconvenience or an irritating scratch. The Mercer episode alienated a lot of people and it changed the horizons of the rivalry completely, and forever. Before, Hibs and Hearts fans could go to games together, whereas that is unthinkable now. I'm sometimes invited to the corporate section at Tynecastle, through work, and I won't go because I know the environment is just not going to be right for me. If Hibs were fortunate enough to score, then I'd find it impossible to sit on my hands and shut up. I don't want to put myself in that position. I'd much rather be behind the goals with the Hibbies, where I'm meant to be, and let everybody else get on with it. The generation of Hibs supporters that were born out of the takeover bid period have a deep-rooted dislike for Hearts. I hate to say it but it's something that has built up within me as well because I can be worrying on a Wednesday night that Hearts aren't getting beaten, even if Hibs aren't playing. Internet message boards have probably increased the animosity that's there because they can argue and insult each other online now as well. You can read it for yourself on any of the Hibs message boards – there's such an anti-Hearts feeling. I think the message boards have probably contributed to changing the culture as well. Nowadays everybody has access to facts, figures, arguments, pluses and minuses... It's never going to go away now is it? There were so many Hibbies online waiting for Hearts to go 'pop', people reading the *Financial Times* before they were reading the *Daily Record* in order to check up on the finances of Hearts. The internet has enlightened people but maybe made them a wee bit more narrow minded as well. On the positive side it has helped the clubs get their message out to a wider fan-base. For the fans, being able to share information on-line is great for sourcing cheap hotels and flights for European trips and stuff like that.

You heard all these things before about Hearts being in such a perilous state and I have to say, hand on heart, that I wouldn't want a supporter of any club to go through that. I think we do need Hearts. The derby has become so important, it's the biggest three games of the season and sometimes four when they creep into the top six, the TV companies are recognising that now as well. There's much more entertainment at a Hibs v Hearts game than there is at a Celtic v Rangers game. I suppose, deep down, I would hate to lose that culture of Hibs playing Hearts consistently. If clubs of that scale start disappearing then Scottish football is in deep trouble. I hate to hear about clubs like Albion Rovers or East Stirling struggling and I'd hate them to disappear – somebody, somewhere supports them.

Centre Stand tickets for European games were scarce and obviously they were expecting a huge turnout for the Hibs versus Leeds game. The tickets went up for sale on sale on a Tuesday morning so my old man was working that day. They were strictly limited to two per person so I got up early, stayed off school and walked round to Albion Road where there was already a queue. Weirdly I remember having toothache that day as I walked round to the old façade of Easter Road. The queue was already down the ramp at the Norton Park School stretching out into Albion Terrace, where I joined it. I must have been in the queue for three hours and the toothache was really kicking in. It was a miserable morning but then, to everyone's excitement, the ticket office opened. It was a really small ticket office at the far right-hand corner of the wall and it was probably just a hut or a garden shed that was behind it. They opened up the hatch and started dispensing the tickets but by the time I got to the hatch I must have been there for three-and-a-half hours at least. I asked for the two tickets and the guy behind the hatch said that I looked under 16 and that they were only selling tickets to over 16 year olds. I was gutted. I burst into tears.

But there was this postman behind me – he had his postman's bag with him, so he was probably going to do his round after queuing for his tickets. Seeing my predicament, he said, 'I'm no having that!' and he dragged me back up the ramp to the player's entrance. They had a suite adjacent to the Centre Stand steps and we just went in, there were absolutely no barriers blocking our way. 'Turnbull!' this man said. 'We're gonnae go see Turnbull about this, I'm no having it!' I'd stopped crying by this time. We got met on the stairs by Cecil Graham, I instantly recognised him. I couldn't have told you what the 'Club Secretary' did at Easter Road but I knew that's what his title was. He asked us what the problem was and this new postman friend of mine explained to him that I had stood in the queue for three hours and that I had 'Nae contact with anybody else,' so it wasn't like I'd been planted there to buy tickets for somebody. He sat us down in his office and the postman was still raging, he had the aura of a 'righteous healer' about him. Cecil Graham came back with two tickets, which I then paid for. He also gave me a couple of Hibs pin badges which I'd never seen in the shop. I hate to say it but I don't have them anymore, I really should have treasured them. The postman got me down the stairs and back along the Albion Road. I never even asked his name, such is the ignorance of an 11-year-old. He said cheerio to me and went off up Easter Road, I couldn't believe what had just happened... I got back and told my old man the story and my mother thought I'd spent the change on these two wee badges but it just wasn't the case. My old man was in despair because he never knew the guy's name and I could only describe him as a postman. It seemed like it was my destiny to get to that game.

Prior to the match, I went round for autographs. You can't really underestimate what an event this was, 50 or 60 per cent of the 1974 Scotland World Cup squad were playing for Leeds. The nucleus of that team was David Harvey, Billy Bremner, Peter Lorimer, Eddie Gray and Frank Gray, so they were pretty phenomenal. There was already a congregation of autograph hunters when I got there but I still managed to got pretty close to the front. It was Billy Bremner I wanted most because he was the man. He elbowed me out of the way so that he could get through crowd rather than just sign my book. Quickly and instantly he alienated himself in my eyes. I did manage to get a few autographs from other players who were nice enough but they didn't have a lot of time for the fans because they were trying to get into the stadium. That was the end for my adulation of Billy Bremner.

I could name the Hibs and the Leeds United teams backwards at the age of 11. The game itself was enthralling and there was a hugely noisy atmosphere. That particular Wednesday night seemed to have an aura about it. There was a faint drizzle and the lights shone down, illuminating pockets of the crowd. The pitch was pristine. Leeds United had star players but Hibs had the better of them – apart from the fact that we just couldn't score. We thought Alan Gordon had scored but it was disallowed and the place went mad in disgust. It was the first game I'd ever been to that went into extra time as I watched Eddie Turnbull, in his big overcoat, barking out instructions to the players and giving them all pelters. I remember Tam McNiven rubbing the players down ready for extra time and all the while I was thinking, God, we're gonnae get another half an hour of this for nothing – it's great, it's great! Then the game went to penalties and I was sitting saying prayers, like that could somehow make a difference. We unfortunately hit the post with our first one, which I'll never forget, and Pat Stanton couldn't bear to even look at the rest of the penalties. Nowadays, the player that misses or scores goes back and joins his mates and they put their arms round each other and watch together, but this was different. Stanton was distraught and he came wandering over to the tunnel near to where we were in the Centre Stand. He was right in front of us. He'd pulled his socks down to his ankles and torn his shin guard ties off. He knew Leeds weren't going to miss any penalties. That wee fucker Bremner took the fifth one, and scored.

The next day my old man bought the *Daily Express*, which I wouldn't even have in the house these days. There was a headline on the back with Bremner saying he thought the Hibees were the best team in Britain. I was fiercely proud going into school, I was saying to my schoolmates, 'Look at that, we done that to Leeds United.' But we just couldn't take it that one stage further. I'm pretty certain that if Hibs had got past Leeds we might have had a European trophy under our belt that season, although beating Leeds United would have been like winning the final in itself.

I saw Joe Baker the second time he was at Hibs, I think it would have been the same season as my first ever game. My cousin Thomas took me and we were in the enclosure under the old stand. Everybody was there for one reason – Joe Baker. He had white boots on, which seems like a strange thing for me to notice, but white boots were few and far between back then. Joe had a lot of hair and those big sideburns. I had seen pictures of him but these had been taken when he was ten years younger and he didn't look the same.

What an atmosphere there was that day. When he scored my cousin Thomas lifted me up and I felt a thump on the back of my head. Thomas turned round and there was this big bloke behind us rubbing his chin. Bobby Clark, the Aberdeen goalkeeper, had a shut out record for something like 11 league games on the trot without losing a goal, but he lost two that day – one to Baker and one to Stanton. We won 2-1 against a good side that had previously won the Scottish Cup. People in my family would talk for years after about the day we went see Joe Baker coming back. What a day it was! I didn't fully realise what a special thing that was to witness at the time.

One of the craziest things I've done was to cycle to Alloa for a pre-season friendly – there wasn't a supporters' bus going. It's at least a 60-mile round trip so that cycle ride would kill me now! Before I set out I couldn't have told you how to get to there, so along the way I had to stop and consult a map. I got into Alloa at about 1pm, ate my packed lunch and went round to the ground. You can't miss Recreation Park because Alloa is about one street long. The groundsman was astonished when I explained that I had cycled over for the game, he thought I was ridiculously keen. I couldn't get the bike through the turnstiles so he opened up the big side gate which they would normally just open for people coming out – I wasn't for chaining it up outside. People still say to me, 'I remember the day you cycled to Alloa, you must have been fucking mad!' It wasn't really worth it because we got beat 2-1, if I remember rightly. Willie Irvine scored, who was a bit of a hero of mine at the time. I would have gone anywhere to see them – you just had to!

As a young man I would always drink copiously prior to the game and after it. Hibs were so bad during that period, I suppose drink helped. You wouldn't have wanted to go and see them sober, that's for sure! My routine's change with the years and nowadays I have a couple of pints before the game. The Four in Hand is my own choice of pub but it really depends on what the people that I go with want to do. After the game I might just go home but if it's Hearts we've been playing or if we've done particularly well then I'll still have a right few pints afterwards. I see a lot of older fellows who have gone full circle and win, lose or draw – hail, rain or snow – they will meet before and after the game and have that same few pints, always at the same table.

I get superstitious about clothes, so much so that if Hibs get beaten then I blame myself. I never wear a scarf to games now, I've gone through so many that I can't wear again because I deem them to be unlucky. I wish I'd kept some of them, they'd be collectable now. If we were in the Scottish Cup Final I doubt if I'd even wear colours now, because if we got beaten I would just blame myself. You also get to the stage where you run out of pairs of underpants. I mean, you have so many pairs of lucky underpants that the minute Hibs get beaten I think, I fucking cannae wear them ones again!

What I would never do is change my seat in the Famous Five Stand, front row of the upper. We have always sat there, Stevie and I, and my wife has a season ticket for a seat in the row behind us (for the past five or six years she has started going as well, which you have to encourage). I can't stand the thought of people changing seats, particularly after the game has started. If Hibs are winning and I see somebody changing seats, and then they lose, I think, That's your fault! Or if I come back and somebody is sitting in my seat I always say, 'Sorry, you're gonnae have to move, I know you're with your mates but I was sitting there.' If I've been sitting in that seat the first half, I've got sit in it for the second half. That will never leave me I don't think. Where do you stop though? You can only blame yourself so much.

Five or six of us went to Dnipro together, including my wife. Like her a lot of people went because they were interested in seeing the Ukraine, not just because Hibs were in Europe for the first time in a long spell. A lot of people had gone to Kiev and then got to Dnipro by train or coach but we got an internal flight from Kiev to Dnipro. The plane was Soviet era and it had obviously been military at some point and it had tables, chairs and lamps so it must have been used for officers previously. There were maybe 30 people on the flight, including about ten Hibs fans. There was only one air hostess. She came out with a pot of tea and poured it into real porcelain cups. I was absolutely intrigued by all this, but at the same time I didn't feel that safe. The runway at Dnipro – if you could call it that – was not the type of runway that we're used to here. It was a bumpy ride and I was pretty glad just to have landed. That flight ended up being the highlight for me because, as everyone knows, Hibs got thumped. Dnipro were a bit physical, they knocked lumps out of Ivan Sproule any time he went near the ball, and I thought that if that tie had been at home with a stronger referee then the game might have turned out differently.

They were worried about the amount of Hibs fans that had arrived, about a couple of thousand in a wee bit of a party mood. I don't think the police were too happy about it, so Dnipro pretty much closed after the game. It was like a ghost town. You couldn't get a drink even at our hotel. We didn't let the result spoil the trip though and we managed to see a bit of Kiev. The Ukranians weren't long out of their 'Orange Revolution' so we went to Peace Square where it all started and it certainly was a beautiful place to be. Hibs might sometimes get thumped on the pitch but you can't let it put you off going to games abroad. The bonus is that you see a bit of the world you might never have seen.

Thinking back to Easter Road, I was gutted when I learnt they were going to demolish the old terracing, so I made a point of getting some photographs. A huge black railing used to split the main terracing from the Dunbar End, it started at the wall near the bottom and went right up to the top. When I went in to take these pictures I ran into Paul Kane, a player I knew because he had got on our supporters bus a few times but I never realised he was now on the ground staff. He was painting these railings and he asked me what I was there for. When I said that I was getting some pictures of the terracing, he said, 'I wish I was doing that instead of painting these fucking railings!' I've still got these pictures and they are very precious to me.

There are wee aspects of the old ground that I loved, like the old half-time scoreboard that kind of diminished at one corner and ran round towards the Cowshed. The walkway that split the two levels and that old rickety scaffolding, calling itself a camera stand, is something I will always remember – and Archie McPherson getting dog's abuse underneath that old camera tower. If the modern-day commentators and pundits were up on that scaffolding I can't even imagine what the abuse would be like.

At Hibs' centenary in 1975 everybody my age was given the book *100 Years of Hibs* for their birthday or Christmas, I made a point of getting as many signatures on it as I could. It was easy enough to get the team and Eddie Turnbull's autograph I got quite easily, even though he was always averse to signing autographs. I tracked down Bobby Combe to a grocer's shop on Leith Walk between Lorne Street and Davidson's Place, he was astonished when I went in. Because I was 12 years old and going in with a bit of knowledge about what he had achieved made him more than happy to sign the book. I never managed to get Willie Ormond before he passed away but I did get Lawrie Reilly's signature and that was a real achievement for me. The number of people that still talk about Lawrie Reilly as their hero is incredible. He was iconic! I fondly remember meeting him. What happened was, when I first met my wife some of the people who worked beside her at the bond went to Lawrie Reilly's pub, The Bowler's Rest, for their lunchtime drink. She turned out to be on first-name terms with him, which pissed me off greatly! I said, 'Right, I'll come down and meet you there one lunchtime.' She was mortified to find I had my book with me when I arrived but Lawrie was there and he was happy to sign it. It was a small spit and sawdust boozer with a snug lounge at the back, which he usually opened for my wife and her friends. While he was signing my book I asked him if he was going to open the back lounge because my wife liked to sit there. There were literally three people in the pub and he said to me, 'I think that's a snob you've got there, son.'

Pat Stanton as the skipper seemed to be integral to that Hibs side, he seemed to have Hibs oozing out of him! His great, great uncle Michael Whelehan, had been the first captain of Hibs so he just seemed to epitomise everything about Hibs. My first confirmation at school required that you had to take a saint's name. There's supposed to be a bit of thought put into it, you would look at the good work a saint had done and then you would adopt his name. Of course

I chose St Patrick. The headmaster and the priests were thoroughly impressed with this because it was St Patrick's School and St Patrick's Church. To take Patrick was going the extra mile! What they didn't know was that there was only one reason for it – he was the main man at Easter Road. Pat Stanton's face adorned my bedroom walls and he is still a hero to a lot of people now. You see him quite a lot nowadays but when I was young Pat Stanton was unreachable. He was literally a god.

George Best joining Hibs was a bit surreal. To this day I love the fact that he played for Hibs, it's great kudos to say that he played for us, even if it was only a dozen games in the Hibs jersey. Even now in some Irish bars there will be a picture of George Best in a Hibs strip. I couldn't put him down as one of my heroes though, because I had a lot of other heroes at that time. I used to say, 'If we had 11 Arthur Duncans we'd be all right.' Arthur Duncan just gave everything for Hibs. He was astonishing, he never let Hibs down once. I loved Ally Brazil as well, because if there's a figure of hate or ridicule I just want them to do well. I was like that with Colin Nish and I fell out with people round about me when I asked them to leave the player alone. If I have a hero in the modern day it would be Franck Sauzee. I love the way he went about his business and he was a gentleman in to the bargain. I think I'm getting too old to have heroes because you look at them now and, in reality, they are just kids.

There was an element of gallus humour when we were going down in 1998, but there were consistently good crowds – Hibs were winning every week in the First Division so maybe that had something to do with it. We have had a fair bit of success over the past five or six years and there now seems to be this kind of doctrine that we have a right to win every week. But essentially we are a club that's born to entertain. Alex Miller didn't really do us much harm and he made us very difficult to beat, he did sign some special players like Michael O'Neill, Keith Wright and Kevin McAllister but jeez, they were horrible to watch and we got beaten off Hearts too much during his reign.

Everybody recognises that a League Championship is beyond us, but not the Scottish Cup. At least two classic Hibs sides have failed to lift the Scottish Cup, although Hearts have done it twice. It's that one major trophy that eludes us in modern times.

Over the years I've encountered some great characters at Easter Road. When I was a boy going with my dad there was an older fellow in the Centre Stand who must have been in his 80s. He had a very bulbous nose and my dad used to say to me, 'Stop looking at the fellow, leave him alone.' He became something of a landmark. Goodness knows what he paid to get in, I'd like to think that the Hibs would just let him in because he'd been alive since 1910 or something like that. At slow parts of the game his frustration would just boil over into an unintelligible rant, probably, 'C'mon Hibernian, get your finger oot,' but it came out like gibberish.

As far as characters go, Maud McFarlane would probably be my number one. She shaped my background from a really early age. I started going to away matches on her bus when I was about 12, a lot of bus operators wouldn't allow people under 16 because there was a drink culture involved. Maud, on the other hand, liked to pack her bus with kids. She looked after them but she also made sure that she got her 'pound of flesh' in terms of ticket sales to help fund the buses. She was a huge character and I was really proud of the fact that I was a Hawkhill member for such a long, long time. I was devout about the bus, I went on it for 14 or 15 seasons, week in and week out.

Maud wouldn't have a word said against the Hibs. If you were complaining on the bus about how poor Hibs had been she would gee you up with something like, 'Never mind that, we'll beat Rangers at Ibrox next week.' If they did, then great, but if not she would say it didn't matter because she believed that Hibs could win any game. She was Hibs through and through, it really was her life.

To sum up Hibs in one word… that word could be 'torture', but no, that's far too negative! Summed up in a name I'd have to say 'Stanton'. And then there's 'Saturday', another word that means so much to me – the day of the week that I associate with Hibs.

Alistair Findlay
Author, born 1949.

❛ I feel privileged to have had a glimpse of the unglamorous, hard work routine of pro-football, the guts behind the glory. ❜

I GREW UP in Bathgate in the late1950s and I remember the news coverage of Joe Baker and Denis Law going to Torino in 1961–62. About ten years later Joe ended up working in Bathgate, in a factory making tractors for British Leyland (as did another ex-Hibbie, John McNamee). He worked alongside my brother Jimmy and told him lots of colourful stories about his time in Italy, which of course Jimmy then told me.

The fact that these players ended up working on an assembly line goes to show how uncertain a future pro-footballers – even the greats – had in those days, compared to now when even average players can be set up for life. Colin Stein, a local West Lothian boy a few years older than me, having starred for both Hibs and Rangers, took up his joiner's tools once again when he finished playing. Awareness of that, combined with my desire to go to university, made me, and my old man, opt to sign part-time rather than full-time forms for Hibs in summer 1965, though this no doubt increased the risk of not making it at all. So I signed for £4 a week plus the same in expenses for Bob Shankly, his first signing following the departure of Jock Stein to Celtic, instead of for Eddie Turnbull's Aberdeen for £2 a week and expenses. I dealt with this in *Sex, Death and Football* in a poem called 'You're Going to the Hibs', which ends with the following stanza on the commercial, hard-edged reality of pro-football, and the less glamorous door 'out' when it's done with you:

> a pub or a sales job and arthritis at the end of it; nae
> sentiment, no, no in this game,
> they'd say, a market-place, where men were bought-and-
> sold like slaves, then 'freed'.

The first senior game I went to was Hearts v Dunfermline at Tynecastle in 1962 when Jock Stein was the Dunfermline manager and the 16-year-old Alex Edwards was playing as was the veteran Hearts winger John Hamilton. That's when I first became aware of 'the crowd', of being 'in the crowd', part of it, this massive, moving, living object. I remember the goalie punting this ball high in the air and Johnny Hamilton – 'Wee Hammy' – standing looking up waiting for it to come down, the crowd silent. Halfway down somebody shouts out: 'I hope Hammy's mooth's shut, it's the only ba' we've goat!'

The first Hibs game I saw was the friendly they played at Easter Road in October 1964, winning 2-0, with Jock Stein as manager. I remember Gento's pace down the left wing and crossing it accurately at full speed without breaking stride. The young Peter Cormack scored a good goal and Willie Hamilton showed his true class. A year later I was on that field training every Tuesday and Thursday evening and going in full-time during school holidays, kicking the ball about with legends, well, trying to get it off them more like. There was a reserve player who gave the players nicknames based on cockney rhyming slang, so Cormack was called 'Gas' (gas-meter/peter) and so on. Pat Stanton was called 'Niddrie', because that's where he came from. He was a tremendous player, a leader, completely non-celeb, chatted to us young players, gave you tips and so on. Years later, in the early '80s when I worked as a social work senior in Craigmillar, one of my colleagues invited Pat, who had grown up in the area, to come along and talk to a group of young offenders. He was hugely impressed by Pat's interest in and ability to communicate with these young men, who were often not willing to talk – or listen – to anybody!

Bob Shankly seemed as dour and taciturn as his brother Bill at Liverpool seemed dour and gregarious. I don't remember him donning a tracksuit like Stein to coach or train the senior players but I was only around on high days and holidays and he had no reason to engage with me. I only ever had one conversation with him in the three years I was there, after training one night and about 18 months into my two-year contract. By then I'd left school and was working, unhappily, as an apprentice quantity surveyor in Edinburgh. I asked him if he would 'call me up' and let me train full-time for the rest of the season to see if I could make it, or just let me go. From silence he barked: 'Newcastle's been at you, haven't they?' The rest of the conversation consisted in me denying any such thing. Much to my surprise, I was offered another year's contract the following April.

It was amazing as a youngster to get glimpses and close-ups of established legends like Willie Hamilton, who looked like Alan Ladd and had the football vision of John White. During pre-season training we used to go down to Seafield and have games on a public park where the pitch was slightly smaller than a senior park. Anyway, we kicked off once and the ball got passed back to Willie, who strode towards it, hooked it up and hit it all in one movement, nearly 40 yards into the roof of the net – that is, if there had been a net to hit it into! In the middle of summer, Willie, towel round neck, would be in a woollen tammy and a full tracksuit with a rubber diving suit underneath. When he got back to the dressing room and unzipped the suit about a gallon of sweat poured out. One guy I never went near was John MacNamee, who took winning against the reserves very seriously. In fact, any time the ball happened to come to me I looked up to see where he was and if he was within a 25-yard radius I just passed it to him. Some of this is in my poem 'Playing the First Team', the final lines of which describe Willie Hamilton:

> too tired to run, he'd hit a ball-forty-two yards from the centre-circle into
> the net; came in, stript off, and enough sweat poured out
> to re-float the Titanic;
> they said Jock Stein slept with him every Friday night so's
> he'd be ready for the match.

The thing that amazed me the most about such players was not just the ability, but their sheer physical power despite their seemingly slight build. Another one in that mould was Alex Cropley. We sometimes played 'third team games' against junior sides made up of part-timers, trialists and full-timers who were not getting regular reserve games. So, we played at Pumpherston one Sunday, my own junior team, and I was up against Cropley, who scored three goals. He just drifted in on the blind side, elbows flying, perfectly timed shots, 30 yards out, brushing through me despite, compared to me, being built like a skelf! A lean, stringy, long-striding, absolutely fearless and tremendously skilful blond battler! No wonder he broke two legs, as Dave MacKay did, and I'm surprised Alex never got more caps. John Blackley also turned out for us, another class player. He had been full-time for a season, playing with Bo'ness Juniors, but when called up couldn't get into the reserves. Word was he was 'on a free' and then Derek Whiteford, the reserve centre half, got injured for the last month of the season and John seized his opportunity with both feet. You have to have the ability to do that, perform, when given the chance, in front of a crowd, not

Pat Stanton.

‘ He was a tremendous player, a leader, completely non-celeb, chatted to us young players, gave you tips and so on. ’

just a near deserted reserve-match, and Blackley had that kind of guts. I think guts and preparedness to kick and be kicked, to be injured, is what separates those who become professionals and those who don't, even if the skill quotient is much the same. Some who were expected to really make it just inexplicably did not – like John Murphy, who was hailed as the new Jim Baxter of my generation, with the same skilful left-foot and slow pace of Baxter. But perhaps it was that lack of pace in the new era of athletic 'total football' beginning in the 1960s that prevented such talent from coming through.

I used to get on the Glasgow–Edinburgh bus at Bathgate for training on Tuesdays to Thursdays at Easter Road and for the first year John Brownlie, a 15-year-old schoolboy, got on the same bus a bit further west at Caldercruix. John would later be taken on as one of the ground staff and he played with me and several other young Hibs full-timers farmed out to Big Vince Halpin, player-coach of Pumpherston Juniors – such as Willie McEwan and Jimmy McPaul. John had the unusual ability for a defender of close ball-control; he used it to get himself out of trouble instead of speed, which I thought he badly lacked. Jimmy McPaul was a powerful left midfielder with a great shot and Willie McEwan an all-round forward player with fine skills. I was a defender with pace who could occasionally pass a decent ball and should probably have signed for Aberdeen to be shouted at by Eddie Turnbull.

Wee Johnny Smart took the evening training. He also worked in the British Leyland factory at Bathgate but lived in Edinburgh. Tom McNiven often turned up and took us for a session, which was absolutely excellent, constant movement and variation of pace and integration with ball-work. Tom himself was a slim, elegant figure with a gentle character and intelligent approach to what he did and how he related. Some 40 years later I would write 'Tom McNiven's Training (Hibs & Scotland Trainer)', a poem that tries to take the reader on an actual training session supervised by Tom, using many of his words and phrases, though also making some stuff up to reflect the times. The final lines are:

Described by many fans as 'Mr Hibs', Pat Stanton made 397 league appearances for the club. It was as captain of Turnbull's Tornadoes that he enjoyed his finest moment for Hibernian, guiding them to a League Cup Final victory over Celtic in 1972. His historical connection to the club becomes even more significant when you consider he is related to the first captain of Hibs, Michael Whelehan. Fans were distraught when he moved to rivals Celtic in 1976.

He gained 16 caps for Scotland before his playing career was cut short through injury, but he enjoyed further success in his subsequent coaching career. Appointed as assistant coach to Aberdeen in the early '80s when Sir Alex Ferguson was manager, he returned to his beloved Hibs as manager in 1982 but resigned two years later over an alleged lack of ambition by the board of directors.

and stretch out your
right-leg behind you and hold it like Nureyev would, he's a dancer,
    two, three –
keep running, same pace, turn, run, thumbs up, point
    them forward, your feet will follow;
skiff the grass with your right hand, jump, head the ball
    left, roll,
keep moving; Nureyev, right foot, up, jump, head,
    keep breathing.

The Easter Road part-timers included the reserve centre half Derek Whiteford, later of Airdrie FC, who was a constant talker and training to be a PE teacher; George McNeil, reserve outside left and future professional world sprint champion, who had a tremendous shot and was a quantity surveyor like myself; and a 14-year-old Peter Marinello, with the face of an angel and as dangerous to full backs as Tony Soprano eyeing up a lasagne.

In my third and final year at Easter Road, a wee guy turned up at the training, a 12-year-old laddie kitted out as best as could be in a droopy strip, oversized gutties, voluminous shorts and hardly enough power in his legs to take a penalty-kick – Alfie Conn. He then grew into thon huge Bear! In those three brief years, I saw recruitment to the senior grade go from mainly junior football to many coming directly from school football, though the juniors, still the resting place for many an old-pro, still being used at some stage to toughen them/us up.

Forty-odd years later I found myself editing the first ever collection of football poetry, *100 Favourite Scottish Football Poems*, for which I managed to get a more accomplished old Hibbie than myself, Tony Higgins, to write a Foreword in which he concludes: 'I was pleased to note a poem from Motherwell great Billy Hunter, who raises many questions about the quality of football today in comparison to the halcyon days of the '50s, '60s and '70s. Who said players' "brains are in their feet"? Alistair I know by his own admission would never claim a place in 'football's hall of fame', but by bringing together this unique collection of poems he has ensured his place in the cultural history of our game.

Willie Hunter came to Hibs 1968–71 and I was very happy to be able to include one of his poems from *Look Back in Amber* alongside some of the greatest names in Scottish modern poetry, from Hugh MacDiarmid to Edwin Morgan and Liz Lochhead. Writing became my life rather than football, which embellished it and I think offered me some of the core values best represented in all the great Scottish managers from Busby, Shankly and Stein through to Alex Ferguson – men who embodied the philosophy and virtues of the game to accompany the spectacle it has always been, and still is.

I never wrote a poem about Bob Shankly but here's one about his brother, Bill. I think the Liverpool poet Parry Maguire says it all in 'The Entry of Shankly Into Liverpool':

From Huddersfield
Driving down in an Austen A40
No palms were thrown at his feet
No sweet Hosannas filled the skies
No heralds announced the saviour's arrival
And beneath Liverpool's sullen grey skies
He walked, the anointed one, in his Jimmy Cagney suit
Football boots in one hand
Football's soul in the other.

I feel privileged to have had a glimpse of the unglamorous, hard-work routine of pro-football, the guts behind the glory.

Derek Dick (Fish)

Singer, born 1958.

' There's a lot of primal scream therapy in football, which I like. I like the explosion of it all and that kind of aarrghh! aspect of it. '

THE REASON I became a Hibs fan is kind of weird. I was a pupil at Kings Park Primary School, which was protestant and consisted mostly of Rangers and Hearts supporters. I was born in 1958 and it wasn't until 1968 that I really started to become aware of Hibs.

My family had a garage business in Dalkeith and my grandad had season tickets for both Hibs and Hearts at the time. As far as I've been told, and I don't know if this is true, my grandad leant more towards the Leith end of town. He used to play football for Dalkeith and would drive the team to the game but that was in the days when most people supported both Edinburgh clubs. Yes there were Celtic and Rangers supporters at my school but they were glory hunters as always. I got involved with Hibs around the time they were going through a lot of managers, there was still the shadow of the Famous Five over the club and people still talked about them.

One of my dad's friends was an architect and he took me to my very first game, in 1971 or '72. It was against St Mirren and we drew 3-3. He was a member of the 50 Club that used to be under the old stand and I remember going along there with him. The place was frequented by a clique of old guys fuelled on cigars and whisky. The football ended up being a bonding thing between me and my dad because he got back into it. He was a workaholic but suddenly he started to take Saturdays off and we started going to the matches together. A friend of his from his army days was a photographer on the *Evening News*, so he used to give me all the black and white photographs from the games. Throughout the whole Turnbull's Tornadoes era I got given all these pictures. I had hundreds and hundreds of these photographs which, to my horror, my mother threw out along with my entire Hibernian programme collection that I had kept for years and years!

The Turnbull's Tornadoes period was when I really got into it, but I was going to see Hibs before Eddie Turnbull became manager. Even though I didn't see him play, I remember Peter Marinello's presence at the club. His exotic name may have had something to do with it because I also remember some of the signings that came across from Scandinavia. But it was with Turnbull's Tornadoes that I consciously embraced the club. Herriot, Brownlie, Black Schaedler, Stanton, Blackley, Edwards, O'Rourke, Gordon, Cropley, Duncan and substitutes Hamilton, Hazel… I can still name that team today!

When I first went to a match at Easter Road I must have been about 12, so I wasn't going to get lifted across the turnstiles. I started off in the Centre Stand – I was straight in at the 'posh' bit. My memories are of cigar smoke and the freezing cold, but it was great, I loved that stand! I actually now own the old boardroom floor from that stand because someone told me 'We're knocking it down this afternoon,' so I quickly got joiners to come in and lift the floorboards from the room. They now proudly reside in my office, in the studio where I live.

When I was at Dalkeith High School I used to go to matches home and away. I remember the big Scottish Cup matches against Rangers and travelling through on Wednesdays to semi-finals, the fear of the danger of violence with Rangers supporters was palpable. At Kings Park it seemed like there were maybe only two or three Hibs supporters in the entire school, it was mainly Jambos and Huns, very few Celtic fans. Dalkeith was still attached to the mining community so you still had those religious divisions. There was a lot of friendly banter but I don't remember any aggression. My grandad was a miner but I was brought up in a very middle-class family. I can remember being slightly caught up in the Protestant/Catholic thing and that I didn't kick about with Catholics. And then I discovered that a guy who lived along the street was a Catholic and that he was also a Hibs supporter, we became friends and we played Subbuteo together. I must have been 13 years old at the time and all of a sudden I just thought, Religion? Eff off! It's got nothing to do with football! Ever since then I've hated sectarianism. We are lucky because with ourselves and Hearts it doesn't really come in to play.

Before the 1980s there was the Turnbull's Tornadoes team. I used to go to the Fairs Cup matches and games against the likes of Leeds and Juventus. My dad got me a season ticket and after every match I phoned to tell him about the match, as I do to this day. Equally, when I'm on tour, I phone up my dad at 5pm every Saturday to get the result. I was never a diehard 'green and white boy' that went to all of the away matches but instead, a very middle class Centre Stand sort of chappie. I joined a band in 1981 and I was down south for seven years, but I still came back to some of the matches. My dad stopped going after I moved away, so a big part of going to the games originally was the bonding experience between father and son.

Turnbull's Tornadoes was about the style of play and the feeling that every time they went up the park there was a going to be a goal, or at least that something exciting was going to happen. I just remember going in and watching a great, fluent football team where there was a lot of emotion, lots of scoring and it was pretty physical as well. Alex Edwards was an absolute firebrand, Alex Cropley was so smooth and silky, Alan Gordon was a great centre forward, and because they were generally from Leith, and all from the East End, I felt part of it all. It's not the same now, just like it's not the same in music. Your relationships with these things change. Is it age? Is it something else? It's perhaps easier to walk away from it all now, although I don't, I still really love seeing them win and getting those three points! Today I was at the game with John Leslie and the two of us were like, 'Yeah!!' when we scored. It's wonderful, it's a good drug! Last season I bought season tickets for me and my dear wife, we went along every week and I got really into it again. I was even reading the *Evening News* and the Hibs online forums, I was interested to read the rumours but when it went into the second half of the season I was like, argh!!!!, but I can still tap in to the big buzz of the football when I want. My problem is that I am away on tour so much, and although I saw the game today, it's probably the last match that I'm going to see this season, which is a bummer. I still follow it, results wise, every Saturday even if I am away. We were in Switzerland doing this festival with the band and we got the promoter to get satellite TV on to the screen so we could watch it back stage before the gigs. I remember being in Paris when we beat Hearts in the cup and I had a roadie sitting back stage on the computer giving me the news: 'Still 0-0.' 'Hibs have just scored!' That kind of thing. It's not as difficult to keep in touch nowadays, with having laptops and wi-fi, so I can just go onto the *Evening News* website every night when I'm on the road, to find out what's going on.

The first strip I ever bought was a Bukta one, a real naff cotton version that shrunk in the wash! When I played Subbuteo, I signed George Best to my Subbuteo team before he signed for Hibs! I was a visionary back then and that was even before I had done acid... I remember, with my Subbuteo team,

'I signed George Best to my Subbuteo team before he signed for Hibs!'

you would invent your own leagues and I had Hibs, Leeds United and Arsenal in the same division. I loved Arsenal, because you could buy Arsenal videos, turn the colour down, and watch Hibs play really well in Europe. My uncle was an Arsenal supporter, so when Alex Cropley went down to join them he would send me the programmes up, so for that reason I am still an Arsenal fan. I used to play Subbuteo myself, commentate and cheat my way through the leagues: 'Hibs are coming forward, here we go! It's Cropley he's going to score!!' so I didn't care, as long as I made Hibs win. My Subbuteo pitch was upstairs in the attic and I had the miniature George Best playing for us, but I remember very little about the real Best because I was away most of the time. I did see him a couple of times though, he was a lazy bastard most of the time but then he would have these moments of sheer genius! When he signed, I initially thought, wow! but then remembered, I had signed him to my Subbuteo team years previously so it wasn't as big a shock as it should have been.

I think football now is not as community or regionally orientated as it used to be. Players come and go all the time. I get depressed watching young players coming up through the ranks and then leaving. You look at the Scotland team now and you see Brown, Whittaker and Thomson and you think to yourself, If we'd only kept them! Add a player like Miller to the mix then we would have had a brilliant team. Much as I respect the financial necessities and the economics of it all, I would still like to think if we hadn't sold those players, and had the right manager, we could have been a major club! I think Scotland is just so parochial. But in saying that, I had a couple of Argentinian friends who came across to visit and we went to watch the game. I was apologising to them beforehand in the Four in Hand pub: 'I'm really sorry, this isn't the standard you're going to be expecting, Scottish football is not that great.' We went along to the old East terracing and they thought it was absolutely brilliant! They were saying afterwards, 'That was the most exciting football game we have ever seen!' and they all bought Hibs strips after the game. They said it was just

The game of Subbuteo with its catchphrase 'flick to kick' has enchanted generations of children from its inception in the post-war Britain of 1947. Conceived by Peter Adolph, this table-top football game began life with cardboard playing figures and instructions on how to mark a football pitch on a blanket. When plastic figures were introduced in 1961, Subbuteo really began to enjoy success. Items such as grandstands, floodlights, limited edition teams and even scaled down policemen added authenticity to the mini-match atmosphere. For many years the Subbuteo Association campaigned for the game to be recognised as a sport and regular world championships still take place in a frenzy of fierce competition. Nowadays Subbuteo remains in production but its market share has been much reduced by the advent of computer football games.

end to end, physical and exciting. So sometimes we forget how good it can be. There's an honest physicality to our football that I just love. I hate feigned injury and players trying to get an angle on the referee. In Scotland it's a more physical game than English football, and especially more than European football, which I suppose is our downfall when we play on the international field.

I went to see Hibs play Liège and it was one of the best times I have ever had in my life, it was incredible! That's the one thing I miss, I wish we went to Europe a lot more, but I'm in the Tartan Army so it makes up for it. Two friends of mine, from when I lived in Brussels, are big football fans and I met up with them when went over to Liège. After the first game I thought, 'Well we might still be able to pull it off' and so we got the tickets, flew down to London and got the British Midlands flight across. There were two planes, the first one was full and the second one was a case of 'Does anyone want to volunteer to get the next flight because this one is full?' So we hung back with these other guys and, in the end, there was only about six of us on this second plane. We got given a shitload of wine and champagne served to us on board and we got off the plane absolutely steaming! I met my mates in Brussels and kicked in with all the Hibbies in the big square, it was just fucking amazing! I even got my face painted green and white. The guys I was with were just sort of gobsmacked, they were saying, 'We've never seen supporters like that, never, ever!' We got beaten but we were still in the stadium because the police had kept us inside and so the place was still bouncing and singing. My mates said, 'We don't understand, why are you still singing when you just got beaten? This is fantastic!' So that's what I like about it, that's why I love supporting Hibs and why I love supporting Scotland as well. We win rarely, but when we do we win, we win big!

When we beat Kilmarnock 5-1 it was just outrageous! At the game against Dunfermline in the League Cup Final, after the club nearly failed to exist in 1991, was the first time I met Alex Cropley. I was in Amsterdam before the game and I flew the entire band back for the final. I simply said to them, 'We're going to the game!' I bought us all tickets, flew us back from Amsterdam and we arrived late to Glasgow Airport more than ready with all our vodka from duty free. We had a few of those and got picked up by the bus. Jay Crawford and a lot of Dunfermline guys were on it, and I remember getting to Hampden late. We were drinking all the way there on the bus which is 'highly illegal' and there were two police motorcyclists who flagged us down and asked us to stop. We all had to get off the bus but one of them recognised me and said, 'Oh, you're Fish!' so I said, 'Look, we've just flown in from Amsterdam, we've come for the final, we're late, it's a mix of Dunfermline and Hibs fans on the bus and we're all having fun!' After a bit of 'negotiation' we gifted them a copy of the album, which was just out, signed it and gave it to the outriders. It obviously did the trick because they gave us a motorcycle escort all the way to the stadium. If that wasn't enough, we got even luckier and got a parking space right next to the Hibs team bus outside Hampden. We got to our seats just as the kick-off happened and I came out, still steaming, met Alex Cropley and said, 'We just won the cup!' because I still had bad memories of the League Cup defeat from years previously. I was there at the finals when we got humped 6-1 by Celtic but I missed the Dryborough Cup finals. I never saw any of those games but I was at the ones we got beaten. But then of course there was the League Cup when Stanton and O'Rourke scored. I will never forget being in Princes Street with my dad underneath the hotel when Stanton was there with the cup. Years later, when we won the cup against Dunfermline we got back to Edinburgh and I remember me and my dad holding on to a lamp post at the top of Easter Road to get our balance, completely pished! You have to remember that that the club was nearly gone a year previously, so we were well within our rights to celebrate. When 'Hands Off Hibs' happened I was in Germany and I was getting faxes every night in the hotel from my dad updating me on developments. He would fax me through press clippings from the Evening News every day reporting on what was going on. I remember thinking that I wanted to be back in Edinburgh but I wasn't and I couldn't be.

I've always been kind of like a Hibs supporter in the background, and even when I go to Easter Road now they still say, 'Are you still singing, big man?' with no idea what I do nowadays! We did a gig at the Supporters Club and we thought, Oh yeah, it'll be easy, but only a hundred or so people turned up. When Marillion happened in 1985 things changed for me because I was still coming to games but I never sat comfortably with the corporate side of Hibs, I think a lot of that feeling has still to do with Gray and Duff. I don't want to get involved in the clubs politics, and I remember Mickey Weir saying to me, 'Once you get involved with that shit it just pollutes you!' You get caught up in all the politics and the shenanigans and I just wanted to be a normal punter but, in the 1980s when I came up to games around the time when we released the song 'Kayleigh', it was like, 'Oh... it's Fish from Marillion.' I got to know some of the players like Andy Goram, and Gordon Ray who is kind of related on my mother's side. It was hard because I would come up to Scotland and drive to the games, get in the car on the Friday night and drive all the way up to a match on the Saturday. I would then drive back on the Sunday or the Monday, but that was when we were really shit! So it was a kind of a strange parallel because when Marillion was really happening Hibs were terrible and were going through some really bad times. I moved back here in 1988 and started getting back into going to the games again but I still never got a season ticket, I just went to the games when I could. This season I have only seen three games, whereas last season I saw 20-odd games.

There's something very different about Hibs – they are very rock'n'roll and arty – it's just a cool fucking club! We ain't brash, we've never been an arrogant club, we've always under-achieved in a cool kind of way and we've never made a big deal about it. Turnbull's Tornadoes were a cool team and I can never forget beating Ayr United 8-1 after winning the League Cup. I always remember Alex Edwards as the ball came across, it was definitely going into the goal but he ran all the way back to the goal line and did an overhead scissor kick, under the bar, to clear it off the line. I just thought, How cool is that?' All of the players were just really cool. John Blackley? Cool as fuck and you could almost imagine the

team having a toke before they went out on the pitch – they were that cool...
I mean we are green and white but we are cooler than Celtic fans because we
don't push the fact that we are Hibs fans, so we're like, 'We're just Hibs fans,
that's all...' Dougray Scott and Bruce Findlay are cool people and there are a
lot of really cool guys who support Hibs. The fans are not like, 'I'll fucking kick
your fucking nab in because you're no a Hibbie,' none of that goes on.

I could never imagine myself being a Hearts supporter, I could never support
that team, never! I'm an Edinburgh guy and there's been times though when you
might look at the 'bigger picture' and think, What if we had a united Edinburgh
club? They could play in Europe to the extent that Man Utd do, so there have
been times when the shadow of Mordor has entered my brain. But it would
never work.

I didn't know anything about the roots of the club when I first became a
fan apart from the fact that they played in green and white. Catholicism had
nothing to do with it and the harp meant nothing to me. I lived in Dalkeith so
it was the eastern end of Edinburgh as far as I was concerned and, essentially,
Leith. My daughter was born in Leith so she's a Leither but I don't think it's
important to remember the roots of the club, it doesn't really bother me. I
mean, I hate religion! I've been in Bosnia so I have seen what religion does
there and I've been in a lot of other countries in the world and seen the effects
of religious schisms. I may support a Catholic football team in some people's
eyes, but I don't think that any player who wears the strip, thinks that he plays
for a Catholic football club. Having roots is fair enough but things have moved
on – we are Leithers and this is the Leith team! I hate the sectarianism between
Rangers and Celtic and I find it, as an international Scotsman, embarrassing...
How can people still go on about that stuff, especially when most of them don't
even understand the real history of it all. It's embarrassing, especially when you
have Rangers and Celtic playing on the international stage and you hear these
songs getting sung, you just think, 'Do you know how Neanderthal that makes
you look?' On the rare occasions that there has been an Irish tricolour flown at
a Hibs match I have thought, 'Since when was the colour orange in our strip?'

I like going to games with the Tartan Army because it's always interesting to
travel with them. There are very few Rangers supporters in the Tartan Army, it's
predominantly made up from Stirling, Aberdeen and Edinburgh people. I love
going to Scotland away matches because it's the only chance I have of getting
to go to Europe these days. It's been really hard to get away to watch Hibs in
Europe because of my job, you just get so caught up in doing gigs. If you went to
one of my gigs, say in Milan, I could guarantee you at least ten people wearing
Hibs strips in the audience, they all know I'm a Hibbie and they all buy Hibs
and Scotland tops.

I was there at the Leeds game when Stanton missed the penalty, I was gutted!
We played Juventus at Easter Road when we got beaten, but I can remember
the ones when we were giving out the humpings. Every time a European team
came to Easter Road it was like, 'Bang! Take that!' At the time there wasn't that
same public awareness of football that there is now, there wasn't the same level

of football on TV, and you didn't have SKY. Football was black and white and Arthur Montford so to see it on TV was rare. When it was on it was one match, you didn't get every game from the SPL so it was kind of like the same as music, because of that scarcity of information, there was a mystery to it. In the same way that there is so much general information out there now it has ripped the mystery away from some things and it's become a little bit passé. In the '80s, you would get interviewed when your album came out and you got a live review when you did a gig, that was all the punters would get. In Edinburgh, when I was in a band, if you got an interview in the *New Musical Express*, *Melody Maker* or *Sounds* then you might get a review from any one of these magazines when you played live, but that was it. You wouldn't hear about a band for another year or two and all you had was the album, so there wasn't this world-wide 'awareness' that goes on now with the internet where you can find out what a bands track list was in Milan, what the guy was wearing on stage in Sweden and what the set list was in New York. You can even talk to the band online now, the interaction is immense, and it's the same with football. I remember back then you might buy *Shoot* if Hibs were in it and it was like, 'bloody hell, Hibs are in the latest issue!' Or if there was a picture of Hibs you were like, 'Wow!' There wasn't even Panini cards back then in the days of Rodney Marsh, George Best and Billy Bremner. It's changed immensely.

When we played Leeds you were still aware that you were playing a big, big team, but I didn't really know all the players, apart from guys like Bremner of course. When Juventus came across to play us we had no information or any idea about them. Sporting Lisbon, Malmö and Hadjuk Split were the same. You might have wondered, Where's Split? The answer was of course Yugoslavia. But then you would think, Where's Yugoslavia? I got married in Croatia and we drove past Split's ground and I said, 'Those were those bastards that kicked us out of the UEFA Cup!' A Norwegian player signed to Hibs and it was exotic. Even if an English player signed to Hibs at the time it still seemed really exotic. That was in the days if someone from Shettleston signed for Hibs, it was also exotic!

I met Joe Baker a lot of times in the '80s and '90s and he was a lovely bloke. I saw him when he came back to play for Hibs, but my memories of that are hazy. I remember him scoring a couple of times but, mainly, I remember everyone saying, 'Joe's back, Joe's back!' and it wasn't really until later that I really appreciated it, kind of like the same way, in music terms, that you discover artists after they're dead and think, Fucking hell... that's some legacy! Like Marvin Gaye, for example. Joe Baker was the equivalent of Marvin Gaye because you thought, jeez, he was brilliant! He did so many things for the very first time, he was a pioneer, and I remember the white boots as well, which were very exotic. I mostly remember the Liverpool match when Steve Highway scored. That was an incredible night. It was in the days when you used to almost have to have to park in Princes Street to get to Easter Road along with 60 or 70,000 other people. London Road would be chock-a-block, it was incredible! Before we played Leeds I thought, 'Oh no... Billy Bremner's playing.' He was the captain of Scotland, but you still thought, 'You little ginger bastard!' because he played the ball off their line about nine times. We were all over them and we should have won that game, that was our game to win and I don't think I have ever been so gutted after a match than at that one.

There's a lot of primal scream therapy in football, which I like. I like the explosion of it all and that kind of aarrghh! aspect of it. I remember people joking that Joe Tortolano was deaf on the left side with people shouting at him, and who can forget that unbelievably shocking tackle that he made in the friendly against Man Utd on Gordon Strachan. You thought to yourself, 'Did that really just happen?' Pat Stanton was the Franz Beckenbauer of Hibs – he was so cool and unfazed. I loved O'Rourke and I loved Cropley's poise and style, he had that elegance. Jim Black was a fire hazard, every time he got the ball it was, Oh no... what's he going to do?' But he was great nonetheless! I loved Scott Brown, I thought he was a phenomenal player. Kenny Miller made a dreadful decision when he decided to leave like many other Hibs players that have made terrible decisions. Kenny Miller should have stayed at Hibs. And Gary O'Connor seemed to have gone missing in action until he came back to us. I wish we had him playing in that semi-final against Hearts. I remember that game because my fiancée saw four single magpies on the way to Hampden – what an omen; and the rest is history! I though Whittaker was better with us than he has been with Rangers. If you look at the players that we have had, the ones that have been poached and nicked, you have to wonder, what if? You've equally got to understand that Scotland is a small country and somebody who is great at football, and wants to go on to the world stage can't be stopped from achieving that, and why should you stop them? We just don't have the infrastructure to keep a lot of those players here. It's something I've come to expect but at the same time it is depressing. I suppose that's part of the way that the game is going. It's a bit like kids, you can't keep them at ten years old all the time, they have got to become teenagers, you are going to have to put up with that. In the same way you have to accept the evolution of the game of football, you can't keep it in the '70s even if it was a great time. I have great memories of that, but at the same time when you talk to Mickey Weir, or Kano, or Pat, they will tell you it was shit in the sense that they were never paid the value of what they were providing. A lot of people made a lot of money out of Hibernian Football Club, and a lot of money out of Scottish football, that they never put back in. It's the same as the music business – musicians in the '60s and '70s were ripped off and grossly undervalued. I think nowadays players have a bit more pizzazz and power, they also have agents, so things have changed. You cannot resist change.

In all honesty, I can't foresee a day when Hibs can win the league again because of the economic factors, even though, OK, comparatively speaking we are in a great economic position, and Rod Petrie's done a phenomenal job, much as he has been decried by a lot of Hibs supporters. I'd rather be in our position than have been in the position Hearts were in when they almost went out of existence.

I think what should have been introduced a long time ago is what happens with American Baseball, where they cap clubs' spending power. The bottom line is that football is entertainment and that's why we have a problem at the moment at Easter Road, because it's not good entertainment. If I wanted to see a band and went to three shit gigs, it would take a hell of a lot of good reviews or albums to make me go back and see that band. I think that's a big part of the pizzazz of football nowadays, and SKY TV doesn't help. For example, watching a St Mirren game on TV usually means you have to be a supporter to enjoy it because it can be dreadful entertainment.

I think a football club has to be integral within its community because it's a part of the whole promotion. Football relies on a 'hardcore' and you've got to treat them fairly, you've got to give them quality and you've got to respect them. You've got to give them what they want and you have to fight hard to validate their support.

Ger Freedman

Honorary Life Chairman of Leith Athletic, born 1958.

' Supporting Hibs is not just about the game of football, it is a way of life. '

I GREW UP down in Pirniefield in the heart of Leith – we were all Hibs supporters down there. My dad and my grandad were originally from the Southside area of Edinburgh where the club originated from. They were both Hibs fanatics so I had no choice in supporting any other team. I was born on 1 March 1958, which is a very relevant day in the club's history. Hibs were playing Hearts in the Scottish Cup quarter-final that day and while my dad waited for me to be born he tuned in to the radio. It was a huge game because even back then we had not won that cup for a long time. As he heard the presenter say 'Hearts 3' he started to get that sinking feeling. But when he heard 'Hibs 4' and that Joe Baker had netted all of the goals in the game, you can imagine how great a day that was for my dad. Of course we got beaten by Clyde in the final but it was a nice way to be brought into the world nonetheless.

The first game I ever went to was on 7 October 1964 and it was equally memorable for me. The score was Hibernian 2 Real Madrid 0. Jock Stein was the manager at the time and had invited them over from Spain to play in a friendly game. I was only six years old, but I particularly remember a lot of English sailors being there for some reason. They must have been docked at Leith and they were all there supporting Real Madrid. There was a fair bit of banter because my dad never liked anyone apart from Hibs supporters. Although I don't remember a lot about the game itself, I do remember Peter Cormack scoring and then Real scoring an own goal, so it was a pretty good introduction to say the least.

My dad took me to all of the home games and I remember going to away games myself when I was about ten or eleven. I hardly missed a game for about 30 years after that. Although I was a decent player myself, I couldn't pass up the chance of seeing the likes of the Turnbull's Tornadoes. So playing football went out the window. We would always stand away at the back of the old terracing on the second tier and my dad would lift me high onto his shoulders so I could see the game. When Hibs scored I was never on his shoulders for much longer.

I would go to all the away games in whatever way I could manage. Usually it was on a supporters' bus and that is how I travelled in 1971 when I went to see Hibs play Leeds in the UEFA Cup. I was only 13 at the time and strangely enough my wife of 31 years to be was actually on the same bus. I didn't actually know her then but when we got together (years later) she told me that she was on that bus with her dad and her uncle. Me and my mates would all go to the away games and make a real day of it. It was a tradition. There was nothing else to do on a Saturday.

It was much more sociable going to the games in the old terracing. Nowadays when you sit down the only person you can cuddle when we score is the person in the next seat to you. Plus you might not even know them. In those days there would be a big group of us standing together and going crazy if we scored. We would always meet up at 12pm in the Coopers Rest. It was managed by Ronnie Simpson [the famous Hibs goalkeeper] and after a few pints around 20 of us would walk up to the ground together. Afterwards we would meet back there for a pint or two as well. Travel to away games was usually on the bus that a guy called Ian MacKay would run from the Marksman Bar in Duke Street. Ian was a big Hibs man and still is to this day. We were just young boys, so Ian would always look out for us. There were many memorable games back then.

Hibs played Napoli in the Fairs Cup in 1967. I remember it especially because Hibs were such rank outsiders after being beaten 4-1 away. I think you could get odds of 20-1 against for Hibs to get through to the next round. We were essentially written off after losing the first game. I have always said that a goal can change any game against any team in the world and we needed to score early that night to have any chance at all. Bobby Duncan hit a thunderbolt after five minutes – what a strike it was. After that goal Napoli simply collapsed and we went on to beat them 5-0. The result sent reverberations all round Europe because Napoli were the typical Italian team who could usually defend for three days and not let a goal in. I always remember the lift that the crowd got from that early goal and to beat them was fantastic. When you think they had Dino Zoff in goals it is incredible – he was acknowledged as the best goalkeeper in the world at that time. We believed we could beat anybody back then and we pretty much did.

In the next round we drew Leeds United. Hibs were one goal down after the first leg and then we got them back to Easter Road. It was also the first season that the four step rule was introduced for goalkeepers. This meant that they couldn't hold the ball for more than four steps before throwing or kicking it away. It was hardly ever enforced in its first season, but typically it was against Hibs and a free kick was given with six minutes left to play. Jack Charlton scored from a header to knock Hibs out, but I still believe we could have gone on to win the Fairs Cup that year.

Six years later we drew Leeds again in the UEFA Cup and I probably witnessed one of the first sweeper performances in football. It was Billy Bremner who was given the role of sweeper for Leeds and even though Hibs battered them that night his performance was amazing. He was knocking and clearing shots off the line all night.

Talking of fantastic European nights, the other game I vividly recall was on 27 September 1972 against Sporting Lisbon when we won 6-1. Jimmy O'Rourke scored a hat-trick and Hibs were absolutely dynamite that night. We had the same team that had just won the League Cup by beating a great Celtic side in the final. Sporting Lisbon were considered to be a marvellous team, so to take six goals off a team like that was unbelievable. No wonder I didn't want to go and play football myself when I had a club to watch like Hibernian. Particularly after his display that night, Jimmy O'Rourke became my favourite player of all time. He was a huge Hibs man and a great goal-scorer. He broke his leg twice and still managed to score a barrel load of goals for the club.

After we got beaten by Celtic 6-1 in the 1972 Scottish Cup final Eddie Turnbull told the papers that the next time we would beat them. As I said, Billy Bremner's performance for Leeds was one of the best displays I have ever seen, but when we won the League Cup later that year Pat Stanton's performance won the day. He outclassed all of those great Celtic players. You didn't realise just how magnificent a player he was until that evening. Stanton simply lived and breathed Hibs. However, a few years later Pat wasn't seeing eye to eye with manager Eddie Turnbull and he so he left Hibs and joined Celtic. In a way I am glad that he won the double with Celtic, he deserved it. He is a good friend of mine and he always tells me the story that when he walked into the Celtic dressing room after signing for them, the rest of the team were all winding him up with stuff like, 'We are glad that you are a Celtic man now.' As Jock Stein arrived in the dressing room Pat said to them, 'I'll never be a Celtic man, I'm a Hibs man through and through.' They call Pat the quiet man but he is certainly not quiet when it comes to Hibernian.

In the early 1990s I was walking to my work one Monday morning on Lorne Street in Leith. I passed a newspaper billboard bearing the headlines 'Who Killed Hibs?'. By the time I got to work the story was all over the radio and it transpired that Wallace Mercer had put in a bid to buy the club. At lunchtime I went round to the stadium. Hundreds of fans had already started gathering outside. Straight after work me, my wife and all the family decided we would go back to the ground. After protesting outside we got stopped and interviewed by a journalist from the *Edinburgh Evening News*. The headline in the paper the next day was 'Meet the Freedman family at War with Mercer'. I meant what I told them that night. If Hibs were not going to exist then there would be no football for me anymore. There was no way I would have supported an Edinburgh United Football team. That possibility was a lie and myth anyway. Everyone knew that the end result was that Hibs were going to be swallowed whole by Heart of Midlothian. It was torture really and I had many sleepless nights because Mercer had essentially won the financial argument for a takeover.

I quickly started doing some fundraising with Kenny MacLean to get the whole Hands Off Hibs campaign moving.

It was a very emotional time for all concerned. I have some vivid memories of events like the rally at Easter Road. There were 20,000 fans at the ground that day and most fans will remember Joe Baker kissing the turf. Even John Robertson of Hearts attended and that was fantastic. He told everyone that the takeover was wrong , remember, he was a paid employee of Hearts at the time. He scored a lot of goals against us so it was incredible for him to get behind the cause. You would read the papers one day and think we are getting somewhere and then the following day we would have another setback. We even used to phone John Gibson from the *Evening News*. He is a great Hibs man and he also went to Leith Academy, as I did. We kept saying to him, 'You will have to use your position to pile some pressure on – lots of people read your column.' He didn't muck around with backing the cause and gave us plenty of coverage. As Leithers and Hibs fans this felt like it was not just the takeover of a football club but also of our community. The whole of Leith was pissed off in 1920 when we merged with Edinburgh against our will, so I imagine that this scenario felt very similar to that. All the worry and the high emotion made you realise just how much you loved your club. I had spent my life going to the games, as had my dad and his dad before him. I wanted to save Hibernian for my boys and for the generations to come. We continued to fight like hell to keep them alive. Even if it had meant they would have to play down on Leith Links, then that would have been enough for me.

Kenny MacLean was leading a fantastic campaign. Many wonderful people and ex-players rallied to the cause. I don't think that Mercer realised the depth of feeling and love that so many people had for Hibs. He was a Glaswegian who had originally supported Rangers and he seemed to think that Celtic and Rangers were the only real rivals in Scotland. He truly didn't realise the depth of feeling for Hibernian and the fact that the Leith community would not give in. When Kenny MacLean appealed to Tom Farmer for his backing it helped us over the line, but it also helped that we had just sold John Collins to Celtic, which gave us a sizeable amount of money. The whole campaign was magnificent, but apparently there was also several threats made against Mercer. It's an awful thing to say, but it seemed to be acts like those which made him give up on his plan. I believe that he eventually left Edinburgh for France to escape the cauldron, claiming that his family had been threatened.

It is a fallacy to suggest that the majority of Hearts supporters did not want the takeover to go through. Around a couple of hundred attended the Easter Road rally, but the vast majority wanted Hibernian to die. When they were in trouble two or three years ago, I was severely disappointed that they survived. I'm not sure that it took the takeover bid to increase my dislike of Hearts – I disliked them all my life. I'm 57 years old now and I wake up every day loathing them a wee bit more, which is quite funny in a way. The first derby after the whole campaign was pretty bitter and a lot of us decided that we would never go back to Tynecastle ever again, simply because we didn't want to give them a penny of our money. It's a shame really, because I loved going to the derby games at Tynecastle. I was even there for my favourite ever game – the 7-0 victory over Hearts.

When we knew that the club was going to survive it was almost like winning the lottery. You couldn't put a price on it and I was so glad that my boys and my grandchildren could still have the chance of watching Hibernian from that day forth.

I organised a celebration night at the Park View Hotel and it was an unbelievable occasion. Four hundred of my mates came along. We could have filled it ten times over. It was funny that night because the one Hearts fan that was in the hall turned out to be the bouncer on the door. He came to me and said, 'There's a guy at the door that hasn't got a ticket.' So I said, 'Just tell him to fuck off,' because I was really busy organising the speeches and trophies etc. But the bouncer just kept coming back to me again and again. Eventually he said, 'His name is Joe,' so I said, 'I don't give a fuck what his name is because he's no getting in.' By the third or fourth time of asking I decided to just go to the door and tell him myself. When I got there it turned out to be no ordinary Joe. It was Joe Baker. So I said to the bouncer, 'I take it you're no a Hibby then? How do you no recognise this man?' Funnily enough, Mr Baker got a bigger cheer on the stage than even Stanton did that night.

The tension was bad after the takeover attempt but I don't remember it really being any different between the clubs before that. When my grandad was on his death bed, he would ask my dad what the Hearts result was first. Naturally he wanted to hear that they had lost and my dad would often oblige by lying and telling him that Hearts had got beaten. He also told him that Hibs had won every time he went in to visit. When my dad relayed this story to me, I said, 'Imagine lying to your dad on his death bed.' My dad passed away nine weeks ago and history repeated itself. For the last two or three weeks of his life he had lost his mental health but would still ask me, 'How did the Hearts get on

‘Napoli were the typical Italian team who could usually defend for three days and not let a goal in.’

today?' So I would say, 'They got beaten today, Hibs beat them.' So I lied – just like my father had to his father.

I think the difference between the two clubs is that Hearts don't have any decorum about them. I think it has been proven in the last few years. They have never once apologised for what happened, many small (and local) businesses suffered badly when they went into administration. All they ever say is, 'We are debt free now and you are not.' If my club had done what they did I can sincerely say that I would have been saying to people, 'I'm ashamed of my club.' I always say to them, 'If your next door neighbour who has never worked in ten years turned up in a Rolls Royce one day and told you he was going on holiday to Florida, you would be pretty pissed off.' I don't think Hibs supporters are glory hunters and I reckon they have more humility about them. Perhaps John Robertson is one exception. I am a great friend of his brother George – who is a huge Hibby. When we used to go to the Coopers Rest. There were two lounge bars. Hearts fans would sit in one, Hibs fans in the other. It was hilarious because there were often horrible songs being sung about John that were actually started by his brother George.

I think it is very important to recognise that the club was started by humble Irish people who settled in Edinburgh. The way that Hibs recognise this history today is spot-on. The manner in which they have changed the badge to represent Leith, Edinburgh and the club's Irish history is also really appropriate. Hibs supporters understand their history now without using it as a reason for division. We acknowledge our Leith identity in equal measures and there is nothing better than when the whole ground sing 'Sunshine on Leith'. In the 1970s and '80s Hibs fans did sing songs about the troubles in Ireland but that has disappeared now. I actually think that Hearts still have problems with sectarian behaviour by elements of their support. They seem to dislike Celtic nearly as much as they do Hibs, I'm not sure where that antagonism stems from.

The most emotional day for me as a Hibs fan was when we won the cup

On 29 September 1967 Hibs faced Italian Giants Napoli in the 2nd round (2nd leg) of the Fairs Cup at Easter Road. Hibs had already negotiated an extremely tough hurdle in the previous round by narrowly eliminating Porto. Hibernian's 1st leg visit to Italy resulted in a comprehensive 4-1 triumph for the Naples club. After the game Bob Shankly (Hibs manager) had boldly predicted that he was confident of ultimate victory in the 2nd leg. It is doubtful whether many fans believed him because Napoli had only conceded five goals in their previous six domestic matches. They also boasted Dino Zoff as goalkeeper, rated as world No. 1 and his heroics are still acknowledged around the globe. Hibernian were as ruthless and inspired as Shankly's seemingly wild prediction. They racked up an incredible 5-0 victory, and as though to further underline this remarkable achievement, Napoli finished runners-up in the Italian league later that season.

against Dunfermline. It was very soon after the takeover bid and all of our emotions came out. There were 35,000 Hibees in the ground and thousands got locked outside as well. People forget it was actually pay at the gate, which would never happen now. I always remember when Keith Wright scored the second goal to win the game, I heard the biggest collective sigh I have ever heard going all the way round Hampden Park. It was quite eerie. I was in the Hibs club for three days after that game – celebrating.

I'm not in love with Tom Farmer now, but what he did for the club back in 1991 was obviously fantastic. Farmer never professed to be a Hibs or a football fan. He is a great Leither. It was great that he realised he had to do something about the takeover, but I think he needs to bow out now. Fan ownership is the way forward but it is going to take time that I am not sure we have much of. At the moment we are in big trouble. If we don't get promoted this year, people that have stopped going will be very hard to tempt back through the turnstiles. We may never get them back. Rod Petrie is the man that has killed us in my opinion. A lot of my friends say that as long as Petrie is at the club they are never going back. He is the greatest threat to the club since Wallace Mercer. I don't blame anybody for not going to games now. It costs a lot of money to watch games in the second tier of Scottish football.

In my opinion, Hibs have actually been in decline since 1975, with some good occasions in between. But if Petrie had resigned then Hibs fans would have come back to watch them in bigger numbers. Most would also have stuck with the club for the next two or three seasons even if we didn't get promoted. I have never felt as angry as I did that day when Hibs got relegated. I knew the trouble that lay ahead. They say that players are not bigger than the club, so the same thing surely applies to chairmen as well. It is quite amazing how so many ex-Hibs managers seem to go on to success after leaving us. Surely that tells you something is wrong with the management of the club? The club should be doing more to encourage the next generation of fans. Let kids in for free – they will spend money on food or merchandise, so the club would still get plenty back. The main problem is that they don't back the managers with money to buy players and so we might even be looking at crowds of only 5,000 if we don't get promoted this year. It shows you how far we have fallen when you think that Hibs signed Steve Archibald from Barcleona in 1988. We were actually prepared to pay more money for him than Liverpool, who were also competing for his signature at the time.

I believe that the problem also lies with some of the fans that do go along every week and say nothing. For example, when we got beaten in the play-offs against Rangers, a lot of supporters were clapping them off the pitch. We were playing one of the worst Rangers teams in history so I wasn't going to applaud them. Show me a good loser and you can show me a loser is the way that I view it. For that first game after relegation we should all have turned up and paid to get in before walking out – then there would have been a real change. You need to win, that is always the most important thing. The Hands On Hibs campaign is good because we need people to stand up and fight our corner. These guys are the same type of people that backed the Hands Off Hibs campaign all those years ago – real supporters who care passionately about the future.

Supporting Hibs is not just about the game of football, it is a way of life. There is nothing better than taking your kids along to support the same team and seeing the joy on their faces when we score. We don't win many trophies but when we do win it makes it all the more special.

Pat Nevin
Writer and broadcaster, born 1963.

❛ There's a huge feeling of belonging we get when we go to the games together. ❜

MY DAD AND the rest of my family were all Celtic fans. They always took me to the games at Parkhead but playing football was a least if not more interesting.

Me and my friends all played football from a very young age. My dad technically trained me from the age of four or five solidly and just about every day. I enjoyed it. I really liked it. At no point from that age to about 17 did I think I wanted to be a footballer but I ended up doing it and it was great fun. Even when Celtic signed me on S-Form I thought it was nice but I still kept on with my education.

When I left Celtic at 16 I thought fine – that's fair enough. I wasn't upset by it because I thought I should go and study, so that's what I did. I kept on playing with mates in the boy's leagues and kind of fluked my way back into senior football one day by playing against Clyde for my boys' club. I was spotted by the then Clyde manager Craig Brown who asked me to play part-time with them while I was doing my degree. Then Chelsea approached Clyde to buy me but I held off for a year and later said 'Oh… alright then!' I still had a year to go of my degree so I said, 'Yeah, I'll do it, but as long as I can get back to my degree after two years.' They agreed and I joined them. I never did go back to complete my degree.

The first football game I went to was Celtic against Dunfermline – I think around about 1969. It was at Celtic Park. For most fans of most teams you tend to migrate to different parts of the ground. So when I got into my teens I started migrating towards 'The Jungle' so that I could feel a bigger part of it all – my family went there. I was 14 at the time so I was watching the dying embers of the same team that had won the European Cup in 1967. It was coming up to 1970, so some of the lads that came in included Danny McGrain, Kenny

Dalgleish, Davey Hay and Lou McCarrie. Quite a good team all in all. I was also fortunate to see bits of Jinky Johnstone before he finished his career. They had some phenomenal players.

At that time I had a second team and that team was Hibernian. It was hard to know why. I had a Hibs strip with a number 4 on the back because I liked Pat Stanton. That Hibs team was one of the great teams of the 1970s. They just happened to come up against a great Celtic team, particularly in cup finals. Hibs should have won a lot more than they did so it was just unlucky because Celtic were possibly the strongest they had ever been. There were scores between the clubs of 6-1 and 6-3 when I was up at the Celtic end supporting Celtic. But I always enjoyed watching Hibs because they were such a great stylish, attacking team. And more specifically I really enjoyed watching Pat Stanton. He was a really classy player. Funnily enough, I already had the strip. I don't know why. Maybe it was just because I liked the design and the colours. It's also quite weird because there were very few strips that I bought as a kid. I obviously had Celtic strips but my first ever strip was a Chelsea kit. That must have been in 1970 or 1971 when I got it for Christmas. It didn't have a badge on it. It was just a plain blue top with white socks and maybe yellow socks. This is made stranger because I went on to play for them. The only other strip I owned until I was about 15 was a Hibs strip. So from a very young age Hibs were my second team and there was always a strong affection for them in the back of my mind. At that point I had no thoughts of switching teams, that didn't happen until much later.

Many years later, if I went to a Celtic game I would be commentating on it, so I wouldn't be on the terraces much anymore. Now and again I would go the odd game when I wasn't working, but I started to feel that the songs been sung weren't really about Celtic Football Club. When I first started going as a kid the songs they sang were probably more political, but that was a different time in the 1970s. People back then would say or sing certain things that a lot of people would never consider saying now. Billy Connolly used to make a joke about singing all these daft songs for 90 minutes, but at full time some of them would walk home together and chat like good mates the next day at work.

After living down south for about 15 years I moved back to Scotland, naively thinking, 'Everyone will have moved on by now'. But on arrival, and going back to watch football and Celtic, I realised, maybe not. It's not an attack on anyone who has certain political views, but I just don't personally have a feeling for that. I met an MSP once who explained to me that I was in the in the minority. She told me 'We're all Irish Republicans.' So I said to her, 'Erm... I'm just a Celtic supporter.' I genuinely didn't go for any other reason than to support my football club. It was made very clear to me by a number of people that this was not the way the vast majority of Celtic fans thought. So I just thought 'that's not me'. I'm not saying I'm for or against it – it's just not what I'm into. I just want to go and watch a football game. If I said the same thing to some people they would accuse me of lying and some fans would start abusing you. I wanted to go to games with my kids and I didn't want to have that around me. So ultimately I decided to find somewhere else to watch my football.

My son was showing a lot of interest in football at the time. Quite often the first game you go to is the team you end up supporting but I actually took him to a Partick Thistle game first. I quite liked the people there, but having been an ex-Clyde player it was never going to work. But the main reason was the fact that we didn't even live near Firrhill, so a few weeks (or months) later I thought I would take my lad along to a Hibs game and that was where it began.

When I declared my support for Hibs I got dog's abuse off Celtic fans. But I should also say it's mainly from a small group within the Celtic fan base. If you walk about on the street, 99 per cent of the time most Celtic fans are good as gold. People tend to be more extreme online and when they see you have changed your team people tend to get a bit nasty. If you go on Twitter you will often get abuse and you can take that really quite personally and really quite seriously. In a way I can understand why people get angry about me supporting Hibs now but I just smile and say to them that there was no offence intended. We do tend to dwell on a lot of negativity about Scottish football fans. I mean I park my car near to Easter Road and quite often I will walk up with fans from the other teams and usually everything is cool as cool can be. So I think we do tend to forget that when fans meet fans from rival teams everything is perfectly civil 99.9 per cent of the time. But all everyone talks about is that 0.1 per cent of the time when there is a bit of trouble. It's important for the rest of society to know that most football supporters are good people but it's equally important for the media to realise this. The media are the worst agents of hype when an incident happens and often imply that there are serious problems there when there are not. They often intimate that trouble happens all the time, sometimes they almost will it to happen. I cover about 120 football games a season through my work and there wasn't one a word last year, from any fan, that was negative towards me – not one. In reality I had lots of really nice words and lots of people chatting to me and, by the way, two of those games were at Celtic Park and they

‘I won't be hanging about the Main Stand, for example, because it's just not where I like to watch Hibernian.’

were brilliant. I love the game and if it gets a wee bit messy and political I stand away from it – I just watch the football.

Every football club has a history and roots but these things have no effect on me personally. I'm more a guy that looks forward than back. I've always been like that. I have nothing against understanding your history as long as you are not bogged down by it. I think that applies to any walk of life. I also understand that it's important to many people. There will always be political viewpoints and theories about Hibs' Irish, Catholic past and that's up to them but it has nothing to do with me. So if you want to partake in that then you will but when I personally go to watch Hibs. It's about supporting the team.

When I was Chief Executive at Motherwell my aim was to make the club totally and utterly inclusive. Whatever your race, colour, creed, sex and sexuality we wanted to make people feel welcome at Fir Park. I tried to promote a much more modern outlook so that if somebody came along to watch the club and other fans didn't uphold this ethos, or were directly offensive, then it would not be tolerated. This was essentially our mission statement and we wanted to make sure that we stuck by it. So the club was a place for the community but it was also a business whilst being something a little bit deeper than that. I think we were even one of the first to have a mission statement.

Reaching out to the community was hard because it's quite different to the East End of Glasgow where I was brought up even though it's not that far away. There was a wee bit of mistrust initially as there always is when new people come into a club. John Boyle threw a whole bunch of money at the club and I will be honest with you, I tried to stop him. In the end Motherwell went into administration, which was dead upsetting for me because I had worked really hard and was really proud of all the things I had achieved. Most importantly, I had run the club on budget (and sometimes under) for four years, brought in a lot of youth from the local area to watch the team and had hopefully started to increase the fan base from a much younger level. We tried everything to make

Easter Road has witnessed Hibs games since 1893 but its largest attendance came in 1950 when a crowd of 65,860 packed in to watch the derby game against Hearts – it is likely that the real figure was considerably higher. During this same period the club had plans to replicate the East Terrace behind both goals. If this had happened, it would have taken the capacity from 70,000 to an incredible 100,000. In modern times the East Terracing was the last section of the ground to be rebuilt. It was previously scaled back from its days as a huge, two-tier open terrace in the 1980s.

Many still mourn its loss, but the new 6,500 seated replacement is an imposing structure greatly suited to greater success on the pitch.

The modern-day stadium has a more modest capacity of 20,250. However, it is still the largest fully-covered, UEFA-compliant football stadium outside Glasgow.

sure it was paving the way for a new generation of fans. Unfortunately, constant success costs a lot of money and a generational change takes time. That's the way it is with most businesses.

I think Scottish clubs like Hibernian do have to reach out more to their community, but then again, I think every club in the world should. Some teams do it in a hell of a ham-fisted way but most people that run football clubs are not that stupid. If there is a disconnect between the fan base and the ownership, then that is a major difficulty. For example, you can have a club that is doing averagely well or ending up mid-table each season. But if there is a real sense of ownership and belonging, and a feeling that you are being respected by the club for being a fan, then supporters will generally put up with average performances from the team. Of course they want to better that but they will still put up with it. Ultimately if you have that disconnect between the fans and the club then you have a big problem. It's one of the easiest things in the world to say, but one of the hardest things to do.

As a child, I always viewed the Scottish League as Celtic, Rangers, Hibs and Hearts in terms of the prestige and size of the clubs. Later, in the 1980s, you obviously had Aberdeen and Dundee Utd coming to the fore. It can be that way again because if you look at the fan base of these clubs then the 'natural order' will probably be restored one day. If you're a Dundee, Dundee Utd or even a Ross County fan, you can't call on the same amount of supporters that Hibs and Hearts can. So Hibs and Hearts are really big clubs within the country. Hibs should be up at the top of the Premier League and now and again should be able to punch a wee bit higher than that. But they are a long, long way from where they should be. This will not happen overnight, because they have taken a big fall. There is not one simple reason for that but a whole variety of reasons. The worst thing is that we got relegated in probably the worst year that you could get relegated. We faced a resurgent Hearts and also had Rangers to contend with. This won't always happen to every club who gets relegated. It was just an extraordinary season. No club is entitled to get promoted in their first year or even the second year, given the circumstances, so it's just an incredibly unlucky state of affairs. Hibs are fighting against teams that would have done perfectly well in the SPL so the main thing is not to panic! It is hard to sit back and think about it in those terms, but it's ultimately true. Hibs didn't do too badly last season when you think about it. At the moment it's like trying to ride the perfect storm.

Hibernian have been a fantastically important thing for me and my son. Especially for him. It's become a massive part of his life now, in the way that he has been accepted and understood by people around him. People don't understand how important that part of his life is and how much of a bonding experience it has been for me and my son. To be able watch to the effect that the highs and the lows of watching Hibs has had on him, as well as watching him learn to deal with that, has been invaluable. He is 23 now, but has gone through all the good times and some of the dull and bad ones as well. I don't get to see them as much as I like but my son is there every second week. He has made great friends there and it's been a great club for him.

The first game we attended together hadn't even started, but as we sat down the decision had already been made. I was chatting to everybody around me and they were chatting back to me. It was all in a really cool way. We were in the East Stand and some of the guys I met that day are still great mates. We went an hour early because my son wanted to be there. Whatever team we played that day or whatever happened in that game really does not matter now. In fact, I couldn't even tell you who it was we played. The whole essence of it was that we felt so at home. Part of it was also being sat in the East Stand and how it made me feel like a kid again like when I stood in the jungle at Celtic Park. It just felt real. Nothing against any other part of the ground but I mean I won't be hanging about the Main Stand for example because it's just not where I like to watch Hibernian. The club felt like it had a real sense of community. I always have a laugh at this (and I do realise that it could happen anywhere), but I was sat there for about ten minutes that day and ended up in a debate with four or five people round us on the relative merits of Iggy Pop and Bowie. So I felt really, really at home in the East Stand because that's one of my favourite conversations.

But there was something else. There was clearly a feeling from the fans that if we'd been beaten 3-2, played well and entertained then we would all walk out the ground feeling uplifted. There was no anger – there really wasn't. There was just a good feeling of 'what a good game that was' and 'we played well'. On the flipside, if we had won 3-2 and played long-ball football, then there would have been grunting and moaning amongst the fans. I was left with a very clear sense of, 'You know what, it isn't just about winning it's about the beauty of the game and playing it in a good way.' It's not just a big part of Hibs but it's also a big part of watching football for me personally. It's how I liked to play the game. So it took a confluence of things to make it very clear to me that I should be a Hibs fan. In reality it was probably always going to happen because they were my second team anyway. It's been a fabulously positive time of life for my son so whatever happens from here on in I am delighted with Hibernian Football Club for the help they have given my family. There's a huge feeling of belonging we get when we go to the games together. The fans and the whole ethos of Hibernian play the biggest part in that. They have helped my son to grow and understand people and life better. He came back from that first game and thought, 'Wow, that was amazing,' so there was never any doubt about supporting Hibernian from that day forward.

Mickey Weir

Former Hibernian player, born 1966.

' To play the next game for Hibs was the most important thing for me. '

MY DAD, MY grandad and my uncles were all fanatical Hibs supporters so I came from a Hibs-supporting family who would go to the games every week.

I was brought up in Pilton and my family would all meet in the Doocot Bar before the games. I would always be sitting outside in the van (with my other brothers) waiting for them to stop drinking. Then they would all jump in the motor and we would head along to the Hibs game.

In those days we had the pleasure of watching players like Alex Edwards, Alex Cropley and Pat Stanton. In attack we had Alan Gordon and Jimmy O'Rourke – they were great players that I loved and will always remember.

But the games that really grabbed me were the European games on a Wednesday or Thursday night. There was something special about those night games with the players illuminated on the pitch by the old floodlights, under the cover of darkness. The atmosphere was always great and even if the game was against a smaller club it still had something special about it at night-time.

In those days it was absolutely choc-a-bloc and you just couldn't get near to the ground. I vividly remember queuing up from the top of London Road all the way down and across the wee bridge on Albion Road – it was unbelievable! If you didn't queue there, you would queue up from the other side of the ground at Lochend. There were usually more than 40,000 regularly going to the games back then.

In those days I was lifted over the gate by my dad or my uncle and we always used to stand under the floodlights at the corner of the Hawkhill end of the ground. This was before they had built 'The Cowshed', so it was just open terracing back then. If Hibs won a corner kick, we would run all the way down the terrace to the corner flag just to see them take the corner from close up. It always seemed to be Alex Edwards who took them. He was our number seven and he became my hero at that time. Ultimately he was the one that brought me closest to Hibs and I wanted to be just like him. Every young kid has a footballing hero but when I think back to watching him play it's the number seven that I remember most.

There were so many characters on the terracing back then and a lot of them were guys from my area, who were all big Hibs supporters. I always remember the sway of the crowd. It wasn't like today with people sitting down to watch the games. You were constantly on the move, you just seemed to get pushed from pillar to post. I remember my dad holding on to me because if you got pulled away you could get lost in the sway of the crowd. I also remember the old guys who would walk around selling pies and Wagon Wheel biscuits, so I would always get money from my dad to run down and buy some food.

I haven't got a clue about the first game I went to because I was very, very young. It's funny because, although the European games really stand out, I still remember Hibs playing teams like East Fife, who were actually quite a prominent club back then. We went to every game that we could get to until I actually started playing football myself, but I don't remember going to a Hibs game when it wasn't absolutely mobbed and jam-packed.

I never got to the stage of splitting away from my dad and watching games with my mates, because by that time I was playing football with my school on a Saturday morning and then I had my boys' club in the afternoon. I couldn't make it to many games, but when I became a Hibs apprentice I would actually go and watch them myself or with pals if we didn't have a game. Even though I was on the ground staff at the time, I would travel with my brother and his mates up to the likes of Tannadice and Pittodrie on a supporters' bus. A few of the team did that so as a young player back then it wasn't unusual. It's very strange when you think about it now.

My dad and my grandad always wanted me to play for the Hibs but I never, ever thought I would be good enough. I wasn't even sure that I would be a football player. I had a lot of things running through my mind. I played a lot of football and then kind of went off the game, because I was constantly told, 'You are going to be too small to play or make it in the game.' So although I didn't completely lose my love for the game, I fell out of love with it a wee bit. If you are told these things at a young age it is very hard to deal with. I was a very full-on person, if I did something I had to do it right or not at all. Once I got a focus and a grasp of my ambition, I gave it everything I had. When I walked into the club for the first time as an apprentice, I vividly remember thinking, 'I've got a chance here and I'm not going to let go of it.'

I was selected to play for the Edinburgh Schoolboys Select and not long after that I got asked to play for Hibs in a one-off trial game at Easter Road. The teams were kind of randomly mixed up and the manager just let us go out and play for the full 90 minutes. It was essentially 'do or die' so you were either good enough or you were not. I felt as if I had done well in the game but I mainly remember being excited about simply playing at Easter Road. To play in front of Pat Stanton, the manager and the legend, was a huge thing as well. My dad and my whole family came along to watch me that day so the pressure was on. As the game started I thought, 'It's a simple case of, if I'm good enough then I'm good enough.' I felt that I did quite well and I was delighted when I got a phone call on the Monday asking me to join the club. It was funny because there were about four or five clubs who came in for me after that game. My dad told me that there was a chance of Manchester City and others clubs wanting to sign me but he said, 'You've got to stay and play for the Hibs'. I always knew that he and my grandad would love to see me playing in the Hibs jersey, but it also helped that I was a bit of a home bird and loved to be round my family and friends, and the Hibs community in general.

That trial game brought a lot of pressure and of course there were other times in my career when I felt that as well. It's a huge part of being a professional player but I always relished the big games in particular. I never, ever worried about failing or playing badly and the reason is quite simple – it's because I practised, practised and practised. I wasn't worried about my first touch, being able to control the ball properly or even being fit. I still felt the pressure of playing but once I got over that first year of my professional career I learnt how to channel it. My one regret is that I didn't play in enough of the big games because of injury problems, but if someone had said to me when I was 21 or 22 that I would play in cup finals or semi-finals I wouldn't have believed them.

I didn't think that I would see my career out because of my injuries. I just knew from an early age that I would have some serious issues. Strangely, knowing this kept me going but there were many games that I probably shouldn't have played in. I was just so hungry to succeed and do well, but I really suffered for it. I have no regrets, although there are times when I look back and think if only I had been fit to play in more games. It haunts me a wee bit that I didn't manage two or three seasons without injury. It was never, ever going to happen though because I just knew in the back of mind that it wasn't possible. In those days players never had regular scans or anything like that. You just had to take each game as it came and the way I looked it at it was – every game I played in was my last game. I was constantly in agony but I kept it to myself – my wife was probably the only one to know about it. I just kept going and kept going. The only clear season I managed was when we won the cup and it was the only season I felt that I had got over my problems. But then at the end of the season I started to fall to bits again. To play the next game for Hibs was the most important thing for me.

People sometimes ask me, 'What was your favourite game you played in?' I always say to them that the first game was my best game, because all I ever wanted was to prove to myself and prove to my family that I could play for the Hibernian – even it was just once. Would you believe that I played left back in that game against Airdrie? I thought to myself, 'Well, you've played for Hibs now so anything after this is a bonus.' To see my dad being so happy for me to play that game for the Hibs was enough for me.

When you are a player the atmosphere and the crowds backing transmits to us on the pitch in a massive way. I was always aware of the fans' backing, especially playing for the team I supported. I always had a great relationship with the fans and they got me through a lot of really hard times, especially when I was injured. They always accepted me, even if I had a bad game. I can honestly say to this day that, no matter how bad a game I was having, I never left anything on the pitch. I always gave everything for the jersey, even if I wasn't well or not quite right physically. That is one thing that I am proud of and I think Hibs fans acknowledged that.

I did feel the burden of being a Hibs supporter and playing for the club but it was different in those days, because there was always about five or six players on every team who were supporters of their club. We had a few of us in that team who were brought up Hibees and that is something that no amount of money can buy. You knew what the club meant very early on in your career and you knew the pressures that came with it. You had to learn how to handle them, but they were still pressures nonetheless. I always think that a lot of players that come into the club do not understand, or know how to handle it; we knew what it meant to play against the likes of Hearts or Rangers. It almost pushed us to a higher level because we were representing the club we supported. I reckon that most of us would have played for nothing. The game has moved on now – there are so many financial rewards and I think that money has taken the true heart out of it.

The people working in the club at that time were also huge Hibees. Guys like Pat Stanton and Jimmy O'Rourke were a huge influence in making me understand the importance of playing for Hibernian. Jimmy loved the Hibs. He always drummed into me how important it was and that has stuck with me until this very day. To walk into to the club and meet guys like Pat (who was my dad's hero) at the age of 17 was simply amazing. George Stewart was a big influence on me as well. If you couldn't listen to their advice as a young man then you had a big problem.

You will never, ever forget playing for your team but to score for your team is something really special. I never felt like the club owed me anything. I always appreciated everything I had and every day I spent there. I knew that I should be happy to play for them and be appreciated in the way that I was. I was very thankful and to score a goal for Hibs was like a dream. If someone had said to me as a kid, 'You are going to score a goal for Hibs one day and you will also win a trophy,' I truly would not have believed it.

To become a professional player you have to have a true belief in yourself and your ability. I worked hard at my game and I never felt that I couldn't make the grade. I knew that if I got a chance I would be able to handle it. It was just whether I would get that chance. Even to score for the reserves in those days was a big thing because it was very much sink or swim. If you didn't produce something for the reserves then you would not get into the first team – it was quite simple. Being an apprentice was essentially a full time job and more. You would be working for 12 hours a day, from about seven in the morning to maybe about seven or eight o'clock at night. We would paint walls, prepare the strips, clean the boots and sweep the terracing. I couldn't paint before that, but I can certainly paint now. The worst task was 'doing the gullies' as we called it. We would draw lots for it on a Friday. It was a horrendous job. We had to clean out the space at the bottom of the old terracing in front of the crowd fence. This was the place where people would piss and drop their litter. You had to wear a pair of these council-type gloves and pick up all of this saturated crap and stick it in a bag or wash it away. It was the most disgusting job you can imagine.

There were many days that we didn't even train. You didn't even have time to worry about feeling hungry. They treated us like dogsbodies at times. But this was our grounding in life and I loved every minute of it. I knew that I had to get through my apprenticeship (and be able to handle it), so jobs like these were a motivation because you thought, 'To get away from this I need to be in the first team'. Sometimes in the afternoon Jimmy O'Rourke or George Stewart would take you in to the gym and play three or four a-side. They would kick lumps out of you and they never took any prisoners. We all had to learn how to handle it. Looking back now, they were definitely doing it to test our characters and toughen us up as well. They wanted to see you have a go at them in return, so they took some hefty challenges as well. There were lots of times when I was very scared and intimidated by Jimmy O'Rourke in particular, because if he didn't like what he saw he would tell you straight away. There were no ifs or buts about it. It taught me a lot about myself. The apprenticeship is one of the best things that have been lost to football.

It was a tough and tiring time. Every morning we had to get the kit ready for the first team and go to training after that. Once training was done, we would go and do more chores. There were many times when we would be in on a Saturday morning, finishing off the tasks that we didn't manage to complete on the Friday. Later that day, we might get picked to play in the reserves or even the first team, so it was often a six day week. But that was the norm and you just accepted it and got on with it. You were never allowed any excuses – it was

❝ All I ever wanted was to prove to myself, and prove to my family, that I could play for Hibernian ❞

UEFA Cup 1989, 1st round, 1st leg.

actually a great way to learn the trade and we all loved it. The rest of the guys like Kano loved it too and it created a great camaraderie among all of us young players.

When I was told I was not on the ground staff any more, it was like being in heaven. It took me about two and a half years to get to that stage. When I got into the first team it was totally different. You would have one training session in the morning and maybe one in the afternoon. Most of the time we would be finished pretty early.

There are so many players and staff that I admire from back then. You could not meet a nicer man than Pat Stanton – he was simply a club legend. He was great with the young players and used to sit us down for hours and tell us about all the games he'd played in. His stories even impressed some of the non-Hibees with how important it was to play for the club. A lot of the time you didn't have actual coaches so the players would teach you the game. For example, Ally Brazil would give you a good kick up the backside when you needed it. Gordon Rae taught me a lot about the game as well. He was a tough guy, maybe not the most technically gifted of players, but he taught me so much about attitude and commitment. All of these guys would encourage me especially because they knew that I had a tough start with being so small. They could see that I had a long battle ahead of me. I knew that was the case as well. Ralph Callaghan was another one who was good with me. I always remember him saying to me, 'It's all about ability and not how small you are, believe in your ability Mickey.' I always tried to remember what he said to me but it was still tough because from season to season you were on a knife-edge never knowing whether you would get a new contract or not. Every year was like that as a professional player.

It was often very brutal when D-Day arrived and the management took you into the away dressing room to tell you whether they would be renewing your contract or not. I always remember seeing some of the guys walking away with tears running down their faces. I instantly thought to myself, 'This is not going

Mickey Weir's debut for Hibernian came in 1983, when he was 17 years old. Hibs were away to Airdrie in a League Cup tie and the team won 3-1 with Mickey playing an unfamiliar role at left back.

He made his home debut in a 3-2 defeat to Dumbarton and in a 16-year career notched up 247 appearances for Hibs, scoring a total of 35 goals.

He joined Luton Town (playing in England's top division at the time) in 1987 for a very short spell before returning to the club he loved.

After finally departing Hibs in 1997, he joined Motherwell for a further two seasons before hanging up his boots in 1999.

Weir was massively popular amongst the fans and he will always be remembered for his magnificent dribbling skills and tremendous work rate.

to happen to me.' I remember sitting in that dressing room one such day, when the manager had just released a young kid and I remember looking at the guy and thinking, 'You know what, you could have done more.' Some of these guys could have had a career – they probably look back now and think, 'If only I had tried harder.' So I was always thinking, 'That is not going to happen to me. I'm going to work and train hard and I am going to practise, practise, practise'. I would go to the gym or do anything I could to improve my game and make it happen. I vowed that if I was going to get taken out of that place then they would have to throw me out. I wasn't going to give in without a fight. It was amazing because it was always the ones that worked hardest who succeeded – regardless of your ability. Attitude is everything and talent is worthless without a desire and hunger to match it.

When the Hands Off Hibs campaign happened it transmitted itself to most of the players who had been there for a while, especially the players who were Hibs through and through. You would see fans outside the ground every day and people losing their jobs around you. Some even lost their jobs because they were seen outside with the fans supporting the cause. My dad always re-assured me and said, 'Nah, we will survive. This is a big club, this is not a club that will just roll over and die.' The real supporters stood up and they were counted. There was nothing fake about those guys who kept the club alive and a lot of them were people that I grew up with.

After knowing the club was saved, we got off to a good start on the pitch and everything just seemed to click for us. It was a great changing room. There were no superstars in that team and nobody thought they were better than anyone else. We were a team of winners and winning was all we wanted to do. I sensed it right away with guys like wee Willie Miller, Gordon Hunter, Keith Wright, Graham Mitchell and Murdo MacLeod in the team. Even during the previous season we had guys like Andy Goram, who was a winner, so it just kind of filtered through to the next generation. Yes, we had good talent, but the most important thing was that we had boys who wanted to be successful. Players like John Burridge – 'Budgie' as he was known – was a good, experienced player who still had a desire to achieve something. I don't remember there being a lot of big talkers in that dressing room though – we just did the business. To me, there was no point in talking about it when you knew what each guy was all about anyway. Money can't buy that.

I hated losing and I think that is what drove me on and kept me going. If I had been playing seven a-side on a Friday morning it would take me a couple of hours to get over it if we had been beaten. I look back now and think 'I must have been horrendous' but I also think that if I had not wanted to win so much then I wouldn't have succeeded in the game.

In the semi-final we were 100 per cent confident that we would beat Rangers because we were a good side and we knew our football. Our manager, Alex Miller, knew his stuff and was a good tactician but we also had players who were hungry and on-form.

Coming back to Edinburgh with the cup was something I will never forget.

Equally, I remember the enormous pressure we were under to win the game. People forget that a year before we were nearly out of business and suddenly we were heavy favourites in a cup final. I kept saying to myself, 'No, we cannae lose here, we have to do it for all my family and my friends and for every Hibs fan in Edinburgh.' It felt like the whole of Edinburgh wanted you to win, apart from Hearts fans of course. We had come so far as a team and I felt like the weight of the world was on me. On that day I thought to myself, 'Just don't fail.' The thought of losing was unbearable. I also knew that I wasn't going to get many chances like that again because my career was on a fine knife edge due to my injury problems. I always remember the first half being very poor for us and we were very nervous because for most of the guys it was their first cup final. But the manager was great with the team at half time by telling us to just go and play our football. He said, 'You are good enough, just relax and play.' So once we got that first goal, I knew there was no going back and we were going to win it. The massive support we had that day made us all the more determined.

I just want the club to be in the right hands and I have said in the past that I don't think it has been. Hibernian are not the club they used to be, but hopefully we will return to that at some point. I don't think the club has been managed properly. Hibs should never, ever be in the situation where we have so many loan players and very few players contracted to the club. We went into a Scottish Cup final against Hearts in 2012 and got badly beaten with a team full of players on loan. That is not good enough for a club like Hibs. I often look back to the time when Tom Hart ran the club. He was the Kings of Hibs and he put the club on a pedestal. People might say, 'Yeah but things have moved on' but why should they move on? It is still Hibernian and I just want them to be in the safest hands with people who do right by the club and the team. I was brought up following a successful club that had an expectation level, but that expectation is not as high as it used to be. I'm not sure how we get back to that – probably the only way is to win matches and get back into the SPL. A club of Hibs' stature should always be looking to challenge for something, whether that be the winning of a cup or playing European football. Even when I played, we were always on the periphery of European qualification and that was the way we were brought up. Until we get back to that, the club will not be the Hibs that I know and remember. You always felt that you were expected to maintain the traditions and the standards that previous generations of players had set. You were not allowed to have an off-day. I'm not saying we always won games, but in general it wasn't acceptable to get beaten by clubs like Dumbarton. There has been a gradual decline in standards. I don't really care who runs the club, I only care about the standard of player that comes to the club. Every year we used to buy two or three good players. For example, when Alex Miller was manager he brought in players like McCallister, O'Neill and Jackson. Before that we had players coming in like Steve Archibald, Andy Goram and Jim Leighton. I have no issues with day-to-day running of the club – it's about what happens on the park that matters to me.

I can never understand why we have scouts travelling to Dundee and Aberdeen when you have areas of Edinburgh like Leith, Drylaw, Pilton and Niddrie on your doorstep. If the club scouted comprehensively in these places they would find good players that want to play for Hibs as well. Once upon a time I was one of those young boys who would have done anything to play for Hibernian – I would even have played for nothing. You should look to your own community first. They are not all going to be great players immediately, but there is plenty of raw material in these places. Some of these kids have a real love for their football team, whether it be Hibs or Hearts. It's not just Hibs that seem to have lost that sense of belonging. Most clubs would rather buy players from France or even England. When I was at Motherwell coaching, the players that I tried to find were within the immediate community. I never looked to Glasgow because I knew that Rangers and Celtic would be the first to get hold of them. I sometimes think that clubs are looking for the perfect and complete player. For example Willie Miller and Gordon Hunter weren't great players when they first came to Hibs but they became good players in time. You've got to give the kids a chance even if they are not the finished article. If you look at any Hibs supporting household, they are just as desperate to see their son playing for the club as they ever were.

Hibs and Hearts are two big clubs and the rivalry between them is great. That is what makes Edinburgh and the derby so special. Hearts are the same as us in the sense that they have always been a club that nurtured their own players. Hearts want to be the best in Edinburgh and so do Hibs, so there is no difference in that respect. When I was a player, I was definitely aware of the tradition at Hibs in how to play the game the right way. I think that is proven by various managers who have left the club because they didn't manage to get the team to play football in that way. However, playing good football is fine but you have to win games at the end of the day. In the 1991 side we had a great team who also played good football. If we didn't play well though we still generally won those kind of games and tried to go back to playing good football the following week. Celtic has a similar tradition I suppose. It's all about getting a happy medium between being a nice football team to watch and a team that can win games.

European football is so completely different to playing league games. I got sent off in the game against Anderlecht and it was just naivety on my behalf. That match taught me a lot about the game. They were so far ahead of us. For that first 15 minutes I hardly touched the ball. Anderlecht had a good pedigree in Europe though and it seemed to take us the first game to get used to their style, although we still managed to get a 2-2 draw at home. In the second game we were very unlucky over in Belgium drawing 1-1 and going out on goal difference. I was also coaching at the time and I remember thinking, 'We are miles behind this team,' and that stuck in my head for years. I remember the ground being packed to the rafters, they had even opened up the Dunbar End up as well. The whole thing was something special, something I will never forget.

I did actually have a chance to go to a European club when I left Hibs, but my wee boy was very young at the time so I didn't think it would have been the right move. Playing abroad didn't really appeal to me – as I mentioned previously, I am a home bird really. In hindsight, maybe I should have taken up the offer because the game over there would have probably suited me better. Our game is more hectic and in Europe you tend have more time on the ball.

When I did move from Scotland to play with Luton, I learnt a lot about myself in a way I wouldn't have imagined. I was brought up in a neighbourhood in Edinburgh where racism was quite prevalent. When a black or Asian person moved into the area they would get a frightening amount of abuse. As a young man I was swept along with it – you didn't think about how the victims must have felt. I met my wife after moving to Luton for a short spell and a lot of her family and friends were Asian or black. I immediately thought to myself, 'I've got to change.' I didn't believe that I was a racist or such, but my views changed so much when I met her. They were such lovely people and meeting them really made me think. I didn't want my kids to grow up with these sort of views and when I played in England it was shocking to hear so much racist abuse from the terracing. So when I came back to Scotland I heard about anti-racist initiatives and decided that I would try and help them in any way I could. I wanted to try and explain to young kids that it is nonsense to abuse black people for the colour of their skin. That whole issue touched me and I'm proud to say that I have contributed something. It's also about putting something positive back into society. I love helping when I can.

I always try to have good manners when I speak to people – my mum and dad brought me up like that. In contrast, when it came to playing football I could be quite horrible, but I think a lot of the players were like that back then. Maybe it takes that wee bit extra to win games and even though I hated that side of me on the pitch, it probably helped me. If Hibs got beaten, as a fan or a player I would suffer badly. But as Eddie Turnbull once said, 'There's class, there's top class and then there's Hibs class.' I learnt so much about myself playing for Hibernian and Eddie summed up exactly what my team means to me.

Also published by Luath Press

Crops: The Alex Cropley Story
Alex Cropley with Tom Wright
ISBN 978 1 908373 97 7 HBK £14.99

More than just the tale of one man and his football, *Crops* is a testament to the passion of generations for the beautiful game, as well as a heart-wrenching account of the sacrifices to which commitment to life on the pitch can lead.

Filled with frank recollections of personal triumphs and despair, *Crops* is also peppered with anecdotes about the footballing legends Cropley played alongside and captures the spirit of football in the seventies. Whether readers remember Cropley's more famous goals with warmth or recognise themselves in the football-crazed kid playing on the streets, this is a must-have for any football fan.

I used to flinch when Studs wound up for a challenge and he feared no-one as he sometimes threw his whole body into a tackle. The meant we also spent too much time together in the treatment room.
ANDY GRAY

Hibernian: From Joe Baker to Turnbull's Tornadoes
Tom Wright
ISBN 978 1908873 09 1 HBK £20

In *Hibernian: From Joe Baker to Turnbull's Tornadoes*, club historian Tom Wright marks a new dawn for the game and the end of an era for Hibs.

Hibernian begins in the turbulent 1960s, when relegation was avoided at Easter Road on the final day of the 1963 season.

The appointment of the legendary manager Jock Stein in 1964 saw an immediate improvement in the relegation haunted side. The Hibs side of the mid-'60s featured an all-Scottish international forward line, and the return of player Eddie Turnbull in 1971 saw the emergence of possibly Hibs' greatest-ever side – the magical Turnbull's Tornadoes.

Packed full of detail and interesting information, *Hibernian* is a must not only for Hibs supporters, but also for the general football fan who is interested in this defining period in the history of our game.

Stramash: Tackling Scotland's Towns and Teams
Daniel Gray
ISBN 978 1906817 66 4 PBK £9.99

Fatigued by bloated big-time football and bored of samey big cities, Daniel Gray went in search of small town Scotland and its teams. Part travelogue, part history, and part mistakenly spilling ketchup on the face of a small child, *Stramash* takes an uplifting look at the country's nether regions.

Using the excuse of a match to visit places from Dumfries to Dingwall, *Stramash* accomplishes the feats of visiting Dumfries without mentioning Robert Burns, being positive about Cumbernauld and linking Elgin City to Lenin. It is ae fond look at Scotland as you've never seen it before.

There have been previous attempts by authors to explore the off-the-beaten paths of the Scottish football landscape, but Daniel Gray's volume is in another league. THE SCOTSMAN

A brilliant way to rediscover Scotland.
THE HERALD

Another Bloody Saturday
Mat Guy
ISBN 978 1 910745 28 1 PBK £11.99

Why do people head out on windswept Saturday afternoons and wet Wednesday evenings watch lower and non-league teams play when they could watch Premier League football from the comfort of their living rooms?

Does an international match between two countries that technically don't exist have any meaning?

Why do some people go to so much trouble volunteering to support clubs which run on a shoestring budget and are lucky to get even a glimpse of the limelight?

Over the course of a season, Mat Guy set out to explore the less glamorous side of the beautiful game, travelling the backwaters of football across the length and breadth of the country – and beyond. He watched Bangor as they were cheerfully thrashed by Reykjavik's UMF Stjarnan, was absolutely won over by the women's game, and found a new team to love in Accrington Stanley.

From Glasgow to Northern Cyprus, Bhutan to the Faroe Islands, Mat discovered the same hope, sense of community and love of the game that first led him to a life in the stands at Salisbury FC's Victoria Park, where his own passion for football was formed.

Details of books published by Luath Press can be found at:
www.luath.co.uk

Luath Press Limited

committed to publishing well written books worth reading

LUATH PRESS takes its name from Robert Burns, whose little collie
Luath (*Gael.*, swift or nimble) tripped up Jean Armour at a wedding
and gave him the chance to speak to the woman who was to be his wife
and the abiding love of his life. Burns called one of the 'Twa Dogs'
Luath after Cuchullin's hunting dog in Ossian's *Fingal*.
Luath Press was established in 1981 in the heart of
Burns country, and is now based a few steps up
the road from Burns' first lodgings on
Edinburgh's Royal Mile. Luath offers you
distinctive writing with a hint of
unexpected pleasures.
Most bookshops in the UK, the US, Canada,
Australia, New Zealand and parts of Europe,
either carry our books in stock or can order them
for you. To order direct from us, please send a £sterling
cheque, postal order, international money order or your
credit card details (number, address of cardholder and
expiry date) to us at the address below. Please add post
and packing as follows: UK – £1.00 per delivery address;
overseas surface mail – £2.50 per delivery address; overseas airmail
– £3.50 for the first book to each delivery address, plus £1.00 for each
additional book by airmail to the same address. If your order is a gift,
we will happily enclose your card or message at no extra charge.

Luath Press Limited
543/2 Castlehill
The Royal Mile
Edinburgh EH1 2ND
Scotland
Telephone: +44 (0)131 225 4326
(24 hours)
Fax: +44 (0)131 225 4324
email: sales@luath. co.uk
Website: www. luath.co.uk